W9-ARG-198

PRAISE FOR
OPEN AND UNAFRAID

"Guided by the inimitable Eugene Peterson, David Taylor has created a winsome, accessible entry into the book of Psalms. He weaves into his exposition his own life experience and vibrant faith. He connects the poetry of the psalms to real-life wonders and struggles. This book offers pedagogical guidance on how to read the Psalter. This is a welcome addition to our literature on the psalms."

> —**Walter Brueggemann,** William Marcellus McPheeters Professor Emeritus
> of Old Testament, Columbia Theological Seminary

"The Psalter is the heart and soul of the Old Testament. It is also a pathway into the presence of God. The human emotions it depicts and the God it encounters help us make sense of life. David Taylor's *Open and Unafraid* not only walks the reader through key themes of the psalms but its practical focus keeps you there, so that you can know God and yourself better. The book is truly a guide into life as it ought to be lived and experienced."

> —**Darrell L. Bock,** executive director for cultural engagement, Howard G.
> Hendricks Center for Christian Leadership and Cultural Engagement; senior
> research professor of New Testament studies, Dallas Theological Seminary

"What encourages me about this book is the way a clear map is drawn to a path to intimacy with the psalmist's God. The author's challenge is to cover the wide range and scope of psalmody. David Taylor has met the challenge by his conscientious exposition of the psalms under thematic headings that open us to an ongoing theme: divine responses to flash points of human need. In every psalm we discover this human-divine contact, and it is because the human voices are so authentic that we feel at home in them. Many of the psalms are personal outbursts in the face of crisis and exhibit raw emotion. Others are cries of gratitude. This book encourages us to pray from what we really experience and who we really are."

> —**Luci Shaw,** writer-in-residence, Regent College; author, *Thumbprint in the Clay*
> and *Eye of the Beholder*

"As a Catholic monastic, the Psalter forms the praying heart of my Christian community. The problematic notions of warfare, violence, and anger in the psalms in the monastic tradition are always addressed as spiritual warfare within ourselves, and not turned outward toward others. But we all deal with praise and discouragement, good and bad, peace and conflict in daily life in Christ. This book helps address those things from a fresh perspective. I am pleased to see another good book on the psalms from a recognized Christian scholar."

—**John Michael Talbot,** contemporary Christian music pioneer; bestselling author; founder and general minister, the Brothers and Sisters of Charity

"There are lots of books about the psalms, so why should you bother with this one? One important aspect of the psalms is that they reflect God's actual dealings with actual people. David Taylor talks about the psalms in a way that shows how they connect with him as a real person. David—I mean this David—talks about his sadness, anger, honesty, and joy, and helps you see how the other David—the David of the psalms—talks about sadness, anger, honesty, and joy, and about how God relates to us and we relate to him as sad, angry, honest, and joyful people."

—**John Goldingay,** professor of Old Testament and David Allan Hubbard Professor Emeritus of Old Testament, Fuller Theological Seminary

"The psalms are at the heart of Scripture and they unlock and express the secrets of our hearts: our deepest fears, longings, and hopes. David Taylor takes us straight to that hidden heart—the hidden heart of Scripture, the hidden heart of the reader—and opens it out fearlessly and beautifully. He is sensitive to the poetry of the psalms and to their original context, but most of all, he unlocks what these psalms can mean for us now. Engaging with this book, and especially with the exercises and prayers at the end of each chapter, could be transformative for many readers."

—**Malcolm Guite,** chaplain, Girton College, Cambridge; author, *Sounding the Seasons* and *Faith, Hope and Poetry*

"Like the psalms themselves, *Open and Unafraid* is rich, both theologically and aesthetically. In these fraught and fearsome days, we need the psalms more than ever. And we need more faithful artists and thinkers like David Taylor to mine the infinite gifts the psalms offer across the ages."

—**Karen Swallow Prior,** author, *On Reading Well* and *Fierce Convictions*

"I have been exposed to different journeys of life undertaken by individuals whose walks through the life pathways have revealed the efficacy of the guideposts and road maps provided in the Scriptures by our Creator, the psalms being one such prominent resource. I also participated recently in a supposed 'mission' seminar in which 'worship' was a major topic, from which I learned that the psalms are 'poems' that express the life encounters the composers had with their (and our) Creator as they lived out the purpose of their creation. Going through *Open and Unafraid* reinforced the insights I have gained so far, as well as provided further clarity and enlightenment to guide my own steps as I continue my life journey along the pathways the Lord has created for me. I, therefore, strongly recommend this book to every one of my fellow travelers on this life journey!"

—**Reuben Ezemadu,** international director, Christian Missionary Foundation, Inc; continental coordinator, Movement for African National Initiatives

"David Taylor takes us on a journey through the psalms, exploring the depth of life's realities: sadness, anger, doubt, chaos, loneliness, even death. He helps readers to face their own human condition with nonnegotiable honesty—open and unafraid. Yet this journey through the psalms also points to God, who is sovereign, gives life and joy, and unites us. You can hear the tender, gentle, and encouraging words from the author as you read this book with a devotional yet challenging message. If you appreciate the books by Eugene Peterson, you will not be disappointed by this book as it bears the same sentiment from the heart of a caring pastor and the mind of a penetrating theologian."

—**Patrick Fung,** general director, Overseas Missionary
Fellowship International

"This David Taylor's book is open and unafraid, because it breathes and sings the grace of God to anybody who reads it, as do the psalms themselves. *Open and Unafraid* is marinated in God's psalms, so its testimony is honest and direct, personal and heart-warming, and both magisterial and humble. The learning underneath the writing is worn lightly, and the conversational tone is engaging, opening up the encyclopedic richness of the biblical psalms (also for governments to hear). The appended questions and exercises for each chapter are truly fruitful and fun. This book has a complete *vade mecum* character."

—**Calvin Seerveld,** professor emeritus of philosophical aesthetics,
Institute for Christian Studies in Toronto; author, *Voicing God's*
Psalms and *How to Read the Bible to Hear God Speak*

"The psalms are an inexhaustible source of comfort and challenge in the life of faith. Thanks to David Taylor for orienting us so compellingly to so many of the psalms' key virtues. But while many books could orient us to the psalms' external excellencies, this one does more, helping us to see how the psalms come into their own as they are used by the Holy Spirit to transform human lives, heal human souls, and enravish us with a deep awareness of the wonder and glory of God."

—**John D. Witvliet,** director, Calvin Institute of Christian Worship; professor of music and worship, Calvin College and Calvin Theological Seminary

"David Taylor's *Open and Unafraid* is a gift for us 'thoughtful' Christians, those of us who through a merely intellectualized spirituality inadvertently find ourselves closed down and made afraid, who have forgotten how to feel and to embody and to inhabit reality with both sides of our brain—with our most honest heart. I have long admired the artists (poets like Eugene Peterson and musicians like Bono) who have helped me on this journey of opening my whole self to God and others. Now that admiration extends to David Taylor, an artist and theologian, who nurtures knowledge of our unabridged personality and thereby disciples us to God by way of the psalms."

—**Todd Hunter,** Anglican bishop

"David Taylor's ambition is that our lives become psalms; that by reading and allowing ourselves to be shaped by the psalms in their powerful emotions, vivid imagery, and enthralling mystery, we should become what we read. I am confident that those who read Taylor's book will share that ambition and themselves become the songs of God."

—**Sam Wells,** vicar, St. Martin-in-the-Fields

"Passion and precision working together are always a powerful force. They served David, son of Jesse, well that ancient day on a battlefield facing Goliath—and they combine equally well here in David Taylor's inspiring new book. Taylor's obvious heart for the psalms, in tandem with his substantial knowledge of them, make him an ideal guide. With a brilliant combination of head and heart, he leads us to study these 150 songs with a fresh intensity—and then to sing them with a new resonance. I have always loved the psalms for their defiant devotion, their deep joy, and their brutal yet beautiful honesty. And after reading this fantastic book about them, I love them even more."

—**Matt Redman,** worship leader and songwriter

"Like the psalms themselves, this book invites us to speak honestly to God about what really matters in our own lives and in the world, and whether or not our words seem fit for church. David Taylor reads these biblical prayers with Dr. Seuss, rappers, and other poets, along with theologians and the daily news. His probing questions and practical suggestions guide readers in tracing out patterns of holy speech that have the potential for healing our hearts and our communities."

—**Ellen F. Davis,** Amos Ragan Kearns Distinguished Professor of Bible and Practical Theology, Duke Divinity School

"Passing on the torch handed to him by Eugene Peterson, David Taylor's *Open and Unafraid* is a gift to the next generation of pastors and leaders as a companion to a journey into the psalms. Honest, perceptive, pastoral, and emotively precise, David's writing takes us into the depth of mystery and charge that the psalms provide for us to come to know our Creator God."

—**Makoto Fujimura,** author of *Theology of Making*

"According to Ellen Davis, the psalms are 'the single best guide to the spiritual life.' Taylor shows us why. He heals and restores our emotions by baptizing us in the book that shaped the humanity of Christ and, as Taylor documents in a remarkable chapter, the church in its history."

—**Bruce Waltke,** professor emeritus of biblical studies, Regent College

"What a wonderful contribution! Dr. Taylor shares his insights as well as his life journey as he offers this rich, informative resource. This work will inspire those who are wondering how the psalms apply to real life, encourage small and large groups to engage the psalms with innovative exercises, and help make us, as Taylor writes, 'not just whole and holy but, by the Spirit, more deeply compassionate to our suffering neighbor.'"

—**Alexis D. Abernethy,** provost for faculty inclusion and equity, professor of clinical psychology, Fuller Theological Seminary

"David Taylor's lovely exploration of the psalms comes to life because he gives serious weight to them as poetry, song, and theology. The grand themes of the Psalter come to life under his careful gaze."

—**Maggi Dawn,** professor of theology and principal, St. Mary's College; assistant director of the Centre for Poetry and Poetics, Durham University

"This honest book is unafraid to tell the truth about human life before God as we see it exhibited in the psalms. It will be a guide for life but even more—it will give you life. It is a hopeful reminder that we have never been alone."

—**Luke A. Powery,** dean, Duke University Chapel; associate professor, Duke Divinity School

"Reading David Taylor is like spending time with an old friend. His writing is both wise and gentle, saturated with love for the biblical prayers that have sustained the life of the church. Like the psalms themselves, *Open and Unafraid* is a book to be savored, pondered, and lived with for years to come."

—**Melanie C. Ross,** associate professor of liturgical studies, Yale Divinity School and Yale Institute of Sacred Music

OPEN

AND

UNAFRAID

OPEN
AND
UNAFRAID

THE
PSALMS
AS A
GUIDE
TO LIFE

W. DAVID O. TAYLOR

NELSON
BOOKS

An Imprint of Thomas Nelson

Published in Nashville, Tennessee, by Nelson Books, an imprint of Thomas Nelson. Nelson Books and Thomas Nelson are registered trademarks of HarperCollins Christian Publishing, Inc.

The author is represented by Alive Literary Agency, 7680 Goddard Street, Suite 200, Colorado Springs, CO 80920, www.aliveliterary.com.

Thomas Nelson titles may be purchased in bulk for educational, business, fund-raising, or sales promotional use. For information, please e-mail SpecialMarkets@ThomasNelson.com.

Unless otherwise noted, Scripture quotations are taken from New Revised Standard Version Bible. Copyright © 1989 National Council of the Churches of Christ in the United States of America. Used by permission. All rights reserved.

Scripture quotations marked CEV are from the Contemporary English Version. Copyright © 1991, 1992, 1995 by American Bible Society. Used by permission.

Scripture quotations marked KJV are from the King James Version. Public domain.

Scripture quotations marked THE MESSAGE are from *The Message*. Copyright © by Eugene H. Peterson 1993, 1994, 1995, 1996, 2000, 2001, 2002. Used by permission of NavPress. All rights reserved. Represented by Tyndale House Publishers, Inc.

Scripture quotations marked NASB are from New American Standard Bible®. Copyright © 1960, 1962, 1963, 1968, 1971, 1972, 1973, 1975, 1977, 1995 by The Lockman Foundation. Used by permission. (www.Lockman.org)

Scripture quotations marked NCV are from the New Century Version®. © 2005 by Thomas Nelson. Used by permission. All rights reserved.

Scripture quotations marked NIV are from the Holy Bible, New International Version®, NIV®. Copyright © 1973, 1978, 1984, 2011 by Biblica, Inc.® Used by permission of Zondervan. All rights reserved worldwide. www.Zondervan.com. The "NIV" and "New International Version" are trademarks registered in the United States Patent and Trademark Office by Biblica, Inc.®

Scripture quotations marked NLT are from the Holy Bible, New Living Translation. © 1996, 2004, 2007, 2013, 2015 by Tyndale House Foundation. Used by permission of Tyndale House Publishers, Inc., Carol Stream, Illinois 60188. All rights reserved.

Any Internet addresses, phone numbers, or company or product information printed in this book are offered as a resource and are not intended in any way to be or to imply an endorsement by Thomas Nelson, nor does Thomas Nelson vouch for the existence, content, or services of these sites, phone numbers, companies, or products beyond the life of this book.

Library of Congress Cataloging-in-Publication Data

Names: Taylor, W. David O., 1972- author.
Title: Open and unafraid: the Psalms as a guide to life / W. David O. Taylor.
Description: Nashville, Tennessee: Nelson Books, an imprint of Thomas Nelson, [2019] | Includes bibliographical references. | Summary: "The creator of the groundbreaking film *The Psalms*, featuring Bono and Eugene Peterson, shows how the Psalms enable us to find a more transparent, resilient, and fearless life of faith"—Provided by publisher.
Identifiers: LCCN 2019027677 | ISBN 9781400210473 (hardcover) | ISBN 9781400210497 (ebook)
Subjects: LCSH: Bible. Psalms—Criticism, interpretation, etc. | Christian life—Biblical teaching. | Faith—Biblical teaching.
Classification: LCC BS1430.6.C43 T39 2019 | DDC 223/.206—dc23
LC record available at https://lccn.loc.gov/2019027677

Printed in the United States of America

20 21 22 23 24 LSC 10 9 8 7 6 5 4 3 2

To Eugene and Bono

CONTENTS

CONTENTS

FOREWORD

I was twelve years old when I discovered the Psalms. At the time, my family lived in Kalispell, Montana. My dad's butcher shop was thriving, and my parents decided to move across town to the east side, which is where all the important people lived. Kalispell is not a very big town, but it was segregated between east and west. In moving across town, I left all my friends. Not having any friends to play with, I bought a Bible. It was the first time I bought a Bible with my own money. I picked it up and started reading it. Somebody told me that the Psalms were important. So I started there.

But I soon became confused. I had grown up in a culture where every word of the Bible was the word of God *literally*. We were not supposed to mess around with it. As I read, though, that God keeps my tears in this bottle, that God is our rock, I thought, *C'mon! Really? This is how you talk about God?* After about two or three weeks of this, I was wholly confused. I thought, *I'm missing something.* Prior to this I had never heard the word *metaphor*. But I quickly learned what a metaphor was, not by knowing the meaning but by just observing what was going on in the Psalms.

I found that the Psalms were chock-full of metaphors: lions, snares, dirt, sun, shade, trees, mountain, lambs. Here I discovered a new way of language—a poetic language—that was imaginative and not literal in the narrow sense of that term. For people like me at twelve years old, the Psalms showed me that imagination was a way *to get inside the truth.* As I have often told my students, a metaphor is a verbal link between the invisible and the visible, between heaven and earth.

As metaphor users, poets tell us what our eyes and our ears often miss, around and within us. Poets use words to drag us into the depth of reality itself; they grab us by the jugular. Far from being cosmetic language, poetry is intestinal language. It's language that helps us to pray. As poetry, the Psalms rehabilitate the intimated imagination so it can grasp the enormous range of the Word of God. They bring us into the large country of God's creation and salvation.

Because they are the devotional poetry of a particular community, the Psalms train us to pray with others who have prayed, and are still praying. They put our knees on the level with other bent knees; they lift our hands in concert with other lifted hands. In the Psalms we join our voices in lament and praise with other voices who weep and laugh. The primary use of prayer, as the Psalter sees it, is not for expressing ourselves but in becoming ourselves, and we cannot do that alone. In praying the Psalms with others, then, we learn to become more and more ourselves in the company of the faithful.

By the end of the summer of 1944, I'd been through the Psalms three or four times. I've been doing it ever since, reading and praying my way through the Psalms. This is what I recommended to my students at Regent College. It is what David Taylor heard from me in class, some twenty years ago, and I am grateful to hear that he took my advice seriously. We cannot bypass the Psalms, as *Open and Unafraid* rightly argues. They are God's gift to train us in prayer that is comprehensive and honest.

Honesty is, of course, very hard to come by in our culture, but I learned how to pray honestly by translating the Psalms for what became *The Message* Bible. What we find in the Psalms is a gritty, no-nonsense honesty, which is why the Psalms are not pretty. They're not nice, but they're honest. And that's what you'll get in David Taylor's book:

a clear-eyed look at the honesty that the Psalms demand of us if we wish to live, as he puts it, open and unafraid—not hiding, not making excuses. It's the honesty to pray who we actually are, not who we think we should be.

As *Open and Unafraid* shows us through a combination of personal stories and careful exposition of Scripture, by praying the Psalms we do not escape the honest truth about our lives or the difficult and troubling truth about our families and cities. We do not get out of the difficult work of sin and forgiveness, of suffering and mortality. We get further into it. Instead of finding our life easier, we find it more demanding. Yet this also becomes the occasion of God's work of making us whole and holy. This is the business of the Psalms. This is also the business of David's book.

With a winsome spirit, David invites us to see the Psalms as necessary—necessary to the life of faith, necessary to our humanity, necessary for learning how to live in the world and how to love God with all our heart, mind, soul, and strength. This is an invitation that we should take seriously, because there is a grace that we will experience in doing so—the grace to bring all of our life to Jesus, in whom the prayers of the psalmists have been fulfilled.

David Taylor has written a very fine book that deserves a wide hearing. *Open and Unafraid* is a book that you will want to read and read again, and yet again, in order to discover the wisdom of the Psalms that shows us how to walk in the life-giving way of Jesus.

Eugene Peterson

INTRODUCTION

A journey through the psalms is the journey of the life of faith.

—Denise Dombkowski Hopkins[1]

The psalms illuminate the mind for the purpose of enkindling the soul, indeed to put it to fire. It may indeed be said that the purpose of the Psalms is to turn the soul into a sort of burning bush.

—Stanley Jaki[2]

Take Up and Read

In the spring of 1996, I took a course titled "Biblical Spirituality" at Regent College, a seminary in Vancouver, British Columbia. The course was taught by the pastor and author Eugene Peterson. In this course, Peterson offered an exposition of the Bible as it intersected church history, theology, poetry, literature, and Greek mythology. It was a spellbinding experience for us as students, hearing him weave together these seemingly disparate fields into a beautiful and coherent vision of the Christian life.

Not once, however, did he offer his students advice, practical or otherwise.

Anybody who is familiar with Peterson's teaching and writing knows he is particularly allergic to how-tos. He rarely tells his readers how to preach, how to witness, how to start a church, or how to lead. At the time a young man, I was unfamiliar with this habit of his and felt myself becoming increasingly frustrated. What exactly were we to *do* with all this insight into what Peterson liked to call "the large country of salvation"?

On the last class of the semester, at the end of the three-hour session, it dawned on me that Peterson had no intention of giving us any practical help to enact his vision of biblical spirituality. I raised my hand. "Dr. Peterson," I said. "This has been a very rich experience. Thank you. I have no idea, however, what to do with it. Could you help us? Could you tell us one thing that we could do, practically speaking, with this scriptural vision that you've presented to us?"

After thinking for a rather longish moment, Peterson answered in his characteristically quiet, gravelly voice. His answer, I felt, was deceptively simple. He said, "Tomorrow, David, read Psalm 1. The next day, read Psalm 2. The day after, read Psalm 3. When you get to the end, start over. Thank you, and good night."

That was it. And that's precisely what I did. The next morning I read Psalm 1. The morning after that I read Psalm 2. And on I went. I read the psalms, one a day, and kept up the habit for several years. In time I found that it slowly changed the way I saw my Christian faith. The language of the psalms began to saturate my sense of self, my understanding of God, my ideas about prayer and worship, and my notion of Scripture and a faithful life.

On the Sunday afternoon of April 19, 2015, nearly twenty years after that exchange in a classroom in western Canada, I found myself sitting across from Peterson and U2's front man, Bono, in the town of Lakeside, Montana. Over the course of an hour-long conversation, I explored ways in which the psalms had shaped their lives and work.

Three months later, on July 29, I found myself in a gallery space in New York City to interview Bono a second time and hear him talk about how the psalms had helped him make sense of art, suffering, mortality, and death.

The result of these two interviews was a twenty-minute short film, directed by Nathan Clarke of Fourth Line Films, and produced by Fuller Studio.[3] Published on April 26, 2016, it has been viewed, to date, more than a million times on YouTube. As I had explained to both Peterson and Bono in our original exploration of the project, my goals were twofold.

My first goal was that audiences of the film would encounter the God of the psalms as a God of healing, justice, grace, goodness, holiness, mercy, and love. My second goal was that people might be inspired to read or pray the psalms for themselves as a way to understand why Christians across time and space, across all denominations and walks of life, have read the psalms and found them to be singularly formative for their faith.

My hope remains the same with this book.

THE HOPE OF THIS BOOK

I've written this book so readers would become excited to embrace a prayer book that has been deeply influential, not just for Jesus and the apostles and for monastic and cathedral practices of prayer but also for the hymns of the Reformation, the spirituals of African American slaves, and the songs of the global church. My hope is that church leaders and laypersons, and even seekers and "nones" (those claiming no religion), would understand that they are never alone in their sorrows, angers, doubts, joys, thanksgivings, or questions about life and death.

Likewise I hope that teachers and students might become curious as to why such a great variety of people throughout the centuries have loved the words of the Psalter: from Saint Augustine to Johann

Sebastian Bach, from the Rastafarians to the Wesleyans, from C. S. Lewis to Charles Spurgeon, from John Milton to Ann Weems, from football players to basketball coaches, and from presidents to creators of movies, such as Peter Weir (*The Truman Show*) and Clint Eastwood (*Pale Rider*).

It would additionally give me great pleasure if readers across ecclesial and cultural lines uncovered in these holy poems the character of a God who meets us as Good Shepherd and Just Judge, as a powerful God of Angel Armies and a comforting God of Refuge. I would hope that readers might explore, for themselves and with others, a life of faith that enables them to be honest to God, and that they would discover afresh, or perhaps for the first time, the heart of the Christian faith.

I should also add, perhaps, that my secret hope is that readers themselves would hear the gentle, encouraging words of Eugene Peterson to take up and read the psalms, one after the other, and find themselves at home with God, from whom no secrets are hidden; each of us is standing alongside saints and sinners, walking with both the faithful and the faithless, open and unafraid, because we all have been marked by the steadfast love of God.

And because the Scriptures encourage us to be not only hearers of the Word but also doers, and because our transformation comes when we have embodied and enacted the good words of the Word, not just read and thought about them, I have included a series of questions and exercises, along with a prayer, at the end of each chapter to put into practice the words of the psalms. My hope is that individuals and groups, even entire communities, might take full advantage of this part of the book.

THE SHAPE OF THIS BOOK

While there are many themes I am not able to explore in this book, my hope is that the themes I do explore offer both a panoramic vision of the Psalter and a detailed view of significant aspects of the landscape of the psalms. Starting with a chapter on the theme of "Honesty," I argue that honesty is the only way we can receive the greatest benefit from the psalms. Standing before a gracious God and before trusted others, without secrets, fully vulnerable, is the way to be made holy, whole, and wholly alive.

In the chapter that follows, on "Community," I show how honesty and community are deeply linked to each other in the psalms, and how it is practically impossible to be truly open and unafraid apart from a community that has fully embraced the grace of God. As the psalms see it, each of us finds our place in the world of faith within the "assembly" of God's people, and in the "company" of friends and neighbors, who keep choosing by grace to remain honest to God and fully honest with one another.

In the three chapters that follow, I introduce the reader to a few basics: a short "History" of the church's use of the psalms over the past two thousand years; a way in which the psalms teach us how to pray by *showing* us "Prayer," which is to say, how to talk to God and how to listen to God; and a brief account of the poetic nature of the psalms as a way to help us understand that we encounter God *through* the wonderful world of "Poetry," not beyond it, nor despite it.

In subsequent chapters I explore a range of themes that come in threes and twos. A triad of chapters—on "Sadness," "Anger," and "Joy"—shows us what it means to be emotionally whole in the presence of God, as well as emotionally healthy in the company of God's people. A collection of chapters that come in pairs—"Enemies" and "Justice," "Death" and "Life," "Nations" and "Creation"—shows us what it means to be faithful to God in the personal and public dimensions of our lives.

In the concluding chapter I suggest that the psalms invite us to pray the words of the Psalter with Jesus and in Jesus' name and in the company of those who follow in the way of Jesus, so that the words might open up a space in our hearts to give and receive the steadfast love of God.

Because I am a theologian by profession and an ordained pastor by the good will of God and the confirmation of God's people, it is impossible for me to read the psalms without seeing Christ in them: on the one hand, how Christ sees them, prays them, and understands his ministry in the light of them,[4] and, on the other hand, how Christians throughout the centuries have perceived the voice of Christ in them as well as how Christ fulfills them, just as he himself said to his disciples in Luke 24:44.[5]

This does not mean that I ignore the historical, literary, or canonical context for the psalms. Understanding these things is essential to a faithful reading of them. But it is equally faithful, I would like to believe, to read the psalms Christologically—that is, through Jesus' eyes. So I end each chapter with a short reflection on how Jesus relates to each theme: to praise as much as to lament, to enemies as much as to justice, to both life and death, to both nations and creation.

WHAT THIS BOOK IS NOT

Because there is such a great variety of books on the Psalms, it may be helpful to state what this book is not. This book is not an introduction to the Psalms (other books do that task quite well and I recommend them to you).[6] This book does not address matters such as questions of authorship, the original liturgical use of psalms, or the variety of forms of psalms (royal psalms, wisdom psalms, historical psalms, and the rest).

Nor does this book presume to settle the debates of biblical scholars, for example, on the historical backdrop for certain psalms, or engage in the lengthy exposition of a psalm text, though I do attempt to give a close reading of a text here and there. This is not because I think these tasks are unimportant, but because for the purposes of this book they would become too distracting. There are also certain elements in the psalms, such as the idea of communal pilgrimage or the centrality of Zion, that remain submerged by the topics I choose to explore.

While I include a range of Bible translations in my explorations of specific psalms, I use the NRSV as my standard translation, and I make extensive use of Peterson's THE MESSAGE translation as a way to help readers *feel* the psalms in ways the other translations may not do. Though much may be lost in translation from the original Hebrew language, I have tried where possible to capture the idea or sense of the psalmic language to help the reader understand it "from the inside," as it were.

Similar to Eugene Peterson's *Answering God*, this book explores particular themes that run across the psalms. And while I have tried to capture a comprehensive vision of the psalms, I have not attempted to be exhaustive about it. Lastly, although I focus on the formative power of the psalms, for both individuals and communities, my hope is that pastors and worship leaders might be inspired to explore ways in which the psalms could be more thoroughly incorporated into their congregational life and worship.

IN THE END: A WAY

The Psalter opens with an invitation to the reader to walk on the way, the faithful way, the way that leads to life. The Psalter closes with an invitation to the reader to join all creation in praise. In the pages in between, the Psalter shows us both how to walk in this way and with whom we walk. We walk in faith alongside the people of God. We walk in hope in the sight of a watching world. And we walk, with our hearts open, before the face of a gracious God.

We walk this way, in the end, with Jesus himself, for whom these psalms are his heart song. And like Jesus, we read and sing and pray the psalms along "the way" (Ps. 1:6; Mark 8:27). With Jesus and with the help of the Spirit of God, we read and sing and pray the psalms, trusting that they will open up a space in our hearts to give and receive the steadfast love of God, from whom no secrets are hidden. And with Jesus, we, too, would confess the words of Psalm 19:7–8:

> The revelation of GOD is whole
>   and pulls our lives together.
> The signposts of GOD are clear
>   and point out the right road.
> The life-maps of GOD are right,
>   showing the way to joy.
>
> (THE MESSAGE)

1

HONESTY

The Psalms as script for the telling of secrets is fully occupied by honest women and men of faith.

—WALTER BRUEGGEMANN[1]

We must speak honestly—but also wisely.

—ELLEN DAVIS[2]

HONEST TO GOD

In February 1995, I confessed my sins publicly in front of five hundred fellow students at the University of Texas in Austin. This took place at a concert of prayer sponsored by a parachurch campus ministry. Standing on the auditorium stage of a large classroom, I confessed the sins of lust, pride, impatience, anger, and others I have now forgotten. While I had previously confessed my sins to a pastor or a group of friends, I had never confessed my sins publicly. (It *is* rather terrifying.) As part of a worship and prayer service, the invitation to confess our sins had offered us a chance to be free from the secrets that distort and oppress us.

Everyone, of course, has a secret of one sort or another. Every family and every community and every country has its secrets too. For some it is an addictive behavior. For others it is an abusive or traumatic experience that may only intensify feelings of shame. For still others it is the fear of being rejected, the lust for power, an uncontrollable temper, emotional infidelity, a vicious prejudice, a program of terror, an insatiable jealousy of others, repeated acts of self-indulgence, or something else.

Whatever they may be, with our secrets we hide. We hide from others and we hide from ourselves. Ultimately, we hide from God. In our hiding, we choose darkness over light; we embrace death instead of life; we elect to be lonely rather than to be relationally at home with others. And the certain result of all our hiding is that we become cut off from our Source of life, strangers to ourselves, and alienated from creation, which, in the end, is pathetic, disfiguring, and an utterly tragic loss of life.

The Psalms understand the human condition. In it we see a mirror of humanity at its best and at its worst. We see our very selves reflected back, "be he a faithful soul or be he a sinner" as Athanasius once described the experience of looking at the psalms, as if in a mirror of the soul.[3] Walter Brueggemann writes that the Psalter "is an articulation of all the secrets of the human heart and the human community, all voiced out loud in speech and in song to God amidst the community."[4]

If we are to be free, Brueggemann argues, our secrets must be told. If we wish to flourish in our God-given calling, our secrets must be brought into the light so we are no longer governed by their corrosive and destructive power. And if we desire to be truly human, we must abandon all our efforts not just to hide our secrets but also to justify them. This is what the psalms help us to do: to tell our secrets faithfully.

To share our secrets with another person naturally requires a great deal of courage. It requires an ability to trust others in ways that few of us feel safe to do. And to tell our secrets to the community requires an extraordinary ability to believe that it will not take advantage of our vulnerable disclosure—by judging us unfairly, by rejecting us, or by gossiping about us—and that we will not be undone by our confession. To be this brave and to trust this readily is a gift that God would willingly give us, if we but asked.

To be open and unafraid with God in the manner that is modeled for us in the psalms is to counter the devastating effects of our primordial sin. When Adam and Eve sinned, their first impulse was to hide. In making clothes for themselves, they hid their bodies. When they heard the sound of their Maker's voice, they hid from God. In their telltale lies, they hid from the truth, and in their mutual accusations, they hid from each other. All the ways in which Adam and Eve hid resulted in one thing: their dehumanization.

Like Adam and Eve, when we hide from God, we become alienated from God and thus spend our strength trying to transcend life's limits: death, dependence, moral laws, God-given boundaries. When we hide from others, we cut ourselves off from the life-giving gift of community. When we hide from creation, we deny our God-ordained creaturely nature and often seek to exploit rather than to care for creation. And when we hide from ourselves, we become strangers to ourselves through selfish, self-indulgent behavior that ultimately does violence to our nature as humans made in God's image.

What the psalms offer us is a powerful aid to un-hide: to stand honestly before God without fear, to face one another vulnerably without shame, and to encounter life in the world without any of the secrets that would demean and distort our humanity. The psalms, then, are for those who know that they spend much of their life hiding secrets; they are also for those who know that standing in the presence of God "is the one place where such secrets cannot and must not be hidden."[5]

The psalms invite us, thus, to stand in the light, to see ourselves truly and to receive the reformative work of God through the formative words of the psalmist, so that we might be rehumanized in Christ.

The Honesty of the Psalms

Psalm 139 is the paradigmatic psalm of the honest person. There is nothing the psalmist hides from God. He invites God to see it all. "You have looked deep into my heart, Lord, and you know all about me" (v. 1 CEV). It is a cleansing and healing self-disclosure. To be known by God in this way, through and through, nothing hidden (v. 15), nothing excused (v. 23), is beyond the psalmist's capacity to fully grasp. "It is more than I can understand," he says (v. 6 NCV). As the poet Laurance Wieder translates verses 1–3:

> *Look in:*
> *My soul is glass*
> *To you, no vein*
> *Or bone unseen,*
> *But you know*
> *All I pass through,*
> *All I do, ahead*
> *Or inside me,*
> *Before I do.*[6]

It is only in standing open before God in this way, naked like a baby and unashamed as the beloved of God (vv. 13–16), that the psalmist discovers his truest identity. "I praise you, for I am fearfully and wonderfully made" (v. 14). In the psalmist's waking hours and asleep at night, the Lord is there (vv. 2–3). No height, no depth, not the darkest night, not a secret thought, neither heaven nor hell, can hide the psalmist from the Lord's searching gaze (vv. 8–12). He cannot escape the Lord's presence (v. 7).

Nor does he wish to. The psalmist feels as precious as all the Lord's thoughts toward him (v. 17). He is secure in the Lord's sovereign care (v. 16). All the days of his life are seen by God. It is for that reason that the psalmist welcomes the (often terrifying) searching gaze of God. "Investigate my life, O God, find out everything about me;

cross-examine and test me, get a clear picture of what I'm about" (v. 23 THE MESSAGE). This is similar to the language we find in Psalm 17:1–3:

> Listen while I build my case, GOD,
>> the most honest prayer you'll ever hear.
> Show the world I'm innocent—
>> in your heart you know I am.
> Go ahead, examine me from inside out,
>> surprise me in the middle of the night—
> You'll find I'm just what I say I am.
>> My words don't run loose.
>
> (THE MESSAGE)

To what end does the psalmist pray in this manner? It is so he might walk in the life-giving "way," echoing the words of Psalm 1.

To walk in this "way everlasting" is to walk in the way that leads to wholeness. We walk it by, among other things, praying in the manner that the psalms model for us: "prayer that is comprehensive (not patched together from emotional fragments scattered around that we chance upon) and honest (not a series of more or less sincere verbal poses that we think might please our Lord)."[7] Said otherwise, to pray the psalms is to pray ourselves *into* wholeness.[8] How exactly do we become whole in this way?

We become whole by praying our honest joys and our honest sorrows. We pray our honest praise *of* God and our honest anger *at* God; we pray also for honest speech in our words *to* God. With the psalmist we pray that God will protect our tongues from deceit (Ps. 34:13). We pray that we not sin with our words (Ps. 39:1). We pray that we resist the urge to gossip and flatter (Ps. 12:3), and that we choose to live with integrity (Ps. 41:12), rejecting words that both inflate and deflate us before God (Ps. 32).

To pray in this way is to keep ourselves open to others and to God. In refusing the temptation to hide from others and from God, we refuse the temptation to use words as a cover-up.[9] We speak instead plainly, trustingly. When we do this, we find ourselves praying freely to God, in a way that *frees* us. The Psalter understands that we do not often succeed at this kind of speech and prayer, and so it repeatedly welcomes the penitent to confess to God, in the hearing of God's people:

> Happy are those whose transgression is forgiven,
>> whose sin is covered.
> Happy are those to whom the LORD imputes no iniquity,
>> and in whose spirit there is no deceit.
>
> (Ps. 32:1–2)

The psalmist describes the experience of "keeping silent" about sin as a kind of disintegration. His bones turn to powder (Ps. 32:3). His energy dissipates, "the very pith of my body decomposed as if baked in the summer heat."[10] He risks returning to the dust (Ps. 22:15). But when he honestly confesses his sin—"Not holding back, not denying, not making excuses"—the Lord forgives him.[11] Instead of "covering up" his sin, God covers his sin (Ps. 32:1, 5), and instead of hiding from God, God becomes his "hiding place." The poet-priest Jim Cutter captures this idea in his translation of Psalm 32:

> *Even in times of overwhelming distress,*
> *With the thunder and force of waters in flood,*
> *Your grace is for me like a temple of rock,*
> *Standing firm in the face of the powers,*
> *Ordering the discord and chaos within,*
> *Preserving my life from utter destruction.*
> *In the eye of the storm I hear the whisper of mercy,*
> *The peace of those who are completely forgiven.*[12]

If honesty is the capacity to speak truthfully to God, sincerely to others, and without any lie about the world in its real condition, then the psalms invite us to honest prayer about all things, not just the things we suffer or regret. We pray honestly about our shame and bouts of depression (Ps. 88).[13] We pray honestly about our hate (Ps. 137).[14] And we pray honestly about our experiences of trust and thanksgiving and joy (Pss. 23; 46; 27; 91).[15]

We pray honestly about God's trustworthy character, the wonder of creation (Ps. 104), the beauty of *torah* (Ps. 119), and the virtue of wisdom (Pss. 37; 49; 112). We pray it all, as Peterson encourages us:

> It is easy to be honest before God with our hallelujahs; it is somewhat more difficult to be honest in our hurts; it is nearly impossible to be honest before God in the dark emotions of our hate. So we commonly suppress our negative emotions (unless, neurotically, we advertise them). Or, when we do express them, we do it far from the presence, or what we think is the presence, of God, ashamed or embarrassed to be seen in these curse-stained bib overalls. But when we pray the psalms, these classic prayers of God's people, we find that will not do. We must pray who we actually are, not who we think we should be.[16]

When we pray the psalms by the empowering and transforming presence of the Holy Spirit, we pray not just who we actually are but also who we *can be* and *shall be* by grace. As Athanasius sees it, the psalms not only enable us to be wholly ourselves before God, they also enable us to be wholly our true selves. This is only possible, he argues, because Christ himself makes it possible. Before coming among us, Athanasius writes, Christ sketched the likeness of true humanity for us in the psalms. In praying them, then, we experience the healing and reformation of our humanity.[17]

The good news for the follower of Jesus is that the decision to be honest to God, which the psalms require of us, does not result in *self-absorption* because we have become obsessed with the cross-examination of our heart and mind. Nor does it result in *self-hatred* because we feel that our sin has the last and most definitive word on our life. Grace has the last word, not sin, as the German theologian Karl Barth rightly reminds us. No matter how great our fault or failure, we cannot sin apart from the grace of God.

"We are forbidden," Barth writes, "to take sin more seriously than grace, or even as seriously as grace."[18] Why? Because God in Christ does not take sin more seriously than grace, even if it remains true that God takes sin with deadly seriousness. We can be honest to God about the best and worst parts of our human condition, because we know that the grace of God precedes our honest confessions, the grace of God undergirds our honest thanksgivings, and the grace of God follows our honest laments.

What happens when we pray the psalms under the light of God's grace? We become free to pray with abandonment because we have abandoned ourselves to *this* gracious God.[19] We have no need to hide from this God, because we are so confident in his grace. And because Jesus comes to us "full of grace and truth" (John 1:14), we can be confident that we shall be found and filled with grace. We, too, can pray daring prayers because we trust that Jesus himself prays them with us and in us by the power of his Holy Spirit.[20]

CONCLUSION

To this day I regret that I failed to keep the piece of paper on which I had written the eleven sins I had originally confessed to both friends and strangers at the University of Texas. I also regret the failure of courage that I experience repeatedly in my resistance to honestly confess my faults. It is for that reason that I return again and again to the psalms. The psalms show me how to be honest to God. They retrain me to be honest with God's people, and they remind me how deeply good it feels to be this open, unafraid, and free.

"The Psalms make it possible," writes John Goldingay, "to say things that are otherwise unsayable. In church, they have the capacity to free us to talk about things that we cannot talk about anywhere else."[21] Ellen Davis says something similar when she writes that the psalms "enable us to bring into our conversation with God feelings and thoughts most of us think we need to get rid of before God will be interested in hearing from us."[22] N. T. Wright offers this general word of encouragement:

> The Psalms are inexhaustible, and deserve to be read, said, sung, chanted, whispered, learned by heart, and even shouted from the rooftops. They express all the emotions we are ever likely to feel (including some we hope we may not), and they lay them, raw and open, in the presence of God.[23]

The psalms welcome all such honest speech in order that we might encounter the "life that really is life" (1 Tim. 6:19). If the common saying within recovery ministries is true, that we are only as sick as the secrets we keep, then the secrets we keep result in the deterioration of our humanity. Kept hidden, our secrets rob us of vitality. But when they are brought into the gracious light of God, they no longer hold a destructive power over us, and a space is made for God, who "knows the secrets of the heart," to rehumanize us (Ps. 44:21).

One of the great benefits of the psalms, Athanasius believed, is that in reading them "you learn about yourself."[24] You see all your failures and recoveries, all your ups and downs. You see yourself as both a saint and a sinner. But the psalms are not only interested in helping us to be open and unafraid before God; they also help us to be open and unafraid with the people of God: vulnerable, porous, freed, fully alive.[25] And in seeing ourselves in this way, honestly, with others, we find ourselves being reformed by the love of God.

There is a reason why honesty and community are deeply linked to each other in the Psalms—and in this book as well. It is virtually impossible to be honest in the way the Psalter invites us to be apart from a community that has fully embraced the grace of God. Likewise, a community that refuses to be honest to God, from whom no secrets are hid, cannot fully live out the faith, hope, and love that the Psalter invites us to inhabit in the name of the one who opens the way to the Father and who generously gives us the Spirit so that we might live without fear.

> But me he caught—reached all the way
> from sky to sea; he pulled me out
> Of that ocean of hate, that enemy chaos,
> the void in which I was drowning.
> They hit me when I was down,
> but GOD stuck by me.
> He stood me up on a wide-open field;
> I stood there saved—surprised to be loved!
>
> (Ps. 18:16–19 THE MESSAGE)

QUESTIONS FOR REFLECTION

1. What things in your life can you be honest about relatively easily? What things are more difficult for you to be honest about?

2. In what ways have your family or community or culture shaped your thinking about honesty—with God or with others? What specific factors in your life make it difficult for you to be open and unafraid?

3. Some of us are people-pleasers, while others of us are utterly indifferent to how people perceive them. For both types, in their own ways, it is difficult to be honest. Assuming you might be somewhere on this spectrum, how might you counter this impulse to hide from others?

4. What are you afraid will happen if you are fully honest to God and with others? What feelings rise in you when you think about no longer hiding from God or from others?

5. What things would help you become honest, vulnerable, porous, and unafraid before God and others? What secrets would the

psalmist invite you to bring openly to God as a trusted friend? What hope or healing might a confession of these secrets to God bring to your life?

6. How do the psalms help you understand the difference between true honesty on the one hand, and self-absorption and self-hatred on the other?

7. What is your response to Karl Barth's comment that we are forbidden to take sin more seriously than grace, or even as seriously as grace, because God in Christ does not take sin more seriously than grace? In what ways have you taken sin too seriously or not seriously enough? In what ways have you taken grace not seriously enough?

EXERCISES

1. Read Psalm 32 or 51. Read it several times. Meditate on it. Pray through it. Consider memorizing a portion of it to carry in your heart as a way to maintain a lively conversation with God throughout the day.

2. Start a journal in which you share your thoughts and feelings with God in a fully honest manner. You may wish to keep this journal to yourself or to discuss it regularly with a trusted, mature, and candid friend. Or you may simply wish to go for a walk and talk honestly to God, instead of writing it down.

3. Adopt a regular practice of confession of sin. This could be done with a pastor or a spiritual director, or it could be done with a friend. And if your community does not already practice it, consider including the regular practice of confession into your corporate worship and giving sufficient time for people to hear the voice of God during their confession.

4. Try doing the Ignatian Prayer of Examen on a regular basis. This includes five things: (1) becoming aware of God's presence, asking

God to bring clarity and understanding to the day's events; (2) reviewing the day with gratitude, trusting that God is present to the details of the day; (3) paying attention to your emotions, trusting that God will speak to you through these emotions; (4) choosing one feature of the day and praying from it, allowing the Holy Spirit to draw from your heart whatever prayer is most necessary for the moment; and (5) looking toward tomorrow, trusting that Christ will be your Good Shepherd who protects and provides for you.

5. As a community, read Psalm 72 several times in several translations and discuss your responses. Consider also praying and singing the words of Psalm 139 together.

6. As a community, choose one person to read Psalm 32 two verses at a time. After each pair of verses, have the group respond with the words, "In your mercy, oh Lord, hear our prayer." At the end of this exercise, take a healthy moment of silence to allow the Holy Spirit to speak to you.

PRAYER

"As I praise you, great God, help me to be both personal and honest. I do not want to parrot generalities I have heard from others, but to witness to your saving help in my life, in Jesus' name. Amen."[26]

2

COMMUNITY

An estimated half of people aged 75 and over live alone—about two million people across England—with many saying they can go days, even weeks, with no social interaction at all.

—BBC News[1]

The psalmist could not see himself as an individual apart from Israel. His self-identity was bound up in his participation in the community of faith.

—C. Hassell Bullock[2]

ONE IS THE LONELIEST NUMBER

"I'm so sorry you were so alone." These are words that many of us at some point in our life have wanted somebody to say to us.[3] For some of us, this experience of aloneness has involved a moment in our life, perhaps during childhood when our parents divorced or in our teenage years when we felt confused about our place within society. For others, the experience of aloneness is something we have felt in our adulthood when, presumably, we should have already figured things out.

When my family moved to the US from Guatemala in 1985, I found myself without any friends. Going into the eighth grade in North Shore Chicago, it felt like I had moved from one cultural galaxy to its opposite: from warm to cold, from emotionally open to emotionally restrained, and from physically expressive to physically muted. At thirteen years old I had no clue how American kids were supposed to behave. I frequently felt nervous and was afraid I would do the wrong thing.

When I said or did something culturally ignorant, I got teased. Being tenderhearted, I cried a lot and that got me teased even more. I visited twenty youth groups in one year and hated every one of them. I felt lonely and disoriented and misunderstood, and I sorely missed my friends back in Guatemala City. Looking back on that period of life, I think of the words that are commonly attributed to Mother Teresa: the most terrible poverty is loneliness, and the feeling of being unloved.

Far more people than we might imagine suffer from loneliness. According to a 2018 CIGNA study, loneliness in America has reached "epidemic" levels.[4] After surveying twenty thousand adults, researchers found that 46 percent felt alone either sometimes or always, 47 percent felt left out, and 27 percent rarely or never felt as though there were people who really understood them. As a point of comparison, the percentage of Americans who reported feeling frequently lonely was between 11 and 20 percent in the 1970s and 1980s.[5]

Chronic loneliness not only results in physical and mental disorders, but it also increases the odds of early death. And it's not something that only Americans experience. Governments from Denmark to Japan have taken loneliness as a serious societal problem. In 2018, the United Kingdom's prime minister appointed a Minister of Loneliness to address what was felt to be a serious health issue. Approximately two million people over the age of 75 across England reported going weeks without any meaningful social interaction.[6] The World Health

Organization now lists the lack of "social support networks" as a deter-minant of health.[7]

LONELINESS AND THE LIFE OF FAITH

Life apart from deep communal life is bad for our health precisely because God did not mean for us to live apart from meaningful com-munity. The Psalter reflects this. It shows us how the life of faith always takes place before the face of the community. This is the terrifyingly good news of the psalms: the community sees it all; it *gets* to see it all.

For the psalmist, the "assembly," the "congregation," the "people," one's "neighbors" and "friends" are always close at hand.[8] There is no hiding from the community; there is in fact no *need* to hide, even if the temptation to hide is always close at hand. The community gets to bear witness to one's praise and one's protest. The community gets to hear one's heartfelt petitions and full-throated thanksgivings. The commu-nity gets to help us be open and unafraid.

More significantly, the community gets to hear the pleas of one's heart far more often than it hears the words of trust or thanksgiving, not because the latter don't matter—they do, very much so—but because the former, the petitions, are what we, like the Israelites, pray often. We don't always see the answers to our prayers.[9] Yet we still pray, and we pray knowing that the community is with us, around us, supporting us, bearing witness to us that we are not alone.

Said more generally, there is no such thing as a modern individ-ualist in the psalms. It is a fundamentally communal book where individuals find their place in the world of faithfulness and faithless-ness within the context of the community. It's "me" in the context of "us"; *their* sins are *our* sins (Ps. 85). It's the "I" because of the "we"; *I* rejoice because *we* rejoice (Ps. 106). It's "my whole heart" with the community, not apart from it, not on the margins of it; *my* lot is bound up in *y'all's* lot (Ps. 111).

Eugene Peterson says it this way:

> We often imagine, wrongly, that the psalms are private compositions prayed by a shepherd, traveler, or fugitive. Close study shows that all of them are corporate: all were prayed by and in the community. . . . It goes against the whole spirit of the psalms to take these communal laments, these congregational praises, these corporate intercessions and use them as cozy formulas for private solace.[10]

For the psalmist there is no autonomous spirituality. There is only a faith that is lived in the company of God's people. This includes those who have come before us as well as those who will follow after (Ps. 78). It's a faith that we have "heard and known" (v. 3), and a faith that "we will tell to the coming generation" (v. 4). Faith happens *with* people (Ps. 40), it happens *in presence of* the "nations" (Ps. 18), and it happens *in front of* all of creation (Ps. 89).

How else might the Psalms shape our vision of community? And how might such a vision of community life inform our faith in practice?

A Psalmic Vision of Community

Psalms 1 and 2 establish a vision for the individual and the community in the Psalter. Here the personal and the social become the ground upon which a life of faith is established. Whereas Psalm 1 opens with a beatitude ("Blessed is the one"), Psalm 2 closes with a beatitude ("Blessed are all"). This signals to the reader that everything that lies inside these two psalms functions like a kind of a frame. It's as if the psalmist were saying, "You get this picture right and you will get the whole Psalter right."

In Psalm 1 the individual is blessed because he rejects the way of the wicked and embraces the way of the righteous.[11] He is blessed, specifically, because he delights in the teaching (*torah*) of Yahweh and refuses the path of the *self*-absorbed. These are two ways of living, two ways of walking, two ways of being in the world. Psalm 1, then, establishes for us the importance of the individual: my prayers matter, my feckless faith and my steadfast faith matter to God, my walking in the ways of Yahweh matters.

But I am not self-sufficient. I do not determine my own worth. God does supremely, but so does the community. Psalm 2, therefore, is a word to the whole community. The community is blessed who trusts the Lord, who trusts the Lord's anointed ruler, who seeks the Lord, who draws near and keeps *torah*, and whose hope is in the Lord. Communities include nations and rulers and cities. They include geopolitical machinations, socioeconomic realignments, family dynamics, and military engagements.

Psalm 2 reminds us that "my" faith always exists in relation to "our" faith. It reminds us that faith is always played out—tested and tried, confirmed and strengthened—on a communal, social, and public stage. In Psalm 1 we encounter the righteous individual. In Psalm 2 it is the righteous king who establishes God's good purposes for all. Faith is mine most certainly, but it is also for *all* "who take refuge in him" (Ps. 2:12), for *all* "who fear the LORD, both small and great" (Ps. 115:13).

Such is the blessed individual. Such also is the blessed community.

In the psalms, a person finds her place within a particular community, not a generic community. This community is marked by tribes and families, by friends and strangers alike. In fact, there is no other way to discover one's identity. This is an important difference between the Psalter's idea of the self and our modern Western idea. Mays explains that difference this way:

> To say "I" meant to speak of one's group as well as one's person. We bring our identity to a group, differentiate ourselves within it, join it, accept its ways and opinions, expect the group to nurture the individual and to justify itself to the individual.[12]

Put more colloquially, "there is no 'I' in team." The personal never devolves to the purely idiosyncratic. Nor do individuals discover their identity in opposition to tradition, to the ways of their fathers and mothers, to the "ancient times" (Ps. 68:33 NASB). Faith is not an individualist transaction between God and me. From the perspective of the psalms, the life of faith involves plenty of personal experiences, but they are never a matter of mere private experiences. Goldingay comments:

> It is unthinkable that expressing gratitude to God should be a private transaction between individuals and God. Thanksgiving is an inherently public act whereby one gives glory to God in the presence of the community for some act, and invites the community as a whole to have its faith built up.[13]

In practical terms, "your" experience of joy was bound up in "all y'all's" experience of joy; "my" sinful actions implicated "our" sinful status as a people; and if the psalmist "was delivered from his troubles and Israel was not, it would be only a partial deliverance."[14]

One of the most painful things for the psalmist is to be abandoned by a friend. We see this repeatedly throughout the psalms: being betrayed or left alone by a friend. Psalm 38:11 says, "My friends and companions stand aloof from my affliction." Psalm 41:9 adds, "Even my bosom friend in whom I trusted, who ate of my bread, has lifted the heel against me." Psalm 88:18 puts it most poignantly: "You have caused friend and neighbor to shun me; my companions are in darkness."

With our friends we say, *I choose you,* because we like the same things, think the same ways, and talk about God similarly. That's why the rejection of a friend is so painful; it's why the hurt caused by a friend feels irreparable. But it's also a friend to whom we can freely confess our sins. It's a friend whom we first choose to tell our good news. Psalm 22:22 says, "Here's the story I'll tell my friends when they come to worship, and punctuate it with Hallelujahs: Shout Hallelujah, you God-worshipers" (THE MESSAGE).

Some of us, as Psalm 107 sees it, have wandered in wastelands, while others have sat in darkness; some have become fools, while others have gone out on the sea in ships; still others are at their wits' end, feeling numb and shut down. Any of these experiences becomes unbearable if we have to bear it alone. But the psalmist shows us that all of it is bearable because the community bears it with us. It's not just for the psalmist to bear alone. Stanley Hauerwas offers this perspective:

> Friendship, if it is the friendship of God, is to be characterized by fidelity in which you are even willing to tell the friend the truth. Which may mean you will risk the friendship. You need to be in that kind of community to survive the loneliness that threatens all of our souls.[15]

We choose our friends, but we do not choose our congregation. This is an additional insight that the Psalter offers to the communal dimension of faith. A congregation is a specific kind of community. We may share certain theological convictions; we may be drawn by particular cultural preferences; we may be united by language or ethnicity. But if it's a healthy congregation, it will include people who don't like what we like, who don't think like we do, and who talk about God in ways that we find weird, dull, or off-putting.

This is a deeply good thing.

When we make our confessions "in the assembly of the people," we learn what it truly means to be faith-filled, because it requires a tremendous amount of trust to be honest to God in front of people who may not particularly like us or understand us. In the Psalter it is such a community that sees it all: our sadness and joy, our hopes and anxieties. Such a community bears witness to the conflicts of life, the finitude of life, the fallibility of life, the suffering of life, and the worst of life.[16]

This is why sympathy and empathy characterize the spirit of the Psalter. We pray prayers *for* others, but sometimes we pray *on behalf of* others who cannot find the words or the will to pray for themselves in the moment.[17] Is it possible to represent in our prayers the hurt, the alienation, the failure, and the discouragement of people who may find themselves on the margins of faith or persecuted for their faith?[18] The Psalter seems to suggest yes.

For some in our communities it is difficult to believe that God has any desire to hear how sad or angry or lost they are. For others it is difficult to believe that the community has any interest in hearing how happy they are; it may feel like an intrusion and they don't wish to inconvenience others. But the psalms welcome all of it. As Peterson translates Psalm 22:26:

> Down-and-outers sit at GOD's table
>> and eat their fill.
> Everyone on the hunt for God
>> is here, praising him.
> "Live it up, from head to toe.
>> Don't ever quit!"

(THE MESSAGE)

In the end, the Psalter believes these things are possible because it believes that God makes such a community possible, a community that makes space for "all the people" (Ps. 106:48) to praise God, and for the "whole anatomy of the soul"[19] (in John Calvin's words) to be given voice in prayer. And for the Christian, it is Jesus who stands at the center of such a community, showing us what it looks like. Drawing on Psalm 22, Reggie Kidd suggests how Jesus, who Hebrews 2:12 presents to us as the Chief Worshiper, sings with many voices.[20]

"One Voice sings above them all," Kidd writes, "and this Voice sings in all their voices, excluding none."[21] What are the songs that Christ sings? He sings the song of all families (Ps. 22:23, 27), the song of those in a place of abundance (Ps. 22:29a), the song of the poor (Ps. 22:26), the song of generations past (Ps. 22:29b), and the song of generations yet to come (Ps. 22:30–31).[22] Jesus sings the songs of ancient times, in ages past, and he sings the songs of the new creation, the songs of the age to come.

Jesus sings all these songs because it is his everlasting pleasure to form a people who, by the Spirit of God, become a communion made up of the like and the unlike, rich and poor, powerful and powerless, the one and the many. Jesus sings these songs "in the midst of the congregation" (Ps. 22:22) because he delights to make a transhistorical, transcultural community that includes every tribe, tongue, and nation, which might bear witness, each in their own unique communal ways, to the life of God everywhere and always.

CONCLUSION

What's the good news of the psalms, then, to our contemporary world? To people who find themselves lonely, living on the margins of community, hiding, feeling shame, misunderstood, or suffering fear and rejection, the psalms make space for them. The psalms show them that they are not alone in these experiences. The psalms offer them consolation and a companionship of sorts. It's certainly what I personally would have wanted when I was a lonely eighth-grader in North Shore Chicago. Though reading the psalms would not have magically produced the kinds of friends I desperately desired, it would have at least shown me that I was not alone in my desires.

For all of us, the psalms show us a picture of true community and invite us to embody such a community, where things can be remembered and not forgotten, and things can be said out loud: joyful outbursts of thanksgiving, testimonies of rescue, confessions of sin, admissions of weakness. The psalms offer us a way for all things to be told in community—both those things that we would gladly announce from the hilltops and those things that we might prefer to keep secret—so that God might heal us and lead us "in the way everlasting" (Ps. 139:24).

Susan Pinker, the social science columnist for the *Wall Street Journal*, gave a TED talk in 2017 titled, "The Secret to Living Longer May Be Your Social Life."[23] In her research she discovered that the Italian island of Sardinia had ten times as many centenarians as North America. Why? It wasn't the olive oil. It wasn't the sunny climate. It wasn't the gluten-free diet or personality types. It was the quality of close personal relationships and face-to-face interactions. She concluded her talk this way:

> Building in-person interaction into our cities, into our workplaces, into our agendas . . . sends feel-good hormones surging through the bloodstream and brain and helps us live longer. I call this building your village, and building it and sustaining it is a matter of life and death.

It's good for your health, it turns out, to be in rich communal relations with others. The psalmists understand this. They understand that God has created a world where life depends on the experience of deep and meaningful community. It's why we can pray with hope the words of Psalm 5, as the Namibian pastor Zephania Kameeta translates it:

> The love and fellowship of the believer is the foretaste
> > of the life together in your kingdom.
> Lord, keep me in this fellowship of those who do your will.
> Strengthen me not to drop out of this way.[24]

QUESTIONS FOR REFLECTION

1. Are there specific times in your life when you have felt especially lonely? What was it like?
2. Have you had experiences of a really good community? If there were an "ingredients list" to good community, what would you include in that list?
3. What makes it so easy for us to hide from our community? More specifically, what dynamics in our society make it easy for us to hide from our community?
4. What might help us to not hide from our community? What might help us to share our secrets and be fully honest with our community?

5. In what ways does the communal culture of the psalms differ from our culture? How does our culture think about the relationship between "me" and "us," "my" and "our," "I" and "y'all"?

6. Stanley Hauerwas describes friendship as the capacity to "tell the truth" to one another. This of course means risking the friendship. Have you had this kind of friendship? What makes it possible? And how might our communities support such friendship?

7. Eugene Peterson translates Psalm 22:26 as the experience of "down-and-outers sitting at God's table and eating their fill." Have you ever felt like a down-and-outer? Do you know people who may feel this way? What might it look like for you to welcome such a person into your community?

8. What comes to mind when you read what Reggie Kidd, drawing on Psalm 22, says about the kinds of songs that Christ sings? What questions does that raise for you? What could you do to make that kind of "song" happen in your community?

EXERCISES

1. Take ten to fifteen minutes to write down specific ways in which you are good at being an individualist and ways in which you are good at being in community.

2. Welcome somebody who is lonely into your community; offer warm hospitality to a "down-and-outer"; or consider building a friendship with somebody who seems to have no close friends.

3. If you are not currently in a community, find a congregation or a small group through a faith-based organization that you might join. Find ways that you might actively participate in the community. Trust that God will give you grace to find, and to persist with, just the right one.

4. Choose two of these psalms: Psalms 7, 22, 26, 35, 40, 79, 89, 105–107, 111, 115, 126. Pay specific attention to how the community

is related to the individual. Share with each other ways in which the community bears witness to the experience of the individual, and vice versa; ways in which your community can make space for those who are not exactly alike; and ways in which your community can practice both sympathy and empathy for all in the community.

5. Taking Reggie Kidd's fivefold song of Christ from Psalm 22 as a model—the song of (1) all families, (2) those in a place of abundance, (3) the poor, (4) generations past, and (5) generations to come—share with each other ways in which these songs, or prayers, might become part of your common vocabulary as a community. In what ways might you regularly bear witness to all these communities, to all the ways in which God is present to them?

6. Write a collection (or litany) of prayers that give expression to both the community and the individual. Include in this collection the things "that our ancestors have told us" and the things "that we will tell for generations to come."

7. Consider using the language of "blessing" from Psalms 1 and 2 in a communal prayer: "Blessed is the community that makes it possible for all thanksgivings to be heard"; "Blessed is the community that makes it possible for all sorrows and confessions to be heard"; "Blessed is the community that makes it possible to bear witness to the finitude and the fallibility of life"; and so on.

PRAYER

Good Shepherd, you who set the lonely in families, who provide care for the orphan and the widow, who give the refugee a habitation and make a home for the homeless, we pray that you would give us the gift of good community, so that we might find our place there, secure in the knowledge that we are deeply loved by others, and in turn generously welcome others, for the sake of the One who calls us brothers and sisters. In the name of the Father, Son, and Holy Spirit. Amen.

3

HISTORY

"Everything written about me in the law of Moses, the prophets, and the psalms must be fulfilled."
—LUKE 24:44

A psalm drives away demons, summons the help of angels, furnishes arms against nightly terrors, and gives respite from daily toil; to little children it is safety, to men in their prime an adornment, to the old a solace, to women their most fitting ornament. It peoples solitudes, it brings agreement to market places. To novices it is a beginning; to those who are advancing, an increase; to those who are concluding, a confirmation. A psalm is the voice of the Church.
—SAINT BASIL THE GREAT[1]

THE PRAYERS THAT KEEP ON GIVING

For over two thousand years, God's people have learned how to hear from God and how to talk to God by praying the psalms. They are the prayers that have been handed down from generation to generation (Ps. 89:1), the prayers that, for Christians throughout church history, keep on giving. For Eastern Orthodox, Roman Catholic, Anglican, Presbyterian, Methodist, Pentecostal Christians, and plenty of others, the psalms suffuse their liturgical and devotional language, linking them to the early church's practice of worship.

For myself, growing up in a free-church tradition, what the American South calls the "Bible Church," I had no regular exposure to the psalms. Scraps of psalmic phrases appeared in our common hymns. Images of the shepherd from Psalm 23 showed up on flannelgraph boards and Bible covers. A preacher *might* make occasional reference to a psalm, but I cannot recall a single sermon devoted to an entire psalm. To my child's mind, the Psalms belonged to the inordinately long list of Old Testament books, tucked between the inscrutable book of Job and the tediously repetitive book of Proverbs.

It wasn't until my twenties that I discovered the psalms as a treasure house of prayers, filled with language for God and for the soul's many cares—for *my* soul's cares. And it wasn't until my late thirties that I embraced the psalms as a kind of nonnegotiable part of my Christian faith. It was then that I also wondered why my particular faith tradition had fallen into a minority position in church history, failing to teach us how to read the psalms or to see them as a normative part of the Christian's life, as members of Christ's body have done for over two millennia, across the global church, and in all contexts of the church's life.

A cursory review of the church's use of the book of Psalms throughout history may be helpful to see why we, too, should see the psalms as invaluable aids to our life of faith, or, as Ellen Davis puts it, as "the single best guide to the spiritual life currently in print."[2]

With poems that would have been composed as early as the tenth century BC, the final shape of the Psalter did not take place until somewhere around what scholars call the Second Temple period (ca. 530 BC–AD 70).[3] When read closely, one of the first things we notice about the Psalter is that these "songs of David" are arranged into five books, each ending with a doxology.[4] This fivefold arrangement is significant to how Jews and Christians have used the psalms. They are:

- Book 1: Psalms 1–41
- Book 2: Psalms 42–72
- Book 3: Psalms 73–89
- Book 4: Psalms 90–106
- Book 5: Psalms 107–150

Each of these five books functions as a kind of mirror to the five books of Moses.[5] For the Israelite, just as the *torah* was to be learned, it was also to be sung. Just as Moses ends his life with a blessing of Israel (Deut. 33:29), so the Psalter opens with a word of blessing to the individual (Ps. 1:1). And just as the Word of God was to be written upon one's heart, so it was to be placed upon one's lips in song, and, across the ages, the psalms have shown Christians how.[6]

THE PSALMS IN THE EARLY CHURCH

At least 196 citations of the Psalter appear in the New Testament, so we can reasonably assume that for the early church, the Psalter functioned as their principal worship book. In the context of the Gospels, for example, both Mary and Zechariah redeploy the language of the psalms in their respective songs of praise, and when John baptizes Jesus, a voice from heaven heard confirming Jesus' sonship echoes the words of Psalm 2 (Matt. 3).

In his ministry Jesus repeatedly summons the language of the psalms. When challenged by the teachers of the law for his actions in the temple, Jesus responds by quoting Psalm 8:2 (Matt. 21:12–17). When the chief priests question his authority, Jesus appeals to Psalm 118 (Matt. 21:23–27). In conversation with the Pharisees, Jesus cites

Psalm 110 as evidence of his Davidic vocation (Matt. 22:41–45). At the end of his Sermon on the Mount, in response to those who might invoke his name in vain, Jesus quotes Psalm 6:8 (Matt. 7:23).

Predicting his betrayal at the hand of one of his disciples, Jesus quotes Psalm 41:9 (John 13:18). A little later he appeals to Psalms 35:19 and 64:4 to show how his ministry is the fulfillment of the Law (John 15:25). On the cross, he gives voice to his terrible pain by uttering the words of Psalm 22:1 (Matt. 27:46). And in his final hours with the disciples in Jerusalem, Jesus instructs them one last time, showing them how all things concerning himself "in the law of Moses, the prophets, and the psalms must be fulfilled" (Luke 24:44).

Following Christ's ascension, when the church has gathered to wait for Pentecost, the disciples choose a replacement for Judas by appealing to Psalms 69 and 109 (Acts 1:12–26). When the Spirit descends on these same disciples, the first Spirit-anointed sermon Peter preaches to the crowds is an exegesis of Psalms 16:8–11, 132:11, and 110:1 (Acts 2:25–35). And after Peter and John have been released from prison, they praise God with help from the words of Psalm 2 (Acts 4:8–12).

In 1 Corinthians 14:26, Paul lists specific spiritual gifts, which members of Christ's body ought to share with one another. One of those gifts is a "hymn," which in the Greek is the term *psalmon*, or "psalm." Colossians 3:16–17 urges the faithful to teach one another with psalms, among other means. Ephesians 5:18–20 underscores this idea, but links the singing of psalms to the work of the Holy Spirit. In James 5, the apostle asks, "Are any cheerful?" His answer, "Sing songs of praise" (v. 13).

In Paul's letter to the faithful in Rome, he alludes to a host of psalms, including Psalms 14, 18, 19, 32, 44, 51, 53, 69, 116, 117, and 140. In the first two chapters of Hebrews, a chain of nine quotations appears from the psalms, in which the royal psalms and lament psalms feature most prominently. And as scholars frequently point out, the last book of the Bible, the book of Revelation, cannot be rightly understood apart from a clear understanding of the psalms.[7]

THE PSALMS IN CHURCH HISTORY

The influence of the Psalter does not, of course, end with the early church.[8] Around AD 200, the African theologian Tertullian writes this description about the liturgy of his day: "The Scriptures are read and the psalms sung, sermons are delivered and petitions offered."[9] Evidence of this is not hard to come by. By the time of Augustine, the psalms were assigned to particular days of the liturgical calendar.[10] Origen (185–254), Jerome (342–420), and Augustine again (354–430) would all write commentaries on the psalms.[11]

Around AD 318, Athanasius, the bishop of Alexandria, said this about the psalms: "under all the circumstances of life, we shall find that these divine songs suit ourselves and meet our own souls' need at every turn."[12] In his *Confessions*, Augustine remarks how churches in the West had taken up the liturgical habits of the church in the East. "Hymns and Psalms should be sung," he writes, "lest the people should wax faint through the tediousness of sorrow."[13]

In the early Middle Ages, Saint Benedict stipulated that all monks and nuns should recite the entire Psalter in the course of a week.[14] Alfred the Great, who became king of the West Saxons in England in 871, was famous for his habit of saying the psalms both at dawn and at dusk. In the late Middle Ages many young clerks-to-be studied their letters by learning the Psalter—by heart. Throughout this era, the only part of the Bible a layperson likely possessed was a copy of the Psalms.[15] It was their "Bible."

For Martin Luther, as Roland Bainton writes in *Here I Stand: A Life of Martin Luther*, the psalms were "the record of the spiritual struggles through which he was constantly passing."[16] Luther once described the human heart like a ship on a wind-driven stormy sea. He believed the psalms functioned like a balm to such a heart. He writes:

> The Book of Psalms is full of heartfelt utterances made during storms
> of this kind. Where can one find nobler words to express joy than in

the Psalms of praise or gratitude? In them you can see into the hearts of all the saints as if you were looking at a lovely pleasure-garden, or were gazing into heaven. . . . Or where can one find more profound, more penitent, more sorrowful words in which to express grief than in the Psalms of lamentation? In these, you see into the hearts of all the saints as if you were looking at death or gazing into hell, so dark and obscure is the scene rendered by the changing shadows of the wrath of God.[17]

In 1529, twelve years after he had posted his "Ninety-Five Theses," Luther penned the hymn "A Mighty Fortress Is Our God" as an adaptation of Psalm 46. A Jesuit priest at the time remarked, not without irony, that "the hymns of Luther killed more souls than his sermons."[18] In the tradition that followed John Calvin, the singing of metrical psalms became one of the singular distinguishing marks of Calvinists in the sixteenth and seventeenth centuries. Historian Horton Davies observes:

It is exceedingly difficult for us to imagine how almost universal the use of the psalter was. Psalms were sung at the Lord Mayor's feasts at city banquets; soldiers sang them on the march or beside campfires; ploughmen and carters whistled or sang them at their tasks; and pilgrims sought a new continent in which to gain liberty to sing only the Psalms. Far from being the songs of the sour-faced, they were sung by ladies and their lovers.[19]

For outside observers, the Presbyterian Puritans obtained the nickname of "psalm-roaring saints." For the Scots, in whose country Presbyterianism originated and flourished, there is a version of Psalm 23 that is so popular that some have called it the "Scots National Anthem." Like the sixteenth-century French Protestants, the Scottish Protestant believers defended their faith, both literally and figuratively, with help from the martial psalms, which invoked God as Just Judge and Powerful King.

The very first book published in the American colonies was *The Bay Psalm Book*, in Cambridge, Massachusetts, in 1640.[20] In 1719, Isaac Watts, who famously sought "to teach my Author [King David] to speak like a Christian," took Psalm 98 and turned it into the hymn "Joy to the World."[21] One can see from the following two excerpts where Watts took his vocabulary from the psalms:

Psalm 98:4, 8

Make a joyful noise to the LORD, all the earth;
Break forth into joyous song and sing praises.

Let the floods clap their hands;
Let the hills sing together for joy.

"Joy to the World"

Joy to the World; the Lord is come!
Let earth receive her King!

. . .

While fields & floods, rocks, hills & plains
Repeat the sounding joy.

Twenty years later, in 1739, Benjamin Franklin noted how "one could not walk through Philadelphia in the evening without hearing psalms sung in different families of every street."[22] Across the Atlantic Ocean, in 1741, George Frederic Handel composed his famous *Messiah* and suffused it with references to the psalms, second only to references to the book of Isaiah. For instance, the oratorio features passages from Psalm 2 at Scene 6 in Parts 1 and 2:

Why do the heathen rage,
and the people imagine a vain thing?

. . .

The kings of the earth set themselves,

> *and the rulers take counsel together,*
> *against the Lord, and against his anointed, saying,*
> *. . .*
> *Let us break their bands asunder,*
> *and cast away their cords from us.*

The first words that John Wesley (1703–1791) learned as a child included portions from the Psalms. And Abraham Lincoln, during his years as a lawyer (1837–1847), spoke the words of Psalm 23 from memory to a woman on her deathbed.

THE PSALMS IN THE MODERN ERA

Moving forward in time, in 1940, one of the last books the German martyr Dietrich Bonhoeffer would write before his execution by the Nazis at the Flossenbürg concentration camp was *Psalms: The Prayer Book of the Bible*. Writing to his parents from a Nazi prison in April 1943, two years before he would be executed by hanging, Bonhoeffer said, "I read the Psalms every day, as I have done for years; I know them and love them more than any other book."[23]

From the Pakistani pastor Eric Sarwar, who has translated the Psalms into Punjabi to make them available to persecuted Christians in Pakistan, to the Estonian composer Arvo Pärt, whose choral composition "De profundis" is a setting of Psalm 130 in Latin, to the Philadelphia-based rapper Shai Linne, whose "Lyrical Theology" project includes an R&B rendition of Psalm 37, to the Soweto Gospel Choir's rendition of Psalm 23 in the South African Sotho language "Ke Na Le Modisa," pastors and musicians all over the world have been making the psalms come alive in all kinds of musical and human languages.

On July 20, 1969, the Apollo Lunar Module *Eagle* landed on the moon. Most people will likely remember the historic words of Neil Armstrong as he first stepped onto the surface of the moon: "That's one small step for man, one giant leap for mankind." Few people, however, will remember the equally remarkable words of Edwin "Buzz" Aldrin on the last evening of the flight, the day before splashdown in the Pacific. Reflecting on the singular events he had just witnessed firsthand, he observed, with help from the words of Psalm 8:

> Personally, in reflecting on the events of the past several days, a verse from Psalms comes to mind. "When I consider the heavens, the work of Thy fingers, the Moon and the stars, which Thou hast ordained; What is man that Thou art mindful of him?"[24]

Four years earlier, on February 1, 1965, Martin Luther King Jr. was arrested in Selma, Alabama, on charges of parading without a permit. While in jail, he proposed a Quaker-style meeting, which meant that anybody could lead a song or give a prayer. His friend and fellow minister, Ralph Abernathy, opened the meeting by reading from Psalm 27:1:

> The LORD is my light and my salvation;
> whom shall I fear?[25]

In 1970, a Jamaican band called the Melodians released a version of Psalm 137, "Rivers of Babylon," recorded as a Rastafarian song. Why did it become the number one song in Jamaica that year? Why did black Jamaicans sing that song then—and still today? Kevin Adams, in his book *150: Finding Your Story in the Psalms*, explains:

> They sing to end what they see as the divine silence on the rape of Africa during centuries of slavery, colonialism, and the oppression of Africa's children. Like the original Hebrews exiled in Babylon, they cry for justice, resonating with the passion of the psalm's shocking ending.[26]

On December 25, 1996, when David Gergen, the former presidential adviser to Richard Nixon and Ronald Reagan, asked Peter Gomes, the minister serving at the Memorial Church at Harvard University, where people unfamiliar with the Bible should start reading, Gomes answered:

> My advice has always been start with an accessible book, and I suggest you start with the psalms. Now people will say, "Oh, but the psalms are so pretty and musical; shouldn't I take something stronger?" If you read the psalms, read them all, and read them at a pretty intense clip—don't spend all year doing it, do it over the course of a couple of weeks—you will find in those 150 psalms such an acute range of human experience you'll think it has been written by your therapist.[27]

Finally, during their iNNOCENCE & eXPERIENCE worldwide tour, which took place in 2015, the Irish band U2 concluded their concerts by dropping pages out of the psalms from the ceiling. This would remain consistent with U2 front man Bono's longstanding love of the psalms, epitomized in his song "40," which is based on Psalm 40.[28] In his own words:

> I was always interested in the character of David in the Bible because he was such a screw-up. It's a great amusement to me that the people God chose to use in the Scriptures were all liars, cheaters, adulterers, murderers. I don't know which of those activities I was involved in at the time, but I certainly related to David. I was writing my psalm.[29]

CONCLUSION

While Christians have made good use of the book of Psalms throughout history, contemporary Christians have unfortunately either neglected it altogether or used it only in piecemeal fashion. This involves a real loss. As we saw at the beginning of this chapter, for Jesus, the psalms frame both his life and his ministry because he has internalized the psalmists' words through a lifelong habit of prayer. It is a habit we do well to emulate if we wish to be formed in the prayer life of Jesus, "the faithful witness" (Rev. 1:5).

But it is not just a Jesus-shaped prayer life that we discover by reading the psalms; we also discover a little Bible, as it were, all that is essential to a faithful life before God at all times and in all circumstances of our personal and public life. As Martin Luther says it:

> The sum of all is that, if you wish to see the holy Christian church depicted in living colors, and given a living form, in a painting in miniature, then place the Book of Psalms in front of you; you will have a beautiful, bright, polished mirror which will show you what Christianity is.[30]

The invitation to be shaped by the psalms remains, of course, always open to us. The psalms invite us, still today, to "hear them, read, mark, learn, and inwardly digest them," to borrow from the words of the *Book of Common Prayer*.[31] The psalms offer to us "the path of life" (Ps. 16:11); they bless us "in the way" (Ps. 1); and they make available to us, no matter where we may find ourselves in the faith, words of life, "better than strawberries in spring, better than red, ripe strawberries" (Ps. 19:10 THE MESSAGE).

QUESTIONS FOR REFLECTION

1. What is something new that you learned about the history of the Psalms?
2. When you review your own personal history, in what ways have specific psalms tapped into your life experience?
3. What is the first psalm you remember? Which is the most recent one you have read and remembered? Compare and contrast your spiritual journey from that beginning till now.

4. As best as you can tell, how has your church tradition made use of the psalms? In what ways would you like your own congregation or community to make more use of the psalms or perhaps use the psalms differently?

5. You might read the list of Christian saints who love the psalms and think, *I'm not like them. I don't really get the psalms.* But everyone starts somewhere. What is one thing you can do to read the psalms more regularly?

6. How does the history of the psalms encourage you in your own personal and communal practices of prayer, worship, discipleship, or mission?

EXERCISES

1. Read Psalm 106 or 107. Read it several times. Meditate on it. Pray through it. Consider memorizing a portion of it to carry in your heart as a way to maintain a lively conversation with God throughout the day.

2. Read Psalm 98 and then read or listen to a recording of Isaac Watts's hymn "Joy to the World." Explore the ways in which Watts interprets and applies the words of the psalmist to the hymn. What does he include? What does he exclude? What meaning might be missed in Watts's partial use of Psalm 98? You could also consider doing this with sections of Handel's *Messiah*.

3. Take one of the quotes in this chapter and print it out. Post it somewhere in your home or workspace to remind you of the truth of God in the psalms as it relates to your life.

4. Find on YouTube or Spotify or elsewhere a recording of "Rivers of Babylon" by the Melodians or "40" by U2. Listen to it together as a group and share your responses.

5. As a community, purchase or borrow from the library a copy of one of these short books, and read and discuss them together:

C. S. Lewis, *Reflections on the Psalms*; Dietrich Bonhoeffer, *Psalms: The Prayer Book of the Bible*; Thomas Merton, *Praying the Psalms*; Eugene Peterson, *Answering God: The Psalms as Tools for Prayer*; N. T. Wright, *The Case for the Psalms*; or Beth LaNeel Tanner, *The Psalms for Today*.

6. If you have a small group that meets regularly, consider beginning and ending your time together by reading a psalm.

7. As a group, watch the short film, "Bono & Eugene Peterson: The Psalms," and discuss your impressions.

PRAYER

Oh Lord, you who have taught your people to pray faithfully from generation to generation, grant that we, praising you at all times and in all circumstances of our lives, might hear your voice in the words of the psalms, knowing that you are pleased to hear our own voice in those same words. We pray this through Jesus Christ our Lord, to whom, with you and the Holy Spirit, be honor and glory, now and forever. Amen.

4

PRAYER

My life is God's prayer.
—Psalm 42:8 the message

Let me hear you sing, let me hear you pray, and I will write your theology.
—Gordon Fee[1]

The Most Honest Prayer You'll Ever Hear

Whatever else they are, the psalms are prayers. They're prayers for people who already know how to pray as well as for those who don't know how to pray at all. They're prayers for those who wish to pray to God with all their heart. The German theologian and martyr Dietrich Bonhoeffer, in a lecture given to students on July 31, 1935, says this: "The only way to understand the Psalms is on your knees, the whole congregation praying the words of the Psalms with all its strength."[2]

My own prayer life comes and goes. At times I have prayed faithfully every morning before starting the day's work. At other times I have managed only tired prayers at the end of the day, and they have often not been very good prayers. At still other times I have found myself without prayer, or, more truthfully, without any desire to pray. What the psalms have offered me then is a beginning. To paraphrase Thomas Merton, the psalms have become my bread of heaven in the wilderness of my exodus.[3] They have nourished my tired heart in my hour of need, and they have nudged me to try again.

In the psalms we find words *from* God, we find words *about* God, and we find words *to* God. And all these words are the very words you and I need to pray well. All such words teach us how to talk to God and are, as such, a grammar for talking with God.[4] In Bonhoeffer's words: "It is not our prayers that interpret the Psalms but the Psalms that interpret our prayers."[5] Said otherwise, in putting the words of the psalms on our lips, we enter into a school of prayer. In such a school we become students, and we never stop being students of such prayers, learning how to talk to God and with God. The psalms in this way are what Eugene Peterson calls "prayer masters." He writes:

> We apprentice ourselves to these masters, acquiring facility in using the tools, by which we become more and more ourselves. If we are willfully ignorant of the Psalms, we are not thereby excluded from praying, but we will have to hack our way through formidable country by trial and error and with inferior tools.[6]

Prayer is a funny thing, of course. In its simplest terms, it is about talking to God and listening to God. In practice, prayer is anything *but* simple. Pentecostals pray in tongues. Korean Presbyterians pray out loud, all at the same time. Benedictine monks pray in Latin or in silence. And little children ramble to God in prayer, while adults struggle to talk to God or talk to God in habituated ways, both off-the-cuff and with scripted words, or at times formally and at other times informally.

The psalms make space for all such prayers, and for all such people too. As the fourth-century pastor Basil the Great saw it, the psalms invite all alike: "To novices it is a beginning; to those who are advancing, an increase; to those who are concluding, a confirmation."[7] Jesus prayed the psalms (Luke 23:46). Paul exhorted the early church to pray the psalms (Eph. 5:18–19). And today both Jews and Christians pray the psalms, along with popes, peasants, and pop stars. The psalms make space for all such people to pray "the most honest prayer[s]" God will ever hear (Ps. 17:1 THE MESSAGE).

If we wish to make the most of the psalms, then, we must not only understand them as prayers, we must also understand how they "do" prayer.[8] The psalms show us the nature of faithful prayer in the following ways.

First, the psalms invite us into a conversation with a very particular God, not a generic deity. This God is not just "Elohim," a divine being common to the ancient Near Eastern world. This is the God of Abraham, Isaac, and Jacob. This is the God of Moses, who delivered Israel from slavery. This God has a story. As such he is a specific kind of Creator (Ps. 104), King (Ps. 5), Lord (Ps. 2), Mighty One (Ps. 62), Shepherd (Ps. 23), Refuge (Ps. 46), Light (Ps. 27), Warrior (Ps. 24), Deliverer (Ps. 81), and Sun and Shield (Ps. 84).

The Psalter introduces us to a God who is near yet who is experienced as absent. Here we find a Just Judge (Ps. 9) who exacts vengeance against all oppressors, as well as a Merciful One (Ps. 86) who inclines his ear to the cries of the afflicted. This God avenges the vulnerable (Ps. 26), heals the brokenhearted (Ps. 147), protects the widows (Ps. 146), provides for the weak and needy (Ps. 68), forgives the penitent (Ps. 32), and redeems the sinner from sin (Pss. 51; 103).

This God is known through his words and deeds, not through a hyper-subjective exploration of the inner life. This God reigns over heaven and earth. This God rules over past and future. This God governs mortals and nations and galaxies.[9] Left to our own devices, we will as likely pray to a god made in our own image—a rational god, a pacifying god, an activist god, an abstract god, or a wonder-working god. Because of our inability to know God truly, fully, on our own, we must allow the psalms, as one of the determinative texts of Holy Scripture, to reveal God to us.

Second, the God of the psalms is both immanent and transcendent. That is, the God we encounter throughout the Psalter is both near and far.

With regard to God's immanence, the Psalter uses a range of images to describe God's nearness. He is presented, for example, as our shepherd, with a particularly intimate phrasing appearing in Psalm 28:9: "Be [your people's] shepherd, and carry them forever." The psalmists repeatedly refer to God as a secure place. In Psalm 46:1 he is described this way: "God is our refuge and strength, an ever-present help in trouble" (NIV).

In Psalm 89:26, the psalmist describes God's relationship to King David as that of a father. Psalm 3:3 uses an intimate image of God as the one who lifts up our head. Psalm 73:28 puts it simply: "But for me it is good to be near God." These images suggest a God who draws near, who stays close at hand, who knows us from the womb. They show us a good Shepherd who knows his sheep by name, who gives his people peace in the midst of trouble, who loves the unlovable and comforts the grieving.

But the Psalter also shows us a transcendent God, a God whose greatness has an inaccessible "otherly" quality about it. In Psalm 80:1 we encounter a God represented as one who sits "enthroned between the cherubim" (NIV). God is the Lord of Hosts (Pss. 103:12; 148:2), the Maker of heaven and earth and everything in between (Pss. 95; 104; 146; 148), the Just Judge against evil and evildoers (Pss. 18:47; 58:10; 79:10), and the GOD-of-Angel-Armies (Ps. 46 THE MESSAGE).

Perhaps the image that most powerfully represents God's transcendence is that of kingship. Psalm 29:10 says, "The LORD sits enthroned over the flood; the LORD sits enthroned as king forever." Psalm 47:2 adds, "For the LORD Most High is awesome, the great King over all the earth" (NIV). This is a God who cannot be manipulated. This

God cannot be reduced to human whims. This God can be known—but not exhaustively. This God is holy (Pss. 22:3; 71:22; 99:5; 111:9).

Third, the psalms model for us a rhythm of call and response. In the psalms, God "calls" and humans answer; God initiates and humans respond. As often as not, humans also call out to God and he replies. It is always, however, a dialogue, never a monologue, even if the initiative ultimately rests with God. In Brueggemann's words, the psalms remind us how "biblical faith is uncompromisingly and unembarrassedly dialogical."[10] Psalm 12 is typical. The psalmist initiates the dialogue this way in verse 1:

> Help, O Lord, for there is no longer anyone who is godly;
>> the faithful have disappeared from humankind.

In verse 5 the Lord responds:

> "Because the poor are despoiled, because the needy groan,
>> I will now rise up," says the Lord.

In Psalm 50 the roles are reversed. Here God initiates the conversation, set up in verse 1 and commenced in verse 7:

> The mighty one, God the Lord,
>> speaks and summons the earth
>> from the rising of the sun to its setting.

> "Hear, O my people, and I will speak;
>> O Israel, I will testify against you.
>> I am God, your God."

The response of the psalmist is implicit in verse 14: "Offer to God a sacrifice of thanksgiving."

As with the rest of the psalms, there is always some form of back-and-forth exchange between the psalmists and God. And the readers are invited to pour out to God all the contents of their hearts and to receive the words of the Lord in return. As the title of Peterson's book says, the psalms teach us how to answer God, who is always calling out to us, always inviting us to know and to love him.[11]

Fourth, the psalms model for us the dialogue of individual and communal prayer. As John Witvliet observes in his book *The Biblical Psalms in Christian Worship,* the psalms not only show us how God and humans talk to each other, but they also show us how individuals and communities talk to God.[12] In this way the psalms protect us from an impersonal collectivism and a self-absorbed individualism. Far from denying the importance of first-person prayer, the Psalter sets such prayers within a communal context.[13] David Ford explains it this way:

> The Psalmist's "I" accommodates a vast congregation of individuals and groups down the centuries around the world today. They are all somehow embraced in this "I." A vast array of stories, situations, sufferings, blessings, joys, and deaths have been read and prayed into the Psalms by those who have identified with their first person. It amounts to an extraordinarily capacious and hospitable "I."[14]

The psalmist avoids many of the idiosyncratic details of an individual's experience, even while working with very concrete imagery, such as we find in Psalm 51:3: "For I know my transgressions, and my sin is ever before me." In doing so, the psalmist shows us what a "capacious" first-person prayer looks like: a prayer that always keeps the community in mind. The psalmist shows that the opposite is true as well. The psalms model for us communal prayers that make ample space for the individual, where a person can find herself represented.

Fifth, the psalms invite us to speak our prayers and they invite us to silence as well. The Psalter includes one hundred and fifty prayers that vary in length. The longest is Psalm 119, with 176 verses. The shortest is Psalm 117, with only two verses. All the psalms involve language that frames and directs our prayers. All the psalms likewise invite us to pray specific words. Psalm 30, for instance, ends this way:

> To you, O Lord, I cried,
>> and to the Lord I made supplication.
>
> You have turned my mourning into dancing;
>> you have taken off my sackcloth
>> and clothed me with joy,
> so that my soul may praise you and not be silent.
>> O Lord my God, I will give thanks to you forever.
>
> (vv. 8, 11–12)

But the goal is not only to be trained in faithful speech and faithful words. The goal is also to be trained in faithful silence. That's part of the idea, scholars suggest, behind the term *selah*. The term functions as a kind of a pause, both in the text and as an invitation to the reader to wait, to listen, to meditate, and to not rush on. Psalm 62:1 says, "My soul waits in silence for God only; From Him is my salvation" (NASB). Psalm 65:1 adds, "There will be silence before You" (NASB). In such a silence there is a fullness.

Sixth, the psalms invite us to say all kinds of things to God in prayer. This may be one of the most surprising things for newcomers to the psalms. The psalms do not invite us to say only a *few* things to God; that is, only the "proper" or "holy" things one supposes God wants to hear from us. The psalms invite us to say *all sorts* of things. This includes such things as:

- You are holy. (Ps. 22)
- We love you. (Ps. 31)
- Help us. (Ps. 12)
- I have sinned. (Ps. 51)
- Forgive me. (Ps. 25)

- Why? (Ps. 22)
- How long? (Ps. 13)
- I am alone. (Ps. 88)
- Defend me. (Ps. 43)
- Have mercy. (Ps. 57)
- You are good. (Ps. 100)
- We shout for joy. (Ps. 98)
- Remember what you've done. (Ps. 105)
- Come again. (Ps. 6)
- Be gracious to us. (Ps. 123)
- Be the God that you say you are. (Ps. 4)
- We praise you. (Ps. 66)
- Bless us. (Ps. 67)
- Lead me. (Ps. 31)
- Thank you. (Ps. 100)

The psalms show us what prayer looks like, what prayer sounds like, what prayer says to God—and it says quite a lot. It says what *needs* saying. It names the joy of good news in full-throated and wholehearted ways. It names—also with full-gutted, wholly honest confession—the sorrow and loss that accompany our pilgrimage on earth. If we would let them, the psalms would show us how to offer to God "the most honest prayer you'll ever hear" (Ps. 17:1 THE MESSAGE).

Seventh, the psalms in this way give voice to the whole anatomy of the soul. This is how John Calvin describes the psalms: "there is not an emotion of which any one can be conscious that is not here represented as in a mirror."[15] No emotion is excluded from such prayer; no topic is out of bounds. This should come as extraordinarily good news for many of us who may worry that God is interested in hearing only a few things from us, perhaps only the "right" things, not all the messy contents of our hearts.

The fourth-century pastor Athanasius, in his letter to a young deacon in Alexandria, Egypt, notes how the psalms "become like a mirror to the person singing them, so that he might perceive himself and the emotions of his soul."[16] The Old Testament scholar Ellen Davis reminds us that God welcomes our emotions. The psalms, she writes, "enable us to bring into our conversation with God feelings and thoughts most of us think we need to get rid of before God will be interested in hearing from us."[17]

Again, this is good news for those of us who believe that we should always have our act together when we pray. The psalms reassure us that a willingness to talk to God is all that matters. With the psalms on our lips, we can be confident that all of our heart can be brought to God. In Tim Keller's words, the psalms "are a medicine chest for the heart."[18] In turn, the psalms provide us with an edited poetic language to give expression to our unedited emotions.[19] Their structure frees us "to let it all out" in faithful ways.

Eighth, in the psalms we bring to God not just our personal concerns but also the concerns of the whole world. The psalms should not be seen as an excuse to pray only about oneself, as crucial as that is for our individual life of faith. The psalms should be seen as an occasion to bring all things to God in prayer: the concerns of history and of creation, of our neighbors and of the world.

In the psalms, history is the proper context for the encounter of God. In prayer we recall the history of God's dealings with his people in order to remember his faithfulness today as we anticipate the fulfillment of his purposes. In the psalms, we also join the praise of all creation as a partner and a poet to that praise. At times creation praises with us; at other times creation bears witness against us, against our failure to properly acknowledge our Creator.

While personal prayer is a basic concern of the psalms, the psalms would also have us pray for our neighbors and for the world. This includes, for instance, the sorrows of our neighbor, the need for justice, the absurdity of evil, the reality of death, the miraculous gift of new life, the care of creation, and the requirement to bear witness to the nations of God's steadfast love. The psalms take us on an outward journey as often as they take us on an inward journey.

Finally, the psalms in doing so train us in the work of sympathetic and empathetic prayer. On certain days a psalm will invite us to pray what we feel in the moment—need, joy, gratitude, hope, fear, anger, doubt. On other days a psalm will invite us to pray despite our feelings of the moment. They will invite us to pray, that is, *in faith.* They will invite us to choose to talk to God even when we'd rather be doing anything *but* that. To pray in these two ways is to cultivate the virtues of sympathy and empathy.

Why do sympathy and empathy matter to our prayer life? Because they are a way that we, like Jesus, can give care and receive care. To pray the psalms, on some days, is to feel *for* others what we may not feel at the moment. It is a way for us to see and know and care for our neighbors. To enter into my neighbor's pain, for example, as I read Psalm 88 (a prayer for the despondent) when I feel joy and might rather be reading Psalm 96 (a prayer of praise), is a way to exhibit the sympathetic love of God.

On other days, to pray the psalms is to feel *with* others what we feel ourselves. To pray Psalm 51, for instance, on an occasion I feel acutely the need for forgiveness, is to enter into my neighbor's need for the forgiveness of God, whether or not his sins are familiar to me. In praying this way, we exhibit the empathetic love of God. To pray in these two ways, in short, is to be trained in self-care and neighborly care, in the kind of care that Jesus offers sinners and saints alike.

CONCLUSION

The psalms teach us how to pray as Jesus himself prayed. On the one hand, to pray with Jesus in this way is to pray with the one who, as the True Human, *enables* all faithful prayers. In praying this way, we are reassured that God attends to every aspect of our humanity. He sees and loves us. *All* aspects of our life, "all its changes, its ups and downs, its failures and recoveries," in Athanasius's words, are carried up in Jesus' own prayers and faithfully offered by the Spirit to the Father.[20]

On the other hand, to pray with Jesus in the psalms is to pray with the one who *embodies* our prayers. With Jesus, we, too, feel forsaken. With Jesus, we, too, feel God's protection against enemies. With Jesus, we, too, feel the grief of loss and the pain of suffering. With Jesus, we, too, feel the life of God's Spirit making us new again and feel our beloved nature as a son or daughter of God. And with Jesus, we, too, find ourselves singing the praises of God with grateful hearts in the middle of the community, free to be vulnerable and fully alive.

The psalms don't ask me to figure out my prayer life alone; they help me to pray and they offer me the company of friends to pray with me. When I pray the psalms, I can be confident that I will hear the voice of saints and sinners in them. I can be confident that I will hear the voice of Christ in them. And I can be confident, in the words of Psalm 66 as Eugene Peterson translates it, that God will come on the double when he hears my prayers, however wholehearted or half-hearted they may be: "Blessed be God: he didn't turn a deaf ear, he stayed with me, loyal in his love" (Ps. 66:20 THE MESSAGE).

QUESTIONS FOR REFLECTION

1. What is your personal experience with prayer? Which parts of your prayer life come easily? Which parts come with difficulty—or feel uncomfortable or confusing or discouraging?

2. In what ways might you start reading the psalms as your own "school of prayer" to get your prayer life started again—or perhaps deepened and expanded?

3. What range of emotions do you experience when you think about approaching God in prayer? How do the psalms help recalibrate both the positive and the negative emotions?

4. What kinds of things did your family or church teach you that you could say to God in prayer? How does the list of things that the psalms invite us to say to God in prayer excite or concern you?

5. When have you felt that God answered your prayers? When have you felt that God did not answer them? How might the psalms echo your experience and help you feel that you're not alone?

6. How might the idea of a "call and response" pattern, or the "individual and communal" pattern, or the "personal and global" pattern of prayer in the psalms inform your own life of prayer?

7. We often pray our immediate needs and feelings. How might the psalms help you to pray beyond yourself, for others, in both sympathy and empathy?

EXERCISES

1. Read Psalms 4 and 5. Read them several times. Meditate on them. Pray through them. Consider memorizing a portion of these two "evening and morning" psalms to carry in your heart as a way to maintain a lively conversation with God throughout the day.

2. Make a list of positive and negative ideas you have about prayer. Note a few concrete ways the psalms might reshape your thinking and beliefs about prayer.

3. Make a list of the emotions expressed in the psalms. Then note the ones you personally identify with. In conversation with a friend or a small group, share your thoughts and feelings about the emotions you don't experience in prayer.

4. Many Christians feel reluctant or intimidated by the prospect of praying out loud in a group. Discuss together how the psalms might help give people words to pray with greater confidence.

5. Explore one way in which your community might increase the use of the psalms in your common prayer and worship. Consider also making more space for silence in your times of prayer, allowing you to hear the voice of God.

6. Acquire a copy of one of these books as a way to support your reading and praying of the psalms: *The Paraclete Psalter: A Book*

of *Daily Prayer*; Timothy and Kathy Keller, *The Songs of Jesus: A Year of Daily Devotions in the Psalms*; Eugene Peterson, *Praying with the Psalms: A Year of Daily Prayers and Reflections on the Words of David*; and Mark Lanier, *Psalms for Living*; *Common Prayer: A Liturgy for Ordinary Radicals*.

7. Commit as a group to pray through the entire Psalter, one psalm per day. Find a time to come together at the end of the 150 days to share your experiences.

PRAYER

Lord Christ, you who taught the disciples to pray, teach me also how to pray. Teach me how to listen and not be overly anxious when I do not hear your voice. Teach me how to be silent long enough so that I might hear your still, small voice in all the noise and conflict of our world. When I am fainthearted in my prayers, strengthen my heart. When I lack the will to pray, grant me the grace to begin again. When I am alone in my prayers, be my companion. When I am afraid or ashamed, may I hear an encouraging word from your people to trust anew. And when I am wordless, let me hear the voice of your Spirit praying in me. In your name. Amen.

5

POETRY

I found that keeping company with poets, men and women who care about words and are honest with them, who respect and honor their sheer overwhelming power, kept me alert—biblically alert, Jesus alert.

—Eugene Peterson[1]

*A verse may find him, who a sermon flies
And turn delight into a sacrifice.*

—George Herbert[2]

THE FAITH OF POETRY

When I was a small child, I loved poetry. I loved it because it belonged to the common language of the books that my mother read to me: Dr. Seuss's *Green Eggs and Ham,* Watty Piper's *The Little Engine That Could,* and Ludwig Bemelmans's *Madeline* series. As a teenager I found poetry intimidating and confusing. It belonged to my required English class—to things *one had to learn*—in the same way that one had to learn the periodic table or the US presidents. Poetry was for poets, I thought, not for me.

In college I grew to love poetry, but not, unfortunately, for the right reasons. My love of poetry was born out of an insecure desire to be perceived as sophisticated. Smart people loved poetry, and even smarter people could quote great chunks of Shakespeare or Dickinson. It wasn't until my thirties that I discovered poetry as something I could enjoy like I did all good things in God's world: as a gift, as something I could *grow* to like without worry or pressure, just as with certain foods or styles of music.

In seminary I discovered the poetry of the psalms. Eugene Peterson reintroduced me to poetry, as I might be reintroduced to an old friend whom I had once feared but I could now enjoy in a companionable way. Poetry was for everyone, he reassured me. Like prose, poetry was part of the furniture of God's world. Like prose, again, it required work to grasp it. But it was also important to remember that poetry could do things that prose could not, and without it, as the psalms see it, we could not be fully human. This is what poets throughout history have always understood—and would remind us repeatedly.

THE WAYS OF POETS

Whatever else poets love, they love the wonder and the ways of words: how they sound in the ear, how they feel on the lips, and how they possess a sensory depth, which is perhaps another way of saying that they love the musicality of words. Few poets have made the most of such linguistic musicality as Dr. Seuss. In his story "Gertrude McFuzz," language crackles with life:

> *Then the feathers popped out! With a zang! With a zing!*
> *They blossomed like flowers that bloom in the spring.*
> *All fit for a queen! What a sight to behold!*
> *They sparkled like diamonds and gumdrops and gold!*[3]

Poets not only love words and the sound of words, they also protect words from being misused and abused.[4] In this way they are like shepherds of words. And they help us feel the truth, as if for the first time. In the hands of an unknown author of a popular spiritual, for instance, the cross is not just a divine act of atonement that the angels observe in a detached manner. It is a cosmic dilemma to the angelic host:

> *Go down angels to the flood,*
> *Blow out the sun turn the moon into blood!*
> *Come back angels bolt the door,*
> *Because the time that's been goin' to be no more.*[5]

In the hands of a poet, the morning sun, which we might take for granted each time we wake up, becomes "a new husband leaping from his honeymoon bed, The daybreaking sun an athlete racing to the tape," as Eugene Peterson translates Psalm 19:4–5. It becomes a perfectly *particular* sun, seen afresh. And as G. K. Chesterton imagines it in his book *Orthodoxy*, "God says every morning, 'Do it again' to the sun." He does it out of sheer pleasure in this one-of-a-kind, nearly perfect sphere of hot plasma.[6]

And while poets are "always telling us that grass is green, or thunder loud, or lips red," as C. S. Lewis once quipped, they are also always telling us that green is *more* than merely green, thunder *more* than simply loud, and lips *exceedingly* red.[7] This is another way of saying that the world is more than just empirically classifiable stuff. It is *wonder*-full stuff. It is stuff that deserves our precious time and our loving attention. Poetry slows us down enough to give God's world the attention it deserves.

THE POETRY OF FAITH

The psalms are poetry through and through. This is, of course, to state the obvious, but sometimes the obvious needs stating. For as the Holy

Spirit, the Author of Scripture, has ordained it, it is *through* poetry, not despite it, that God is encountered in the psalms. It is through poetry, not beyond it, that a faithful life is formed.[8] And if we wish to get the most out of the psalms, we need to have some sense of its poetry. As C. S. Lewis reminds us:

> Most emphatically the Psalms must be read as poems; as lyrics, with all the licenses and all the formalities, the hyperboles, the emotional rather than logical connections, which are proper to lyric poetry. . . . Otherwise we shall miss what is in them and think we see what is not.[9]

Yet this raises a host of questions. How does poetry work? How does it inform our reading of the psalms? And how does it form a life of faith? These are questions we must answer if we are to experience all that the psalms have to offer.

Poetry is a kind of language that says more and says it more intensely, more densely, than does ordinary language. Biblical poetry does this through similes, metaphors, parallelisms, rhythm, and hyperbole, among other literary devices. These are the ways a poem "means" a thing. Take, for example, the sound of words in Psalm 8:1–4:

> O LORD, our Sovereign,
>> how majestic is *your name* in all the earth!
> You have set your glory above the heavens.
>> Out of the mouths of babes and infants
> you have founded a bulwark because of your foes,
>> to silence the enemy and the avenger.
> When I look at *your heavens*, the work of your fingers,
>> the moon and the stars that you have established;
> what are human beings that you are mindful of them,
>> mortals that you care for them?
>
> (emphasis added)

In the original Hebrew language, "your name" and "your heavens" sound almost the same.[10] The sound of words shows us how the heavens—with its stars, moon, and sun—spell out the name of the Lord, an intimate, personal presence. But even without knowing the original Hebrew, we might still catch this nuance if we observed carefully the repetition of the term *your*.

In most English translations the term appears six times to describe the Lord, as if the poet were purposefully striking a single key on the piano over and over. The work of the Lord, by "your fingers" and "your hands," which results in the creation of "your heavens," is a reflection of "your glory" and of "your name," the latter of which is repeated at the beginning and end of the poem to frame the psalm. Everything that happens inside this frame, from the poet's perspective, is intended to communicate something specific about the personal name of God.

Or take the sky above us as another example. According to scientists, the atmosphere of Earth is comprised of nitrogen (about 78 percent), oxygen (about 21 percent), and argon (about 0.9 percent), with carbon dioxide and other gases in trace amounts. The atmosphere has a mass of about 5.15×1018 kg. The principle layers of the atmosphere are the exosphere, the thermosphere, the mesosphere, the stratosphere, and the troposphere.

According to the psalmist, through his use of theologically informed poetry, the sky is perceived rather differently:

> God's glory is on tour in the skies,
>> God-craft on exhibit across the horizon.
> Madame Day holds classes every morning,
>> Professor Night lectures each evening.
> Their words aren't heard,
>> their voices aren't recorded,
> But their silence fills the earth:
>> unspoken truth is spoken everywhere.
>
> warming hearts to faith.
>
> (Ps. 19:1–4, 6 THE MESSAGE)

This is how Psalm 19 describes the sky, in language that is denser, more musical, more poetic. It is a sky, to be sure, but so much more than what scientists might tell us.

Poetry accents the musical textures of human language. A stanza from a nineteenth-century spiritual, for example, makes generous use of the sound "s." It does so to give the hearers of the song a feel for Satan's sinister and seductive ways:

> *Ol' Satan's got a slippery ol' shoe*
> *And if you don't mind he will slip it on you*
> *Ol' Satan's like a snake in the grass*
> *Waitin' to bite you as you pass.*[11]

W. H. Auden once remarked, "I like hanging around words, listening to what they say."[12] This is what poets love about their work, but it is also how God has hardwired all of us: to love the musicality of language. Our love of rhythm and meter, in fact, is directly "related to the beat of our hearts, the pulse of our blood, the intake and outflow of air from our lungs."[13] It's no wonder, then, that the psalmists find poetry to be a suitable vehicle to express themselves before God.

As a poet himself, Eugene Peterson translates Psalm 24:9–10 in a way that captures its sonorous quality:

> Wake up, you sleepyhead city!
> Wake up, you sleepyhead people!
>> King-Glory is ready to enter.
> Who is this King-Glory?
>> GOD-of-the-Angel-Armies:
>> he is King-Glory.
>
> (THE MESSAGE)

For any reader of the psalms, the invitation is to savor the words of the Word. Psalm 119:103 describes God's word like honey: "How sweet are your words to my taste, sweeter than honey to my mouth!" Psalm 19:10 describes the psalmist's love of the *torah* similarly, so it is no wonder that the psalms invite us repeatedly to taste and to see, to hear and to delight in the Word of the Lord.

Poetry brings us into metaphor-rich territory. What is a metaphor? A metaphor is a figure of speech whereby we speak of one thing in terms of another, usually in surprising ways; for example, Juliet is the sun, the church is a temple, God is our rock. In the Psalter, the truth about God does not exist on the other side of a metaphor. It exists *through* the metaphor. Take "the Lord is my shepherd," for instance.

The Lord is not, of course, an actual shepherd by profession, like a Tunisian goatherd or an Australian sheepherder. Nor is the point simply to say that the Lord generically cares for his people. The metaphor of shepherd involves much more. As the Old Testament scholar John Goldingay points out, in the context of Israel's life, the image of a shepherd was not a gentle one. Shepherds were rough characters who at times became ruthless killers.[14]

The metaphor of a shepherd evoked memories of Moses. It evoked associations with Israel's exodus. It evoked an image of a wilderness, where sources of water were scarce and wild animals endangered the safety of sheep. It evoked non-cozy pictures of great kings as sovereign lords, who treated their people as vassals. Evoking all these images, the metaphor of the Lord as shepherd involves a surplus of meaning.

It's not that metaphors tell us things we already know, just in a spruced-up way. Nor is it that metaphors function as decorative, but ultimately unnecessary, elements. Metaphors disclose things about God and the world that could not be known any other way, because a metaphor explained is different from—and less than—a metaphor experienced. To encounter the Lord as shepherd, therefore, is to encounter him in a richly meaningful way. No other image will do the job quite the same—not God as caretaker, not God as protector, only "the Lord is my shepherd."

Poetry draws our attention to the particularity of things. Good poets are always interested in the concrete over the abstract, the particular over the generic. This is because poets, like God, love the details of life. Like God, again, poets delight in the unique quality of things and persons. The English poet Gerard Manley Hopkins captures this idea in his 1877 poem "As Kingfishers Catch Fire."

> Each mortal thing does one thing and the same:
> Deals out that being indoors each one dwells;
> Selves—goes its self; myself it speaks and spells,
> Crying What I do is me: for that I came.[15]

As poets see it, their work is "to distinguish one life from another; to illuminate diversity; to light up the least grain of being, to show how it is concretely individual, particularized from any other; to tell, in all the marvel of its singularity, the separate holiness of the least grain."[16] In doing this work, poets remind us that there are no "dittos" in God's world; there is nothing that can be dismissed as "just another thing."[17] Every particular *thing*, every particular *person*, demands attentive care.

Fir trees and storks, Leviathans and Lebanon, rock hyraxes and desert owls, sycamores and slugs—the psalms bring to our attention the particular things of God's world so that we might love them as God loves them.

Poetry invites us to slow down and to pay care-filled attention. We cannot pay attention to the things of God's world if we are in a rush. We have to slow down. Poetry helps us do this. What may feel frustrating to those of us who are not poets is, in fact, the gift of poetry: namely, that we cannot speed-read a poem. To read a poem properly we have to slow down. Eugene Peterson helps us understand what is involved here:

> A poem requires re-reading. Unlike prose, which fills the page with print, poems leave a lot of white space, which is to say that silence takes its place alongside sound as significant, essential to

the apprehension of these words. We cannot be in a hurry reading a poem. We notice connections, get a feel for rhythm, hear resonances. All this takes time.[18]

How does this experience of poetry relate to the life of faith? Peterson explains: "This attending, this waiting, this reverential posture is at the core of the life of faith, the life of prayer, the life of worship, the life of witness."[19] A faithful life is not like a grocery list—something to get through as efficiently as possible. A faithful life isn't simply reciting the right ideas about God. A faithful life is an invitation to contemplate God, to linger in the presence of God, to *be* with God, not just to *do* for God. Peterson translates Psalm 27:4 this way:

> I'm asking GOD for one thing,
> only one thing:
> To live with him in his house
> my whole life long.
> I'll contemplate his beauty;
> I'll study at his feet.
>
> (THE MESSAGE)

Poetry, then, makes it possible for us to pay careful attention, and as the psalms see it, poetry also gives us permission to take the time we need to attend to God, to people, to things. Poetry retrains our muscles of listening so we might have a chance to hear from our Maker. Poetry slows us down enough so we can discern what it means to live our lives, here and now, in light of our Maker.

The psalms originate in a communally oriented oral culture. As such, they should be read and heard out loud if we wish to discern how a psalm *means*.[20] Its meaning occurs *through* its orality, not despite it, which, of course, is what all good poets will tell you.[21]

The point is this: We could write a theology book about justice (and we need such books), but it's in reading Psalm 10 responsively, for example, that we get a *grasp* of justice; we get a "feel" for it, with its vivid images of a God who does not turn a blind eye to the activities of the "wicked," who "boast" and "curse" and "lurk" and "crouch" and "persecute the poor" and "murder the innocent." We could preach a sermon about the loss of a friend (and we need sermons like those), but when we sing a rendition of Psalm 88, as with the eighteenth-century hymn "To Thee, my God and Savior," we know it *from the inside*. We say, yes, it's just as intensely bitter and tragically sad as that which we see described in the hymn's third verse:

> *Remov'd from Friends, I sigh'd alone,*
> *In a loath'd Dungeon laid, where none*
> *Vouchsafes to visit me,*
> *Past Hopes of Liberty.*
> *My Eyes from weeping never cease,*
> *They waste, but still my Griefs increase,*
> *Yet Lord, to thee I've pray'd,*
> *And still invok'd thy Aid.*[22]

We could talk about the majestic character of God, or we could put Charles Wesley's Trinity hymn, drawn from Psalm 33:6, on the lips of a congregation and let the people taste it for themselves.

> *Jehovah the Almighty Lord,*
> *Father of Jesus Christ, and ours,*
> *The heavens created by his word,*
> *And by his breath the heavenly powers:*
> *And that essential Spirit divine*
> *Whom Jesus breathes into his own,*
> *Doth in the new creation join*
> *With God and his eternal Son.*
>
> *To Father, Son, and Holy Ghost*
> *Be equal adoration given,*

> *Maker of the celestial host,*
> *Maker of the new earth and heaven!*
> *Joint-Authors of our glorious bliss*
> *We soon shall sing the Three in One,*
> *And God beholding as he is*
> *For ever shout around his throne.*[23]

In all these examples, the meaning of a thing—justice, friendship, God—is discovered *through* poetry, not *despite* poetry. And there's a good chance we will also understand a thing more truly and more fully through the experience of our senses, whether through speaking or singing or showing, in a way that a silent reading of the psalms might not make possible.

The psalms exist both within "the tradition of David" and within a community of poets. We find three kinds of poets in the Psalter: (1) those who are named and known, (2) those who are unnamed and unknown, and (3) those who are unnamed but known by the guild to which they belong. In the Psalter we have poems by David and in the spirit of David.[24] We have poems by the guilds of temple musicians: Korahites and Asaphites.[25] And we have poems by individuals who remain anonymous.

Whether known or unknown or otherwise, the poets we find in the book of Psalms give voice to both their own concerns and the concerns of the community. It is not one or the other. It is both. The heartbreaks of moms and dads, the hopes of young and old, the fears of the working class and the anxieties of the ruling class, the little people and the famous people—everybody somehow, somewhere, gets a voice.

The characteristic mark of poetry in the Psalter is parallelism. One of the features of biblical poetry is that it says things in the tersest way possible; it is not a flowery or a rhapsodic style of poetry.[26] The most recognizable characteristic of biblical poetry is what scholars called "parallelism," rather than the more common characteristic of rhyme in popular poetry.[27] It is like the fundamental call-and-response device of the ancient biblical world. One line calls out to another, expecting it to respond—positively, negatively, or otherwise.

Four examples of typical Hebrew poetry are these:

> I will call to mind the deeds of the LORD;
>> I will remember your wonders of old.
>
>>> (Ps. 77:11)

> Weeping may linger for the night,
>> But joy comes with the morning.
>
>>> (Ps. 30:5b)

> Let all the earth fear the LORD;
>> Let all the inhabitants of the world stand in awe of him.
>
>>> (Ps. 33:8)

> When the waters saw you, O God,
>> When the waters saw you, they were afraid;
>> the very deep trembled.
>
>>> (Ps. 77:16)

Psalm 77:11 represents what's called *synonymous* parallelism, where the second line basically restates the first line. Psalm 30:5 is an example of *antithetic* parallelism, in which the two lines express opposite thoughts. Psalm 33:8 involves what scholars call a *grammatical* or *lexical* parallelism, where verbs and nouns play off each other in some fashion. And Psalm 77:16 is an example of *synthetic* parallelism, where the second line heightens or specifies the first line.

Each of these examples together constitutes Hebrew parallelism.[28] What it is not is *mere repetition*; it is instead like a dialogue between lines or sections of a psalm. Such a dialogue results in dense expression— from the heart of the psalmist to God, and from the psalmist to the community. As it relates to prayer, parallelism makes it possible for the heart to sink itself deeply into the psalmist's words, to chew on them like a dog on a bone, to linger in prayer, and to hear the voice of others in our common prayer to God.[29]

Conclusion

Poetry, it should be stressed, is not a mere forerunner to propositional speech or the dispensable companion to practical language. While propositional and practical talk belong to the constellation of media by which God reveals himself to us and by which we communicate to God in response, they do not exhaust it. That constellation also includes poetic language, which we find not just in the psalms, but also in Joel and Job, Acts and Song of Solomon, Proverbs and Isaiah, Exodus and Ezekiel, Luke and Hebrews, and Zechariah and Revelation.

Poetry is a native language of God and of the people of God. It is a mother tongue of the Word Incarnate on whose lips the psalmist's words came naturally. And it is the medium of art by which the Author of Scripture, the Holy Spirit, instructs us to address God by way of the prayers and praises of the psalms.

At its best, good poetry makes the familiar strange, and the strange familiar. As a work of poetry, the psalms make what is familiar to us about God, life, faith, and prayer strange again, reminding us that these things cannot be domesticated or absolutely mastered. But they also make the things that are strange to us—like God, life, faith, prayer—familiar again, reminding us that these are things we *can* know and do. No credentials or professional degrees are required.

Like prayer, finally, poetry is a way to love people by paying careful attention to their lives. When I pray nightly with our daughter, we pray specific things. We pray slowly and deliberately about health, travel, friends, troubles, food, rabbits, nightmares, grandparents. Instead of rushing through our prayer, we pay attention to the things Jesus would want for them. And the poetry of the psalms is like that: a way to help us pay attention to the things that matter to God—and to my neighbor and the world as well.

QUESTIONS FOR REFLECTION

1. How do the Eugene Peterson and George Herbert quotes at the beginning of this chapter inform your perception of the psalms as poetry?
2. Some of us love poetry, others frankly do not, and plenty of us find ourselves intimidated or confused by it. Where do you put yourself on this spectrum? How might the psalms invite you to understand poetry as something any person could appreciate?
3. What do you wish poets would tell you to help you understand poetry and how it works?
4. Consider one of the primary metaphors in the psalms: "God as shepherd." How has God been your shepherd over the course of your life (or not)? What other metaphors resonate with your experience of God?
5. How does reading the psalms as poetry slow you down? Does this encourage or discourage you? In what ways would you like to be able to slow down more and pay more careful attention? How might the poetry of the psalms strengthen the muscles of paying attention and help you see God as the one who cares deeply about the details of your life?
6. Is the idea of parallelism in Hebrew poetry new to you? How does this style help you re-see the psalms and what they're doing through poetry? What might this style say about how we can talk to God, both personally and as a community?

Exercises

1. Read Psalm 8 or 148 in a paraphrase version of the Bible, like *The Voice*, *The Living Bible*, or *The Message*, which captures the poetic feel of the psalm. Read it several times. Meditate on it. Pray through it. Consider memorizing a portion of it to carry in your heart as a way to maintain a lively conversation with God throughout the day.

2. Read Psalm 19 in *The Message*. First silently, then out loud. How does the psalm feel different when you read it out loud?

3. Read Psalm 4 responsively in your favorite translation. Have one person or group read the first verse, then the other person or group read the second, and so on. How does this manner of reading help you understand the meaning of the psalm differently?

4. Discuss with others the specific metaphors in the psalms that catch your attention. Share which metaphors do not resonate and why.

5. Convert a specific metaphor in the psalms into a prayer that you might share out loud with a group. For example, God as:
   - king
   - shepherd
   - rock
   - refuge
   - fortress
   - dwelling place
   - judge
   - light and shield
   - song and strength
   - help

6. Try writing your own psalm using the guide below, and consider sharing and discussing it with a friend or a small group:
   - Choose a theme or a topic.
   - Keep your phrases succinct and avoid long sentences.
   - Be specific and concrete in your statements, rather than abstract and generic.

- Choose evocative imagery and concrete metaphors to help you see what you're praying.
- Use the biblical poetic style of parallelism to create a rhythm in your psalm.
- Title your psalm.

PRAYER

Dear Jesus, you who loved the sounds and ways of words as the Word made Flesh, show me where my story fits inside your big Story. Help me to feel your care as the Good Shepherd, your nourishment as the Bread, your comfort as the Light, your welcome as the Door, your guidance as the Way, your sweet sustenance as the Vine, and your hope as the Resurrection and the Life, so that I might become a living poem of your beautiful ways and words in the world. Amen.

6

SADNESS

Blessed are you who weep now.
—LUKE 6:21

Unless those who proclaim the Gospel acknowledge honestly that darkness . . . they might as well save their breath for all the lasting difference their proclaiming will make to anybody.

—FREDERICK BUECHNER[1]

A BROKEN WORLD

We live in a broken world. Divorce fractures a family, a child abandons the faith, a friendship sours over a word that has wounded and refuses to be healed, or a prolonged loneliness leads to a crippling depression. The loss of meaningful work provokes suicidal thoughts, while the burden of unpayable debt plunges a family into poverty. An unexpected death leaves one heartbroken, even as experiences of chronic pain rob the joy from life's simplest pleasures.

And feelings of emptiness, quiet despair, or repeated failure characterize particular seasons of our life in an acute and painful way.[2]

Other experiences of brokenness occur at a societal level. A city is yet again ruined by floods, which leave its citizens displaced and bitter. Forest fires devour homes and animal life. A terror attack decimates a public market. Systemic racism leads to a nightmarish cycle of violence. Religious persecution turns an entire community into a refugee people without a home. Volatile oil prices put entire industries at risk. And the outbreak of a viral infection causes the death of millions.

Poverty, oppression, disease, genocide, and environmental decay—they all mark our world in some way.

On April 17, 2010, my wife and I lost our first baby to a miscarriage. This took place on my thirty-eighth birthday. For months afterward we carried around a gnawing pain—a pain that slowly ate us up from the inside, leaving us profoundly disoriented. On September 11, 2011, our daughter Blythe came into the world. Hope again surged in our hearts. Other children would now come easily, we thought. Our dream of a big family—five children!—could still be achieved, our advancing years notwithstanding.

Two days shy of Christmas 2014, after months of fertility treatments, we lost our second child to miscarriage. After this our marriage suffered considerably. Our communication repeatedly broke down, and our capacity to meet each other's needs dissipated. Small hurts flared up into angry conflict, and each of us resorted to surrogates that we hoped might dull the pain but that only made things worse.

There are still days when the pain feels almost unbearable. Neither of us is getting younger, our parents are growing older, our friends' children are reaching their college years, and the train, so it feels, is passing us by. What we needed then was language to say out loud what our hearts can only grasp at with inarticulate groans. What we needed, quite desperately, was a community to bear witness to our sadness. Above all, what we needed was to know that God can handle our broken hearts and our raging words of protest.

This is what the psalms would offer us—then and now. Here are prayers of lament that furnish us with language for the seemingly unspeakable. Here are songs to name the sorrow in the company of the faithful. Here are poems that give coherent shape to our incoherent feelings in the presence of our Maker, who has, it often feels, seemingly abandoned us to our inconsolable pain.

> Give ear to my words, O Lord,
> Consider my groaning.
> Heed the sound of my cry for help.
>
> (Ps. 5:1–2 NASB)

> Turn to me and be gracious to me,
> For I am lonely and afflicted.
>
> (Ps. 25:16 NASB)

What the lament psalms have offered us in our hour of need, they offer to all who find themselves in need: edited language to give expression to our unedited emotions.

What then is the basic pattern of psalms of lament? What are their thematic concerns? And what is the good news they offer to each of us?

THE BASIC SHAPE OF LAMENT PSALMS

A careful reader of the Psalter will soon discover two types of lament psalms. One type gives voice to an individual's concern, such as Psalms 5, 6, 17, 22, 41, 88, and 109. Here topics include experiences of abandonment, sickness, abuse, loss, and so on. While wholly personal, these individual laments have been incorporated into the public life of Israel's worship through communal discernment of the final editors of the Psalter, and they hereby become any given person's lament. Psalm 6:6–7 is illustrative:

> I am weary with my moaning;
>> every night I flood my bed with tears;
>> I drench my couch with my weeping.
> My eyes waste away because of grief;
>> they grow weak because of all my foes.

A second type gives voice to communal experiences of lament, such as Psalms 44, 74, 83, 85, and 89. The topics that occupy these public events of loss include drought, famine, epidemic, national devastation, war, and so on. Psalms 44:13–14 and 74:1 offer us good examples of this type:

> You have made us the taunt of our neighbors,
>> the derision and scorn of those around us.
> You have made us a byword among the nations,
>> a laughingstock among the peoples.

> O God, why do you cast us off forever?
>> Why does your anger smoke against the sheep
>> of your pasture?

The majority of the lament psalms end in affirmations of hope or confessions of praise, as Psalms 5 and 7 vividly show us. Others, like Psalms 44 and 88, end on a grim note. Both kinds, however, belong in Holy Scripture; and, for that reason, they belong in our practices of personal and corporate devotion too.

With psalms of lament—individual and communal—there is a recognizable pattern. Psalm 13 represents the typical pattern of such a psalm: a complaint, a petition, a resolution.

A Complaint (vv. 1–2)

How long, O LORD? Will you forget me forever?
How long will you hide your face from me?

How long must I bear pain in my soul,
>and have sorrow in my heart all day long?
How long shall my enemy be exalted over me?

A Petition (vv. 3–4)

Consider and answer me, O LORD my God!
>Give light to my eyes, or I will sleep the sleep of death,
and my enemy will say, "I have prevailed";
>my foes will rejoice because I am shaken.

A Resolution (vv. 5–6)

But I trusted in your steadfast love;
>my heart shall rejoice in your salvation.
I will sing to the LORD,
>because he has dealt bountifully with me.

While there are plenty of variations on this pattern, the complaints are directed chiefly to God. Psalm 3:1 says this: "Oh LORD, how many are my foes!" Psalm 10:12 adds, "Arise, O LORD; O God, lift up Your hand. Do not forget the afflicted" (NASB). What are the complaints about? They may be about God, about one's life, or about a presumed enemy. Psalm 38:3 states, "There is no health in my bones because of my sin." Psalm 72:4 asks of God, "Save the children of the needy and crush the oppressor" (NASB).

The kinds of petitions the psalmists make of God range widely. They include requests for healing, deliverance, vindication, provision, and protection, and, in the cases of confession of sin, forgiveness. The final resolution of a psalm of lament may involve a confession of trust; it may involve a resolve to praise or a promise to obey; or it may involve a confident affirmation of God's own faithfulness, even if there is no empirical data to prove it. Eugene Peterson observes:

[The primary language of prayer is people] calling out their trouble—pain, guilt, doubt, despair—to God. Their lives are threatened. If they don't get help they will be dead, or diminished to some critical degree. The language of prayer is forged in the crucible of trouble. When we can't help ourselves and call for help, when we don't like where we are and want out, when we don't like who we are and want a change, we use primal language, and this language becomes the root language of prayer.[3]

THE PSALMS OF SADNESS

One of the most striking things about these lament psalms is that they include the interrogation of God. This, as it turns out, is a divinely approved form of address.[4] Psalm 121:4 confesses that the Lord is the one who neither sleeps nor slumbers but watches over us. But in Psalm 44:23, the psalmist dares to say, "Awake, Lord! Why do you sleep? Rouse yourself! Do not reject us forever" (NIV). Here, the psalmist sounds like Elijah, who taunts the priests of the god Baal:

> Shout louder! . . . Surely he is a god! Perhaps he is deep in thought, or busy, or traveling. Maybe he is sleeping and must be awakened.
> (1 Kings 18:27 NIV)

Is this the way one speaks to the Maker of heaven and earth? Is this how you talk to the Holy One? Is this how we ought to address the Sovereign God? According to the psalmist, the answer is, at times, yes.

It is a daring theology on display. Finding himself in acute pain, the psalmist mouths off. He presses the Lord for an answer, but the Lord keeps silent. "Do not be silent!" the psalmist responds (Pss. 35:22; 109:1). It is yet again evidence of the kind of visceral honesty that belongs in the place of faithful worship. This is no faithless cry against the Almighty. This is not the attack of an atheist. This is the wrestling-out of faith *in the presence of the Lord.* For the psalmist, there is no "civilized" speech; there is no stiff upper lip or quiet resignation. There is only more intense address *before the face of God.*

It is not only the psalmist's life that is at stake; it is also—and more importantly—the Lord's name that is at stake. It is God's reputation that is in question. It is God's character and capacity to fulfill his promises that are at issue. "Deliver us . . . for your name's sake," the psalmist exclaims in Psalm 79:9. Brueggemann comments that while such prayers may trouble us, and we may resist praying this way often, they are thoroughly biblical:

> The speaker is *honest enough* to know that yearning, and the speaking is *faithful enough* to submit the yearning to God.[5] (emphasis original)

The psalms of lament are full of imperatives: forgive (Ps. 79:9), heal (Ps. 6:2), vindicate (Ps. 43:1), deliver (Ps. 31:15), sustain (Ps. 119:116–117). The most frequent imperative is *remember* (Ps. 74). These psalms invite the faithful to speak out loud what needs to be confessed in the assembly of God's people: *Remember me! Remember us! Remember your promises!*

Whether God responds or not in the moment or much later or beyond the life of the psalmist is another matter. Whenever the psalmist voices his complaint, it is the sign of an active, not a passive, faith. In Brueggemann's words, "Such prayer is intense, dangerous, and urgent. It moves deeply beneath our usual innocuous prayer in which nothing is at stake, because in this kind of prayer, everything is at stake."[6]

Plenty of these psalms lead to silence or to the dust (Pss. 4:4; 28:1; 39:9). For some the silence may be oppressive. For others it may further confuse their idea of God. For still others the silence becomes an occasion to hear the still, small voice of the Lord. This voice cannot be heard in the clamor of protest. It cannot be heard in the whirlwind of busyness that distracts us, if only temporarily, from our pain. It can be clearly heard only in the silence. It is the voice of the one who sees and hears. Psalm 55:17 is representative:

> Evening and morning and at noon
>   I utter my complaint and moan,
>   and he will hear my voice.

A number of psalms of lament lead a worshiper to the dust. Psalm 22:15b says, "you lay me in the dust of death." Psalm 44:25 says, "We are brought down to the dust; our bodies cling to the ground" (NIV). Within the context of the psalms, "the dust" represents the opposite of voluntary worship. It is a place of misery and exhaustion. It is a place for the depressed. The dust is as low as it gets for *nephesh hayah*, living beings.

Yet here, in the dust, in lowliness, a window of hope opens up for the faithful. For if it is from the dust of the earth, the *adamah*, that God forms our primeval parent, Adam, then it is also from this place of divine creativity that something new can be born. Carroll Stuhlmueller remarks, "Silently lost in adoration within the dust before God is preparation for the ultimate answer to all questions: one's becoming a new creature in Christ Jesus."[7]

The dust, under this light, becomes good news for the faithful. In Christ's economy, things do not die without reason; they die in order to be resurrected. In fact, it is the Lord's pleasure to raise the poor from the dust (Ps. 113:7). The psalmist writes:

> As a father has compassion for his children,
>> so the LORD has compassion for those who fear him;
> for he knows how we were made;
>> he remembers that we are dust.
>
>> (Ps. 103:13–14)

In this place of lowliness, we are delivered from the damaging idea that our happiness rests in our self-sufficiency. Our happiness rests instead in utter dependence on our Father in heaven. In the dust we receive the Holy Spirit, who renews us in the life of Jesus, the firstborn from the dead.

This, of course, does not mean that everything will be resolved in our acceptance of silence or lowliness.[8] Faith is a gift, yes. Faith certainly frees us to embrace the goodness of God in the face of suffering. But it does not mean that happiness will always mark our lives. For those who experience systemic injustice, there is often no clear resolution. For victims of abuse, who may still have painful scars in their bodies and psyche, there are often unanswered questions. For the broken and the powerless, there is frequently only one option: the need to endure.

Yet for people such as these the psalms give a voice. They, too, have a place in the company of God's people. The psalmist prays, "Deliver me from my enemies, O my God; protect me from those who rise up against me" (Ps. 59:1). In Psalm 88:1–4, the psalmist cries out:

> O LORD, God of my salvation,
>> when, at night, I cry out in your presence,
> let my prayer come before you;
>> incline your ear to my cry.
>
> For my soul is full of troubles,
>> and my life draws near to Sheol.
> I am counted among those who go down to the Pit;
>> I am like those who have no help.

The psalms offer yet another gift. In the face of incoherent experiences, they offer us a coherent poem. This may seem like an odd gift. Who needs a poem when you need justice or a livelihood? Who wants a rhyme when we want a family member back from the dead? But when nothing makes sense, the lament psalms give coherence to the incoherence of our world.

They offer a beginning, a middle, and an end, instead of a seemingly meaningless narrative. They present a rhythm of sounds instead of a cacophony of noise. They suggest an orderly world of metaphors, instead of a disordered mess of thoughts and feelings. And in offering these things, the psalms reframe our sense of life. And they do so in light of a particular history.

It is important to remember that these psalms do not resolve to pure subjectivity; they reside instead within a tradition. Frequently the psalmist takes upon his lips the familiar words of Israel's confession: "For you, O Lord, are good and forgiving, abounding in steadfast love to all who call on you" (Ps. 86:5). Here the psalmist declares in faith the creedal words of his forebears, the words of the Law and the Prophets (Ex. 34:6; Num. 14:18; 2 Kings 19:19; Isa. 37:16).

We are not the first to experience doubt, the psalmist reminds us. Our experiences of anger and depression are not original, even if they are personally felt as if for the first time. Others have been there. Others have crafted words in faith that bear repeating. We stand in a tradition as the people of God, and that tradition hands over to us good words.

These words need to find themselves on our lips and said out loud, again and again, in the company of others with whom we can share our pain so they can work their healing power on us. They heal us by offering us an opportunity to become whole, rather than leaving us fractured by our losses and disoriented in our sadness. They heal us by offering us hope in the form of words that name realities, helping us to make sense of often-senseless things. And they heal us by bringing us face to face with a God who is compassionate and gracious, abounding in love, faithful till the end (Ps. 86:15).

CONCLUSION

In the end, to ignore these words or to choose more "polite" words is to believe that God cannot handle our broken humanity. It is to believe that God has forgotten how we are made. But God has not forgotten. God has not run out of compassion. In Christ he suffers with us. In Christ he shares our brokenness. He, too, knows what it is like to pray with loud cries (Heb. 5). He, too, grieves and feels distress (Mark 13). He, too, weeps (Luke 19). He, too, has felt abandoned and forsaken (Mark 14–15).

What we find in these psalms of lament, it is important to stress, is never *mere* sadness. We find instead sadness before the face of God. For here there is never mere complaint; here there is complaint brought *to* God, rather than kept *from* God. Here there is no victim mentality, even if the psalmist is a real victim of violence who requires vindication. Here there is a wholly honest reckoning of pain *within the community* of those who seek to be wholly human, as hard as that may be, wrestling with God, not apart from God.

John Calvin sums up well these psalms of lament: "[Here] we have permission given us to lay open before [God] our infirmities, which we would be ashamed to confess before men."[9] This is an incalculable gift. It is a gift that Phaedra and I receive as we mourn all the small and big things in our life, alongside a community of those who seek to walk with Jesus, trusting that these psalms are God's chosen vehicle for making us not just whole and holy but, by the Spirit, more deeply compassionate to our suffering neighbor.

QUESTIONS FOR REFLECTION

1. What is one thing from this past week that you feel needs to be lamented in your own life? What is one thing that calls for lament in your own community? What is one thing that deserves to be lamented at a national or global level?
2. What is one thing that is hard for you to lament? What are things that might be easier for you to lament?
3. What kinds of experiences help you to feel your sadness? What makes it hard for you to feel sadness? Do you feel embarrassed by it? Ashamed? Scared? Does it feel wrong, like you might be the only one to feel what you feel?
4. What do you think might be lost by not sharing our sadness and our laments as a community? What do you think might be gained by sharing these feelings as a community?
5. What is one passage in the psalms of lament (Pss. 5; 7; 13; 22; 35; 42–43; 59; 88; 109) that resonates with your experience of lament?

6. In what specific way do you wish for God, or for others, to be present to you in your lament today?

EXERCISES

1. Find a moment to be silent. If all you can manage is five or ten minutes of silence, thank God for it. In this moment of silence, be present to whatever it is that has caused you to feel sad or upset. What is one thing that comes to mind as you reflect on this experience? In what ways do you feel that your sadness is bearable—or unbearable? In what ways do you feel that your experience is seen or unseen by others, or even by God? Give yourself permission to feel the sadness without the need to apologize or explain it. Trust that God is with you in your sadness. Invite God to be present to you in your sadness. If you feel the need to give expression to your sadness, consider praying one of the individual psalms of lament, such as Psalms 6, 11, 17, 26, 38, 41, or 86.

2. Write out your own psalm of lament, following the basic pattern presented in the chapter on poetry. Write your complaint to God. Write a specific petition of God. Write a resolution to trust that God will hear and heed your petition in a timely fashion, even if it is not according to our timetable. Give yourself permission to end, like Psalm 13, on a tone of hope, or like Psalm 88, in the dust and darkness that may feel all too real. Trust that you are not alone in this experience, but that God in Christ is with you, that the Spirit of God intercedes for you "with sighs too deep for words" (Rom. 8:26), and that others are in a similar place.

3. Study a specific psalm of lament. As you go through the study, consider memorizing parts or the whole of a psalm to carry in your head and heart those words that might enable you to name reality and to embrace what is true—or at least to stumble toward the truth.

4. Share with one another a personal or corporate occasion for lament. Consider also praying Psalm 41 antiphonally—that is, back and forth, as a kind of call and response. Consider ways in which you might be intentionally present to one another's laments throughout the coming week. Consider ways you might walk with one another through laments without feeling the need to offer immediate practical solutions.

5. Craft a prayer based on one of the communal psalms of lament (Pss. 44; 74; 77; 79; 80; 83; 85; 89). Consider using this prayer in your communal times of worship and prayer.

PRAYER

Merciful God, you who weep with those who weep, who rescue those who have been oppressed, who incline your ear to the needy, who draw near to the abandoned, who bind up the brokenhearted, who raise up those who are laid low, and who feel compassion for those who are broken in body or in spirit: hear our prayer. Do not be deaf to our pain. Have pity on us in our affliction. Bring an end to our distress. Preserve our lives. Rescue us. Heal us. Be near to us this day. We pray this so that we might join the company of those who take refuge in you and praise your holy name. We pray this in Jesus' name, a man of sorrows, acquainted with grief, on whom we cast all our cares. Amen.

7

ANGER

*And so I continued to bear the crippling weight of anger,
bitterness, and resentment toward those who caused my
suffering—the sea/ring fire that penetrated my body;
the ensuing burn baths; the dry and itchy skin; the
inability to sweat, which turned my flesh into an oven in
Vietnam's sweltering heat.*
— KIM PHUC PHAN THI[1]

*I am grateful, too, to Lewis for having the courage to yell,
to doubt, to kick at God with angry violence. This is a
part of healthy grief not often encouraged.*
— MADELEINE L'ENGLE[2]

THE ANGERS OF THE WORLD

I have struggled with anger my whole life. In college I would walk
around the campus with anger simmering just below the surface. Any

number of things might provoke me to an outburst—a careless comment, a missed bus, a lost opportunity, an unwanted interruption, an unexpected failure. Usually those closest to me, family or dear friends, experienced firsthand my eruptions of anger.

After our daughter Blythe arrived, I found myself driving around the streets of Durham, North Carolina, with an infant in the back seat. Like a protagonist in a revenge-themed movie, I perceived all cars as a threat to my only child's life and, therefore, to my well-being. I would sit at traffic lights, a surplus of anger churning inside me, and imagine a scene where I would beat an attacker into unconsciousness with a baseball bat—a bat that I didn't actually own.

A few years before this, when I was a young pastor in Austin, Texas, I blew up at a fellow pastor. I had nursed resentment against him for things I believed he had failed to do that I felt he ought to have done. During a staff meeting he said something that touched a sore spot in me. One moment I was listening; the next moment I was yelling. I yelled at the top of my lungs. I shook my fists at him and bludgeoned him with a litany of slights. It was ugly, and it was embarrassing. I'm still embarrassed about it.

But I know that I am not the only one who struggles with anger. Plenty of things make people angry around the world: the state of the economy, the outcome of a sporting event, recurring sickness, the betrayal of a friend, the experience of domestic violence, the abuse of power by those in authority, or the killing of innocent people.

In 2018, Rebecca Traister released her book *Good and Mad: The Revolutionary Power of Women's Anger*. In it she argues that anger at repeated experiences of injustice has fueled movements like Black Lives Matter and #MeToo. The Catholic faithful have been angry for a long time at the failure of bishops to address the problem of clergy abuse, of both children and nuns.

In the 2018 movie *The First Purge*, a lead character declares: "If we want to save our country, we must release all our anger in one night." In the context of the movie, this involves allowing citizens to use violence in whatever way they wish for one night of the year.

In the *Time* magazine article "The Las Vegas Shooting and Our Age of Anger," editor-at-large Jeffrey Kluger writes this:

> Americans have made something of a fetish of our rage of late—a fact that's even been leaking into our language. The base is never just "animated," it's always "enraged." Health care debates are never "spirited," they're always "furious." In the run-up to the 2016 election, a CNN/ORC poll found that 69% of Americans reported being either very or somewhat angry at the state of the nation.[3]

What Bernie Sanders actually said was this: "I am angry and millions of Americans are angry."[4]

People get angry at themselves too. They say things like: *I'm so stupid; I'm fat; I'm ugly; I always fail.* Some people nag. Others erupt in sudden fury. Still others simmer in passive-aggressive behavior. Unrighteous anger destroys, while righteous anger fuels the work of justice and peace. God gets angry. Jesus gets angry. Saint Paul says plenty of things about anger, not all of them self-evident.

What exactly then are we to do with our experiences of anger—or the experiences of those nearby? Suppress it? Deny it? Indulge it? How do we keep from "losing our head" when we feel used by people? How do we forgive someone who is unwilling to own up to their harmful actions? And what do we do with emotions that threaten to turn revenge fantasies into reality? It is questions such as these that this chapter seeks to answer.

THE PSALMS OF ANGER

One way forward is to take advantage of the psalms of anger, sometimes called the imprecatory psalms or the curse psalms, which include Psalms 5, 6, 11, 12, 35, 37, 52, 54, 69, 79, 83, 109, 137, and 143, among others. It begs the question, of course, that Christians have been asking since the early church era: Can we *really* pray the curse psalms?[5]

Aren't these prayers diametrically opposed to the "Spirit of the Gospel," as Isaac Watts once asserted?[6] Didn't Jesus forbid us to curse our enemies? Did he not command us to pray for those who persecute us? Isn't anger one of the seven deadly sins? And is C. S. Lewis right, in the end, that "one way of dealing with these terrible or (dare we say?) contemptible Psalms is simply to leave them alone"?[7]

I would like to think that Lewis is wrong on this account. We do not leave them alone. We trust instead that God has given us the angry psalms to help us feel angry without being undone by our anger. We trust that God has given us these psalms to rescue us from the desire to do violence to others. And we trust that God has given us these psalms to heal and unite us, and to show us the possibility of a faithful anger.

Within the context of the Psalter, a curse psalm is a psalm where the psalmist prays angry prayers against his enemies and those he perceives to be God's enemies. The psalmist curses his enemy because he is hurt. The hurt is so acute, the wound so deep, that it provokes the psalmist to anger. And, as my counselor would often remind me in our sessions together, while the movement from "sad" to "mad" in our experiences of profound pain is a natural one, the movement from "mad" to "bad," where we commit sin against our neighbor, is always a choice. And it is from this decision to do violence, either to another or to ourselves, that the curse psalms rescue us.

Along these lines, because sadness always lies at the core of our experiences of anger, the basic shape of curse psalms follows the basic shape of psalms of lament, because they, too, are a lament. Psalm 12 is typical of such psalms. It begins with a complaint by the faithful, transitions to a petition to God, and ends with a response by the faithful.

A Complaint (vv. 1–2)

Help, O LORD, for there is no longer anyone who is godly;
　　the faithful have disappeared from *humankind*.
They utter lies to each other;
　　with flattering lips and a double heart they speak.

(emphasis added)

A Petition (vv. 3–6)

May the LORD cut off all flattering lips,
>   the tongue that makes great boasts,
those who say, "With our tongues we will prevail;
>   our lips are our own—who is our master?"
"Because the poor are despoiled, because the needy groan,
>   I will now rise up," says the LORD;
>   "I will place them in the safety for which they long."
The promises of the LORD are promises that are pure,
>   silver refined in a furnace on the ground,
>   purified seven times.

A Response (vv. 7–8)

You, O LORD, will protect us;
>   you will guard us from this generation forever.
On every side the wicked prowl,
>   as vileness is exalted among *humankind*.

>   (emphasis added)

With this basic shape in mind, what are some of the thematic concerns of the psalms of anger? Let me suggest four.

First, whatever else the curse psalms are about, they are about God. The Psalter opens with language describing the God who judges the wicked, and it closes with language describing the God who judges the wicked. This is evident from the beginning to the end of the Psalter:

>   For the LORD watches over the way of the righteous,
>   but the way of the wicked will perish.

>   (Ps. 1:6)

>   The LORD lifts up the downtrodden;
>   he casts the wicked to the ground.

>   (Ps. 147:6)

From the psalmist's perspective, it is ultimately not all about us. It is not all about our experience of the wicked, which in the Psalter stands as a shorthand for individuals and societies and powers that stand in some way opposed to God's good order. It is not about our need to punish and to give "bad people" what they deserve. Ultimately it is about God. It is about the character of God. It is about the faithfulness and goodness and holiness and mercy of God.

It is important to be clear, moreover, that the vengeance language in the psalms is not about personal vengeance. It's about God's justice. What the psalmist longs for is God's vindication. "In the Hebrew tradition, the execution of justice is the divine prerogative. God is the one who knows and embraces pain, and the plea is that God will act on the side of the faithful. . . . Faith in the Psalter is not idealistic but disturbingly realistic."[8]

As hard as it is at times to resist the desire to get revenge and to give people who have done wrong "what they deserve," this resisting is exactly what the psalms invite us to do. They don't deny our anger at being wronged, but they do deny us the right take vengeance into our own hands (Rom. 12:18–20). It is in this sense that the psalms of anger are essentially prayers of relinquishment. To pray this rhetoric of violence is to cede to God my desire to become violent: "Your will be done, on earth as it is in heaven" (Matt. 6:10).

Second, where people are oppressed, the character of God is at stake. When violence is done against human creatures made in the image of God, then, from the psalmist's perspective, that divine image is susceptible to defacement. When human community is ruptured by injustice, then the purposes of the Holy Trinity are jeopardized. When tribe slaughters tribe and nation wars against nation, then the God who made every tribe and nation will need to step in and save what is his.

When damage comes to creation, then the Creator's work is threatened.[9] Psalm 139:19–20 illustrates this sentiment:

> O that you would kill the wicked, O GOD,
>   and that the bloodthirsty would depart from me—

> Those who speak of you maliciously,
>> and lift themselves up against you for evil!

For the psalmist the language of vengeance is a way to say: This world is *your* idea, God. This human life is *your* doing, God. If you don't do something to stop the wicked from destroying it all, it's *your* reputation that's at stake! Don't let it come to nothing! Don't let this suffering be meaningless! Deliver us—for *your* name's sake (Ps. 54:1–3).

When the psalmists experience human injustice or a terror of nature, they feel acutely that the character of God is at stake. This is, of course, what Christians have felt for centuries—whether in the recent massive exit of Christians from the church because of failures by pastors to properly care for the flock, or in the massive earthquake of 1755 in Lisbon, Portugal, that prompted the French writer Voltaire to write his novel *Candide*, in which he attacked the notion that "all is for the best."

Third, the cursing language of the psalms is akin to profane language. The psalmist's experience of violence inevitably provokes hyperbolic language as a way to express the shocking violation of the good order of God's world. In Psalm 35:1, as Peterson renders it in *The Message*, the psalmist cries, "Harass these hecklers, GOD, punch these bullies in the nose." In Psalm 109 the psalmist says this about his enemies:

> May his children be orphans,
>> and his wife a widow.
> May his children wander about and beg;
>> may they be driven out of the ruins they inhabit.

> May there be no one to do him a kindness,
>> nor anyone to pity his orphaned children.
> May his posterity be cut off;
>> may his name be blotted out in the second generation.
>>>> (vv. 9–10, 12–13)

This is cursing language. It's harsh and unnerving and, quite frankly, very cruel. *May his children wander about and beg?* Let me suggest here a hypothesis that might make sense of this language. The hyperbolic, outrageous, exaggerated, and perhaps even obscene language of the curse psalms occupies the same basic territory as profane language. Let me explain.

In her book *Purity and Danger,* the anthropologist Mary Douglas argues that every society arranges itself around an orderly system of symbols that enable it to thrive.[10] She calls this system of self-organization "purity." As Douglas sees it, purity is fundamentally about what enhances life (justice, honesty, clean water, the making of hospitals) and what hinders life (injustice, deceit, unsanitary bathrooms, the making of sex slaves).

The opposite of purity is disorder, or chaos.[11] While purity is related to order, it is also related to holiness. The "holy" space is the space of wholeness and, thus, also of life. To step outside of this holy space is to step into a profane space. In technical terms: inside is pure, outside is impure; inside is order, outside is chaos; inside is clean, outside is dirty.

This inside/outside language points to the importance of boundary lines. Boundary lines separate what is perceived to be the "good" from the "bad." In Israel, for instance, a leper is excluded from the inner spaces of the temple, the architectural symbol of Eden, because he represents an image of disorder. Because of his physical "mis-picturation," he poses a threat to the "good," the integral condition of bodily health. On specifically religious terms, he belongs "outside."[12]

The term *profane,* from the Latin *profanes* (*pro,* meaning "before"; *fanum,* meaning "temple"), suggests the idea of being "outside the temple." Profane space is the opposite of sacred space. In this light, profane language can be regarded as language that lies outside the boundaries of the sacred. In technical terms, it is *dirty* language because it transgresses the holy order.[13]

The function of profane language, then, is to facilitate expression of *uncommon, disordered,* and *undesirable* experiences.

When a carpenter hammers his thumb, he may scream a "curse" word, because his mishap does not belong to the good order of carpentry.[14] The profane expression corresponds to a profane experience. When a tornado destroys an entire town, its people may resort to "expletives" to describe their God-awful experience of tragic loss. Or when the rich and powerful prey, yet again, upon the poor and vulnerable, we may find ourselves using "swear" words to express the unholy, damnable nature of this obscene treatment of the weak in our society.

This, I believe, is partly what is at work in the cursing psalms. The psalmist uses a kind of profane language to give expression to profane experiences—experiences that violate human dignity and that desecrate God's good purposes for the world.

Fourth, curse psalms point the way to healing. In this last point, let me focus on one particular, and rather challenging, psalm: Psalm 137. While the first two sections of the psalm have generated vast numbers of musical and poetic settings—such as Antonín Dvořák's 1894 composition *Biblical Songs*, Op. 99, no. 7; Hasidic rapper Matisyahu's "Jerusalem," released in 2006; and Elizabeth Smart's 1945 poem "By Grand Central Station I Sat Down and Wept"—the third section has been removed from worship contexts throughout church history.[15]

But we're wrong to do so, argues the Croatian-born theologian Miroslav Volf, who insists that psalms such as these should remain within our devotional practice. "Such psalms may point to a way out of slavery to revenge and into the freedom of forgiveness."[16]

That's easier said than done, of course. But Christian practices that are devoid of demanding language, like the kind we find in the psalms, leave us vulnerable to theologies and pastoral practices that are incapable of dealing with the experience of anger that so easily leads to violence, with its systemic, multigenerational reverberations played out on the public scene and in the privacy of our homes.[17]

Christians should read Psalm 137, Volf argues, because it reminds us that by placing unattended rage before God, we place both our unjust enemy and our own vengeful self, face to face with a God who loves and does justice. Hidden in the dark chambers of our hearts and nourished by the system of darkness, hate grows and seeks to infest everything with its hellish will to exclusion. In the light of the justice and love of God, however, hate recedes and the seed is planted for the miracle of forgiveness.[18]

Where is our anger safe, then? Volf answers:

It's not safe simply bottled up in my own heart. It's not safe in some public space of venting our collective feelings. It is safe in the space where it is placed before the one God of both those whose children have been dashed against the rocks and of those who did the dashing of those children against the rocks.[19]

This being said, it is never easy to know how to incorporate a psalm like 137 or 88 or 109 into our life of faith. But it is important to remember that the Holy Spirit, as the Author of Scripture, keeps these psalms in the Bible for good reason: they lead us to Jesus. As Dietrich Bonhoeffer says:

The imprecatory psalm leads to the cross of Jesus and to the love of God which forgives enemies. I cannot forgive the enemies of God out of my own resources. Only the crucified Christ can do that, and I through him. Thus the carrying out of vengeance becomes grace for all men in Jesus Christ.[20]

CONCLUSION

Aristotle once said, "Anyone can become angry—that is easy. But to be angry with the right person, to the right degree, at the right time, for the right purpose, and in the right way—this is not easy."[21] This is another way of saying, perhaps, what Saint Paul said in an echo of Psalm 4:4 a few centuries later: "Be angry but do not sin" (Eph. 4:26). This, again, is easier said than done.

Thankfully, the psalms show us a way forward: how to pray angry prayers without being overcome by our anger; how to curse in context; how to hate without sinning; or, as Eugene Peterson once put it, how to "cuss without cussing."[22] The difference between a right and a wrong response to anger, I suggest, is the difference between a humble heart and a hardened heart.

A humble heart is honest to God about one's feelings. A hardened heart wants only to exact an eye for an eye. A humble heart entrusts one's enemies to God. A hardened heart demonizes one's enemies. A humble heart is angry *before the face of God* and in the presence of the community. A hardened heart hides from God and perpetually finds the community wanting. What the psalms invite us to choose is a humble heart.

This is, of course, easier said than done, especially for someone like myself who still struggles with anger. I struggle against the temptation to curse reckless drivers. I indulge imagined situations where I put a colleague "in his place" who has hurt me. And I fight to resist giving in to outbursts of ungodly anger at home. This is why I'm so grateful for the psalms of anger. For myself, they help me to speak before God and the people of God the angers of my heart—and to trust that, in this act of faithful and forceful speech, God will also heal my heart.

To pray them, in the end, is to trust that Jesus prays these same prayers in us and for us, and by his Spirit does something much better than "managing" our anger: he sets our hearts free to love our enemies in a way that we never imagined possible. In praying these prayers with Jesus, we likewise acquire the heart of Jesus and so discover the seemingly impossible: how to be faithfully angry.[23]

QUESTIONS FOR REFLECTION

1. What is one thing in recent weeks that has made you feel angry? It might be something relatively small, like being cut off in traffic, or something big, like experiencing a form of violence, or something that's happened to others.

2. In what way might it be hard for you to be honest about your feelings of anger? What are things from your family background, or personality type, or community culture that make it difficult for you to express anger? Do you feel embarrassed by it? Ashamed? Scared? Or like it feels wrong?

3. Do you know someone who expresses anger in healthy ways? What do you admire about them? Do you know someone who expresses anger in unhealthy ways? How do they express their anger—blow up, give the cold shoulder, shut down?

4. What is one passage in the psalms of anger (Pss. 5; 11; 35; 40; 54; 69; 79; 83; 109; 137; 143) that resonates with your experience?

5. In what specific way do you wish for God or for others to be present to your anger today?

6. What would it look like to create a hospitable space in our communities for people to express their anger faithfully, trusting that God is with them, rather than against them or removed from them? What would need to change in the culture of our communities for this to happen?

7. What practices in your personal and communal life—preaching, singing, prayer, testimony, mission, and so on—might cultivate a habit of faithful or righteous anger?

EXERCISES

1. Write down specific things that have caused you to become upset or angry. These may be things that have happened in the

past or just recently. Then write down in as much detail as you can how these experiences have made you feel. Again, try to be as honest with yourself about how you felt, not how you *wish* you felt or think you *should* have felt. Welcome God into this process.

2. Ask God to show you one person with whom you'd feel safe to share these experiences. It's important to know that your anger can be shared and shouldered by others, rather than you being alone, left to your own devices, and therefore vulnerable to further suppression or self-deception. Trust that speaking these things aloud in the presence of safe, trusted others, and in God's presence, is a step toward healing.

3. Pray one of the psalms of anger. Trust that God is able to receive your anger, including your anger at him. Trust that God welcomes your sometimes-incoherent prayers—your painful prayers; your helpless, doubt-filled, tearful prayers. Trust that Jesus welcomes it all and, by his Spirit, wishes to transform it into something redemptive and beautiful.

4. Study a specific psalm of anger or group of psalms together. This might include Psalm 5, 6, 11, 12, 35, 37, 40, 52, 54, 56, 58, 69, 79, 83, 109, 137, 139, 143, or 149.

5. Share with one another a personal or corporate occasion for anger. Consider also praying together Psalm 109 antiphonally—as a kind of call and response. Consider ways that you might walk with one another through feelings of anger without feeling the need to offer instant practical solutions.

6. Craft a prayer based on one of the communal psalms of anger. Consider using this prayer in your communal times together.

PRAYER

To the God whose holy anger heals;
to the Messiah whose righteous anger overcomes evil;

to the Spirit who keeps our angers from turning violent and destructive:
  receive our wounded hearts;
  take our burning words;
  protect us from the desire for revenge.
May our faithful angers become fuel for justice in our fractured world,
and for the mending of broken relations in our neighborhoods and homes.
For God's sake—and ours.
Amen.

8

JOY

Whenever I felt the beauty of the world in song or story, in the material universe around me, or glimpsed it in human love, I wanted to cry out with joy. The Psalms were an outlet for this enthusiasm of joy or grief.

—Dorothy Day[1]

Praise generates more praise; glory adds to glory. Praise works by overflow and contagion; it invites others to join in.

—Catherine La Cugna[2]

THE SONG OF THE SEA AND THE DANCE OF THE TREES

During my years as a pastor in Austin, there was a young man at our church whom I will never forget. His name was Tim. At the time, he was an MBA student at the University of Texas and had joined our congregation during his sojourn in college. As I remember him, Tim was the perfect image of the conservative business student: khaki pants, button-down dress shirt, soft-spoken, polite, gentle, measured, clean-cut, and smart as a whip.

But Tim was also a complete surprise of a human being. While our church was theologically charismatic, practically we were a rather moderate charismatic bunch. Hand-raising and the occasional holler of praise to God would not be uncommon. We were not, however, the stereotypical nonstop tongues-speaking, miracle-generating, Spirit-slaying, baptizing-in-the-Spirit, high-energy singing, Pentecostal two-step hopping congregation. People rarely, if ever, danced extravagantly. But Tim did.

At a certain point during our extended time of congregational song, Tim—usually standing at the end of a pew—would launch into what can only be described as part hopscotch, part hand-windmill, part Maria-von-Trapp-at-the-hills-that-are-alive-with-the-sound-of-music movement. It was an utterly unselfconscious and pure-hearted expression. For Tim, the words of Psalm 150 were to be taken literally: "Praise him with dancing!" He fully embodied the spirit of Psalm 30:12:

> I'm about to burst with song;
>> I can't keep quiet about you.
> GOD, my God,
>> I can't thank you enough.
>
> (THE MESSAGE)

I would often watch Tim with a combination of delight and envy. *That's what praise looks like*, I thought to myself. *That's how it goes, without affect, uninhibited by others' judgment. That's its free and full-hearted spirit.* I never once joined him, much to my regret today. But I did eventually ask him why he danced. His answer humbled me. He danced, he said, out of obedience. Dancing in this way did not come naturally to him. It was instead his sacrifice of praise to God.

"In singing praise," writes Walter Brueggemann, "all claims for the self are given up as the self is ceded over to God."[3] This is why in the psalms the sea "roars," the field "exults," and the trees "sing" (Ps. 96:11–12). This is why human beings yield themselves fully to God in dance and song. Such is the nature of self-abandonment as the unqualified response of our lives to God. Tim understood this fact well; and it is why, with the psalmist, he laughed often. The goodness of God overwhelmed him.[4]

The entire Psalter is called the *Tehillim*, the "Book of Praises," for a reason. It is here that we see what praise looks like, what praise sounds like, and what praise says to God. It says what creatures need to say to God. This includes the praise of God in history and the praise of God's creation. It involves praise of God's far-reaching redemption as well as the praise of God's intimate work of care and protection. It embraces the praise of saints and sinners.[5] It starts in praise and it yearns toward praise.

Because the psalms of praise feature the experience of joy, it is this collection of psalms that I explore at length in this chapter, without completely ignoring the Psalter's hymns and songs of thanksgiving.

THE PSALMS OF JOY

There are two basic shapes of a psalm of praise. The first involves a summons and a reason. Psalm 47:1–2 is a good example of this shape:

A Summons (v. 1)

Clap your hands, all you nations;
    shout to God with cries of joy. (NIV)

A Reason (v. 2)

For the LORD Most High is awesome,
    the great King over all the earth. (NIV)

The second involves the structure "because X, therefore Y." Psalm 27:5–6 illustrates this pattern well:

Because (vv. 5–6a)

For in the time of trouble he shall hide me in his pavilion: in the secret of his tabernacle shall he hide me; he shall set me up upon a rock.

And now shall mine head be lifted up above mine enemies round about me: (KJV)

Therefore (v. 6b)

therefore will I offer in his tabernacle sacrifices of joy; I will sing, yea, I will sing praises unto the LORD. (KJV)

All psalms of praise describe in some fashion who God is by telling the reader what he has done, and they invite the reader to bear witness to such a God and to yield oneself to this faithful God. It is a twin invitation to testimony and self-surrender, so that we might fully give ourselves over to God in praise.[6] But because the psalms bring praise and joy into a relationship that may surprise us or run counter to our common practices, it is important that we study this relationship carefully.

Psalms of praise assert and assume that God is the ultimate source of joy. This involves not just his character and deeds but his very presence as well. Psalm 16:11 says, "You will fill me with joy in your presence, with eternal pleasures at your right hand" (NIV). Psalm 43:4 describes the experience of going "to the altar of God" as the experience of joy and delight in God. In Psalm 21:6 the figure of the king receives God's "unending blessings" as the gift of gladness, "with the joy of your presence" (NIV).

Psalm 145, the first of the "Hallelujah Psalms," perhaps best captures the heart of a psalm of praise. In verse 4 the psalmist says, "One generation shall laud your works to another, and shall declare your mighty acts." Then follows a litany of praise characterized by terms of abundance: "The LORD is good to *all*" (v. 9 NIV, emphasis added); "*All* your works praise you, LORD" (v. 10); "The LORD is trustworthy in *all* he promises" (v. 13); "The LORD upholds *all* who fall" (v. 14); "The LORD is . . . faithful in *all* he does" (v. 17); "The LORD watches over *all* who love him" (v. 20).

Within the Psalter, the experience of joy is grounded in the work of God, but not in any generic sense. It is grounded in the economy of abundance that marks the life of God (Pss. 36:8; 78:25; 105:40). Praise is inevitably an experience of the overflow of God's faithful generosity.[7] Eugene Peterson, in his introduction to the book of Philippians in *The Message*, describes the life of Christ this way:

> It is this "spilling out" quality of Christ's life that accounts for the happiness of Christians, for joy is life in excess, the overflow of what cannot be contained within any one person.[8]

While sin may tempt us to live in an economy of scarcity, where any number of things are found to be wanting, a psalm of praise invites us to experience the joyful presence of God as a presence of abundance, in fact and in faith. In praising God with the words of the psalms, explains Thomas Merton, "we can come to know Him better. Knowing Him better we love Him better, loving Him better we find our happiness in Him."[9]

Joy is what the whole creation does. All throughout the Psalter, creation raises its joyful praise to God. The rivers clap their hands and the mountains sing for joy (Ps. 98:8). Both sunrise and sundown ring out with songs of joy; or, as the NASB translates it, "You make the dawn and the sunset shout for joy" (Ps. 65:8). The pastures and the meadows and the valleys shout for joy (Ps. 65:12–13), the heavens rejoice, the earth is glad, the trees sing and the fields make merry (Ps. 96:11–12).

As the psalms see it, all of creation would instruct us in the practice of joy, if we'd let it. This is certainly what John Calvin thought. God, he believed, wants to ravish us by his creation, and by it, to ravish us with himself. "If one feather of a peacock is able to ravish us," Calvin preaches, "what will God's infinite majesty do?" If a hawk can ravish and amaze us, "what ought all his works do when we come to the full numbering of them?"[10] Creation both exhibits the joy of the Lord and summons us to join its praise.[11]

In the Psalter it is not just "heavens and earth" that rejoice in God. It is also human beings and human bodies that rejoice in God. More pointedly, it is not just hearts that leap for joy in the psalms, it is bodies too: the mouth, the throat, the lungs, the hands, and the feet. All throughout we find the language of "shouting," "bursting," "reveling," "resounding," "clapping," "thundering," "crying," "exulting," and "dancing." These are not internal and invisible words; these are body words, physical and expressive.

While some communities may shout only tepidly or might never get caught dead "dancing with the tambourine," other communities clap and exult without restraint. For certain congregations, such visible expressions of praise might feel embarrassing or foolish. For others, there might be no felt need to express oneself to God in this physical manner, for all requirements of proper worship have been presumably met by intellectual, verbal, or practical means.

But from the perspective of the Psalter, both hearts and bodies get to leap for joy. Both spontaneous and formal expressions of physical praise have a place in the common worship of God. At times our bodies may need to lead the heart and mind in acts of joyful praise. At other times our bodies may need the heart and mind to lead it in acts of joyful praise. But for the psalmist, it is the heart *and* mind *and* body *and* soul *and* spirit at all times; it is the whole self that is offered up to God.

God's work of rescue invites joy. In the psalms, joy is not just a tonic for the embattled soul. Joy is also, and perhaps most fundamentally, a response to the experience of God's rescue. When God offers the psalmist refuge in the storm, the response is joy (Ps. 5:11). When God gives victory in the face of defeat, the psalmist shouts for joy (Ps. 20:5). When God forgives sin, joys wells up in the heart (Ps. 51:8). When God consoles the anxious heart, joy slowly but surely takes its place (Ps. 94:19).

For the people of Israel, the need for rescue was constant. It was needed before the years of exile, during the years of exile, and after the years of exile. In Psalm 126, the psalmist praises God for his miraculous rescue of Israel, which brought them back home: "When the LORD restored the fortunes of Zion, we were like those who dreamed. Our mouths were filled with laughter, our tongues with songs of joy" (vv. 1–2 NIV). Whenever we experience God's rescue, it is always a kind of coming home.[12]

Psalm 126 continues in verses 5–6: "Those who sow with tears will reap with songs of joy. Those who go out weeping, carrying seed to sow, will return with songs of joy, carrying sheaves with them" (NIV). The three movements here are significant:

- Sowing → reaping
- Weeping → shouting for joy
- Going away → coming home

This is where God always seeks to take us: from hard labor to the fruit of our labor, from sorrow to gladness, from exile to home. And for the psalmist, there is always a sense in which joy retains a poignant residue of sorrow, a kind of happy-sadness that marks our earthly pilgrimage.

Throughout the Psalter joy precedes and follows sorrow, and as often as not, joy exists alongside sorrow. In Psalm 86:2–4 the psalmist writes:

> You are my God; be gracious to me, O Lord,
>> for to you do I cry all day long.
> Gladden the soul of your servant,
>> for to you, O Lord, I lift up my soul.

Because of the sorrow that dots our lives, joy is often a choice. While a song of praise may erupt from a spontaneous outburst of affection for God, it may also require a decision. In Psalm 107, despite the immediate experience of grief and loss (vv. 4–28), the psalmist offers to God a sacrifice of praise in the presence of God's people (v. 32). In verse 22 he says, "let them offer thanksgiving sacrifices, and tell of his deeds with songs of joy."

The psalmist praises God despite his feelings. But he also understands that we cannot do this alone. Left on our own we will often give up. We need others to help us. In the Anglican *Book of Common Prayer*, the priest prays the following prayer: "Give them an inquiring and discerning heart, the courage to will and to persevere, a spirit to know and to love you, and *the gift of joy and wonder in all your works*"[13] (emphasis added). This is what we, too, can pray for one another: that we would be given the gift of joy in the midst of all the things that rob or squelch our joy. As the apostle writes in 1 Peter 4:13, "But rejoice insofar as you are sharing Christ's sufferings, so that you may also be glad and shout for joy when his glory is revealed."

In 1942, on Advent Sunday, Dietrich Bonhoeffer wrote a letter to the "brethren" who had once been students at the underground Finkenwalde Seminary, which he had directed from 1935 until its forced closure by the Gestapo in 1937. He begins his letter by naming those who had been killed in action. He writes, "Everlasting joy will crown their heads."[14] Yet that joy, he clarifies, is not for the dead only; it is for the living too. And it is not an artificial joy, a joy that, like a drug, numbs the pain. It is true joy.

> The joy of God has been through the poverty of the manger and the affliction of the cross; therefore, it is indestructible, irrefutable. It does not deny affliction when it is there, but it finds in the very midst of distress that God is there; it does not argue that sin is not grievous, but in that very place of sin is found forgiveness; it looks death in the face and it is just there that it finds life.[15]

In November 1937, five years before Bonhoeffer would write this letter, twenty-seven pastors and students were arrested by the Gestapo. Many others would only be able to minister illegally. On April 5, 1943, Bonhoeffer would be arrested and incarcerated at Tegel Prison in Berlin. On April 9, 1945, he would be executed at the Flossenbürg concentration camp. And yet he would remain unwavering in his conviction about joy. With Psalm 100, he would say, "For the Lord is good and his love endures for ever."[16]

For the Christian it is not just that "the joy of the Lord" describes our experience of God, it is also that "the joy of the Lord" describes God's own joy (Ps. 35:27). We see this most clearly in the person of Jesus. His life and ministry are marked by joy, and his resurrection, as Patrick Kavanagh describes it, is a kind of "laugh freed for ever and ever."[17] Jesus is the supremely joyful one. The author of Hebrews writes this in 12:1–2:

> Therefore, since we are surrounded by so great a cloud of witnesses, let us also lay aside every weight and the sin that clings so closely, and let us run with perseverance the race that is set before us, looking to Jesus the pioneer and perfecter of our faith, who for the sake of the joy that was set before him endured the cross, disregarding its shame, and has taken his seat at the right hand of the throne of God.

All that Jesus does he does for the sake of joy (Matt. 25:21; Luke 15:7). And he offers that joy to us too. In John 15:11 he prays that his joy might be in his disciples, so that their "joy may be complete." Jesus echoes the psalmist when he says, "you will have pain, but your pain will turn into joy" (John 16:20). And it is the Holy Spirit who gives us Jesus' own joy (Rom. 14:17; Gal. 5:22). In Acts 13:52, Luke describes the in-filling of the Holy Spirit as the in-filling of joy. To be *full* of God, in short, is to be *full* of joy.

For this reason, we can know that joy is our true end. Just as the Psalter is filled with lament psalms in its first half and marked by a steady increase of praise psalms in its latter half, so the movement of faith is ultimately from lament to praise. We are always "moving *towards* praise"[18] (emphasis original). While Psalm 1 shows us what it means to walk in the way of God's Word as a way of life, Psalm 150 shows us the goal of walking in this way: unencumbered praise.[19] All prayer, in the end, becomes praise. As Eugene Peterson remarks:

> All prayers, by definition, are directed to God, and this aim brings them, finally into the presence of God where "everything that has

breath" praises the Lord. Praise is the deep, even if often hidden, eschatological dimension in prayer.[20]

But as Ellen Davis reminds us, although lament always hopes to grow into praise, "it does not forget where it came from."[21] Praise arises out of contexts of suffering, and it does not ignore that suffering. It declares itself in hope, not in a denial of reality. As Paul himself writes in Romans 12:12, "Be joyful in hope, patient in affliction, faithful in prayer" (NIV). This is why, as the psalms see it, joy always makes space for sorrow, while happiness, as it is usually understood in our society, cannot. This is why our acts of praise often involve a sacrifice of praise, with our eyes set on the fulfillment of praise.[22]

CONCLUSION

In December 2015, after three years of unsuccessful attempts to have another baby by natural means, my wife, Phaedra, and I decided to switch gears and begin the process of adopting a baby. We were excited, but also cautious. We felt worn out from all our fertility "adventures" and knew that the experience of adoption would offer its own adventurous journey. But as we said to each other repeatedly, neither of us had the grace *not* to have a bigger family.

During these months of preparation, we prayed for joy to surprise us in the midst of what felt like a complicated space in which to be. We still grieved our infertility, we felt fearful of all that could go wrong, we felt sober in light of what adoption meant for a child and the birth parents, and we felt a general sense of uncomfortable stretching as we let go of control. So many things about our life felt hard and lonely.

But on the afternoon of March 28, 2017, Phaedra and I arrived at the Woman's Hospital of Texas, in downtown Houston. At 6:21 p.m. our son Sebastian was born, all 7.8 pounds and 19.6 inches of him. The doctor, the nurses, the birth mother's grandmother and best friend—all expressed such joy at the arrival of this beautiful boy. The joy of holding him in our arms wholly overwhelmed us.

Our daughter Blythe, five years old at the time, could not stop beaming from ear to ear. The day before, she had held both of our hands and exclaimed: "God has answered all our prayers!" He had indeed. Blythe told us she wanted to care for Sebastian in every way possible: changing diapers, feeding milk, singing lullabies, making jokes. After all the years of waiting for a sibling, the look on her face brought us to blubbering happy-sad tears.

In the psalms, praise is the final word. This means that joy also is our final end. While we wait for the new creation, however, our joy is experienced now as a kind of stab or pang, as C. S. Lewis describes in his autobiography, *Surprised by Joy*. Biblical joy, he writes, is always marked by an "inconsolable longing."[23] We rejoice, yes, but with a painful yearning for the sweet fullness of joy. In our case it meant that our joy with Sebastian intermingled with the pain of his birth mother; and our longing for a son included a painful yearning for him to be without any separation from his birth mother.

What the psalms of praise offered us, then, was "a vehicle for realistic but jubilant joy in God, taking up the good and the bad into a faith that always (even if it takes a struggle) results in praise of God."[24] And they offer to all of us an antidote to all the things that would tempt us to become a joyless people.[25] They invite us to live in God's economy of abundance and to refuse an economy of scarcity. They take our shriveled, hardened hearts and open them out to God again. And they offer us the grace to become a people who, like the mountains and hills, sing together for joy so that we may bear witness to the weeping that comes in the night and to the joy that comes in the morning.

QUESTIONS FOR REFLECTION

1. Recall the three times in your life when you have experienced the greatest joy. What was that like for you?

2. What is one passage in the Psalms that resonates with your experience of joy?

3. What things make it hard for you to practice joy? What things make it hard for people in your congregation to practice the kind of joy that the psalms show us: joy inexpressible, effusive joy, quiet joy, shouting joy, or convivial joy?

4. How does C. S. Lewis's description of joy as "longing" resonate with you? How would you explain to a neighbor or friend the difference between happiness and joy? And how might the practice of the psalms of joy become a subversive witness in our culture today?

5. What do you think we as a community are losing by not participating in the kind of joy the psalms show us? What is one thing you might do to cultivate a spirit of psalmic joy in the life of your community?

6. In what specific way do you wish for God or for others to be present to you in your experiences of joy?

7. The pastor and novelist Frederick Buechner once said that our calling in life exists at the intersection of our deepest joy and the world's greatest need. What might that be for you?

EXERCISES

1. Read Psalm 47 or 98 or 126. Read it several times. Meditate on it. Pray through it. Consider memorizing a portion of it to carry in your heart as a way to maintain a lively conversation with God throughout the day.

2. Describe a time in your life when lament and sadness turned into joy.

3. Share with a friend your thoughts on the idea of a "sacrifice of praise" in the midst of grief and loss. Has there been a time when you were able to offer that kind of sacrifice? Share what would help you to do that more easily or frequently.

4. Read Psalm 96 or 100 or 148 out loud as a community. Read it with

fervor. Where the text uses the language of "roaring" or "shouting," consider allowing yourself to join the psalmist by roaring and shouting the good news for all to hear. Raise the roof! Don't hold back!

5. As a group, respond to this prompt: "Joy and praise are our final end."

6. Craft a prayer based on one of the psalms of praise (Pss. 8; 19; 33; 66; 67; 95–100; 103; 104; 111; 113; 114; 117; 145–150). Consider using this prayer in your communal times together.

7. Acquire a copy of the hymnal *Psalms for All Seasons: A Complete Psalter for Worship*, ed. Martin Tel, Joyce Borger, John D. Witvliet (Grand Rapids, MI: Brazos Press, 2012), and read, sing, or pray together as a group from the psalms of joy, such as Psalm 27, 35, 47, 95–100, or the "Hallelujah Psalms" (Pss. 146–150).

PRAYER

God of joy unspeakable, you have not created us so that we should merely endure existence. You have created us rather for delight and you have filled our mouths with laughter. Turn our tears into songs of joy, change our wailing into dancing, and make our wilderness blossom with life, so that with the morning stars we might sing for gladness and with the festive throng we may come to your house with shouts of praise. We pray this in the name of the One who endured all things for the joy set before him. Amen.

9

ENEMIES

Deliver me, O my God!
For you strike all my enemies on the cheek.

—Psalm 3:7

Only the person who is totally free of his own desire for
revenge and free of hate and who is sure not to use his
prayers to satisfy his own lust for revenge—only such a
person can pray with a pure heart: "Shatter the fangs
of the young lions, O Lord, break the teeth in their
mouth."

—Dietrich Bonhoeffer[1]

UNIVERSAL ENEMIES

Many within our communities fall within one of two camps: those who
see enemies everywhere and those who deny the reality of enemies. For
one camp, anybody who opposes them—whether a family member, a

stranger, a neighbor, or "those people"—is regarded as an enemy. For the other camp, the language of enemy is avoided because it is regarded as impolite or unbecoming of a "spiritual" person.

According to the book of Psalms, both camps get it wrong. For the psalmist, enemies are real but they're not everywhere. They're often flesh and blood but not always. They are to be named, but they are also to be relinquished to God.

From Latin *inimicus* (*in*, meaning "not"; *imicus*, meaning "friend"), the term *enemy* describes any person or group whom you experience as actively hostile or a force that harms you in some fashion. Enemy language is native to human beings. Policeman, poets, pathologists, psychologists, pastors, border patrol, and pastry chefs all use enemy talk to make sense of things in the world.[2]

For those on the far right in the United States, comments about the media as "enemy of the people" feel fully justified. As one conservative commentator has remarked, "with exceptions, liberals are among the worst enemies American freedom has."[3] For those on the far left, such language induces outrage and fear. But it has not prevented them from using enemy language, too, with essay titles like "Republicans Are Enemies of Human Civilization."[4]

In 2019, Iran is America's enemy.[5] For certain political leaders, the demonization of Iran serves to advance America's interests in the Middle East.[6] Likewise, for the supreme leader of Iran Ayatollah Khamenei, calling America "the Great Satan" strengthens Iran's religious identity and revolutionary character.[7] Enemy talk, apparently, works; not just for politicians but for artists too.

In 1882, the Norwegian Henrik Ibsen wrote a play called, "An Enemy of the People." In it he chastised both the conservatives and liberals of his day. In 1982, a group of college students at Adelphi University, in New York, formed the rap group Public Enemy.[8] They chose their name to protest the dehumanization of black people. Explained Chuck D, its front man:

The United States Constitution once considered black people to be three-fifths of a human being. If this is a public document, obviously we must be the enemy.[9]

Athletes make enemies of a sort. This includes figure skaters Tonya Harding and Nancy Kerrigan, boxers Muhammad Ali and Joe Frazier, and the US versus Russia in pretty much any sport. Artists talk about the enemy between their heads, philosophers talk about the ego as the enemy, marketers talk about the perfect as the enemy of the good, cooks talk about oil as the enemy of air, and the Bible is chock-full of enemy language.

When Saul summons the prophet Samuel from the dead, Samuel says to him, "the Lord has turned from you and become your enemy" (1 Sam. 28:16). In Numbers 10:35 Moses prays, "Arise, O Lord, let your enemies be scattered." Paul uses enemy language to describe death (1 Cor. 15:26), the magician Elymas (Acts 13:10), himself (Gal. 4:16), and all of us sinners (Rom. 5:10) and "friends of the world" (James 4:4).

It is also how Jesus describes his mission, which inevitably splits families: "a man's enemies will be the members of his household" (Matt. 10:36 NIV).

But isn't all this enemy language antithetical to the gospel? Isn't it sub-Christian—or, at best, pre-Christian? Hasn't Jesus himself forbidden us to curse our enemies? Did he not *command* us to forgive them? And isn't all this enemy talk how we get into trouble, by dehumanizing our opponents, justifying our hatred, defending our refusal to love, and excusing our acts of violence?

Looking at the book of Psalms, it seems that enemy talk does, in fact, have a place in the life of faith. Enemy language belongs to faithful living, not because the Psalter comes out of an ancient culture that didn't know any better, but because enemy language is faithfully honest about life in a fractured and often cruel world. It's honest about other people and their capacities to harm, wittingly or unwittingly. It's honest about oneself—about the heart of darkness that lies within. And it's honest to God.

What else would the psalms say to us about enemies?

Enemies are everywhere in the psalms. If we take the psalms seriously, rather than tidying them up, we must reckon with the fact that enemies are real. As Brueggemann remarks, the Psalter is "awash in enemies."[10] Peterson describes it this way:

> People who are looking for a spiritual soporific don't pray the Psalms, or at least don't pray them for very long. The Psalms are full of unsettling enemy talk. God is the primary subject in the Psalms, but enemies are established in solid second place.[11]

Psalm 18 is illustrative. The psalm opens with a note to the worship leader, which includes language of enemies: "A Psalm of David the servant of the LORD, who addressed the words of this song to the LORD on the day when the LORD delivered him from the hand of all his enemies, and from the hand of Saul" (v. 1). The psalmist finds himself in danger and pleads to the Lord for help: "I call upon the LORD, who is worthy to be praised, so I shall be saved from my enemies" (v. 3).

Following a vivid description of his harrowing condition, the psalmist exclaims at mid-point: "He delivered me from my strong enemy, and from those who hated me; for they were too mighty for me" (v. 17). The psalmist professes his commitment to follow the Lord's ways faithfully, with integrity (vv. 20–23). He confesses God's protection and provision (vv. 24–36). And he asserts God's power to save (v. 37): "I pursued my enemies and overtook them."

The psalmist ends his testimony with an acclamation of praise to the Lord (vv. 46–48):

> The LORD lives! Blessed be my rock,
> and exalted be the God of my salvation,

the God who gave me vengeance
and subdued peoples under me;
who delivered me from my enemies;
indeed, you exalted me above my adversaries;
you delivered me from the violent.

This isn't a psalm for polite company. It isn't a psalm for people who only want things to be nice and for people "to get along." Nor is it a psalm for those who wish to remain indifferent to the harsh realities of the world or to deny the visceral desires of the human heart. It's a psalm for people who look at the world for what it is: full of broken people, dark forces, and harsh conditions.

The world is full of fractured relations and hostile dynamics. Evil infects the human heart and people do bad things. Women get gang raped, the elderly fall victim to scams, workers are cheated out of their pension, a child is lost to a drunk driver, a pastor abuses his authority, a man is profiled because of his skin color, a Christian is persecuted because of her faith, millions are displaced from their homes.[12]

One could call this "the challenges of life." One could soften it by calling people "opponents" or "adversaries." But for the psalmist, reality demands that we use the language of enemy to describe things truthfully. J. Clinton McCann writes, "In the face of monstrous evil, the worst possible response is to feel nothing. What must be felt is grief, rage, and outrage. In their absence, evil becomes an acceptable commonplace."[13]

Faith happens in a hostile world, not in the mystical ambient light of a gothic cathedral. Faith works itself out in the middle of enemies, not in the silent chambers of the soul or only in the company of folks who were "poorly intended."[14] Erich Zenger summarizes it this way:

The people who pray the psalms feel themselves surrounded, threatened, and shot at by a gigantic army; or they are like an animal pursued by hunters and trappers; or they see themselves surrounded and attacked by rapacious wild beasts, trampling bulls, or poisonous snakes.[15]

Anybody can become an enemy, and the harm that comes from our enemies is real. The German scholar Othmar Keel has counted ninety-four terms that the Psalter uses to describe enemies.[16] This list includes predatory beasts, bulls, snakes, armies, evildoers, cities, profit hunters, and death. It includes friends who turn into enemies, such as in Psalm 55:12–13:

> It is not enemies who taunt me—
> > I could bear that;
> it is not adversaries who deal insolently with me—
> > I could hide from them.
> But it is you, my equal,
> > my companion, my familiar friend.

Other tribes and nations can act like enemies. The duplicitous are enemies. The bullying and the brutish are enemies. Enemies are those who despoil God's good earth, who take advantage of the vulnerable, who pillage defenseless neighborhoods, who deceive the elderly, who treat children like objects to be discarded on a whim. Psalm 56:2 says, "My enemies trample on me all day long." And if the psalmist is to be believed, I, too, can become an enemy.

For victims of violence especially, their enemies are not "occasional transgressors who harmed out of ignorance or whose abuses were casual rather than premeditated and repetitive but on those who chronically and violently flaunted their position contrary to God's righteousness."[17] The harm that some experience demands language that fits. Enemy language fits.

The vivid, visceral prayer language of the psalms corresponds to the vivid, visceral nature of human reality. In Psalm 109, the psalmist uses especially shocking, almost obscene language to describe his enemies:

May his posterity be cut off;
> may his name be blotted out in the second generation.

May the iniquity of his father be remembered before the LORD,
> and do not let the sin of his mother be blotted out.

Let them be before the LORD continually,
> and may his memory be cut off from the earth.

For he did not remember to show kindness,
> but pursued the poor and needy
> and the brokenhearted to their death.

He loved to curse; let curses come on him.
> He did not like blessing; may it be far from him.

(vv. 13–17)

For some of us, this kind of language does not roll off the tongue easily. It unnerves us—makes us intensely uncomfortable. It might even revolt us. For others, this enemy talk excites us. It gets the blood boiling; it trips off the tongue. We relish the hope of retribution: the righteous judgment of God against the "wicked." We welcome Jim Cotter's translation of Psalm 109:

> Woe to the traders in arms,
> woe to the traffickers in drugs,
> woe to the poisoners of minds,
> woe to the serial killers,
> woe to the men of cold eyes,
> woe to the remorseless hearts,
> woe to those with no pity.[18]

But it is important that we be clear about the purpose of enemy language in the psalms.[19] Its purpose is to remind us that the violent and sinful ways of human beings—including our own violent, sinful ways—need to be named so that *God* can step in and do something about it. Praying against one's enemies is most emphatically *not* a license to do violence to others; nor is it an invitation to indulge our irresponsible desires to call anybody we do not like an enemy. It is instead a way to get us to talk to God. Its goal is healing, not self-gratification.[20]

It is equally important to stress that praying against one's enemies is not a matter of mere venting or throwing a tantrum. We're not "sticking it to the man." Praying these prayers, rather, is a matter of honestly naming our experience of enemies—the rage, the sorrow, the feeling of utter helplessness, the acute sense of injustice, the irrationality of it all—in order to entrust one's enemies to God.

Psalm 139 suggests a paradigmatic pattern for prayers against enemies. It begins with anger:

> O that you would kill the wicked, O God,
>> and that the bloodthirsty would depart from me—
> those who speak of you maliciously,
>> and lift themselves up against you for evil!
> Do I not hate those who hate you, O LORD?
>> And do I not loathe those who rise up against you?
> I hate them with perfect hatred;
>> I count them my enemies.
>
> (vv. 19–22)

This is unadulterated, quintessentially angry enemy prayer. It can be hard to read, and it can be even harder to believe that this is language that a Christian would put on his lips. "Kill the wicked"? Hating "those who hate you"? A "perfect hatred"? Can we really say this as followers of Jesus? But soon after this imprecation, the psalmist prays a prayer of relinquishment:

> Search me, O God, and know my heart;
>> test me and know my thoughts.
> See if there is any wicked way in me,
>> and lead me in the way everlasting.
>
> (vv. 23–24)

This is the prayer of self-examination, and it belongs at the heart of psalmic prayer against enemies. The movement from one statement to the other—from angry prayer to relinquishment prayer—does not come easily, and it rarely happens in the moment. In fact, it often takes a good deal of time before one can move from verses 19–22 to verses 23–24. But that's where the psalms invite us to go. In praying these prayers, we entrust ourselves to God.

Enemy prayers also invite us to petition God. *Act now, oh God!* Defend the weak. Rescue the needy. Vindicate the innocent. Fight against the law keepers who twist the evidence, the bullies who hide behind their cowardice, the drug-traffickers who prey upon the weak, the sexual predators, the warmongers, the abusive religious, the advertisers who care only for profit and not for the dignity of human beings. In petitioning God this way, we seek *God's* righteousness.[21]

We seek God's righteousness by seeking it in the way that Jesus taught us to seek it. Speaking to the crowds in Matthew 5, Jesus says, "You have heard that it was said, 'You shall love your neighbor and hate your enemy.' But I say to you, Love your enemies and pray for those who persecute you, so that you may be children of your Father in heaven" (vv. 43–45). But Jesus also tells Peter in Matthew 16:23 that he is behaving like Satan and, therefore, like an enemy.

In Matthew 23, Jesus rebukes the Pharisees. Echoing the language of Deuteronomy, he accuses them of willingly harming the people: "Woe to you, scribes and Pharisees, hypocrites! For you tithe mint, dill, and cummin, and have neglected the weightier matters of the law: justice and mercy and faith" (v. 23). Yet on the cross, Jesus looks out on his accusers and says, "Father, forgive them; for they do not know what they are doing" (Luke 23:34).

Underscoring Jesus' command in Matthew 5 to love our enemies, Paul exhorts the believers in Rome to reject all desires for vengeance. He writes, "if your enemies are hungry, feed them; if they are thirsty, give them something to drink" (Rom. 12:20). But Paul also echoes Jesus' own words when he tells the Corinthian faithful that Christ "must reign until he has put all his enemies under his feet" (1 Cor. 15:25). This includes both Satan (Rom. 16:20; Heb. 2:14) and death (1 Cor. 15:26).

In Luke 1, Zechariah rejoices at the birth of his son, John, because it anticipates the arrival of the Messiah who will save God's people from their enemies (Luke 1:71). And yet Paul reminds the faithful that their struggle "is not against enemies of blood and flesh, but against the rulers, against the authorities, against the cosmic powers of this present darkness, against the spiritual forces of evil in the heavenly places" (Eph. 6:12).

CONCLUSION

I once worked for a company where the mid-level manager repeatedly threw me under the bus in order to save face with the CEO. He never had my back, and he never fully supported my efforts to serve the company. All too often he took credit for things that I had accomplished. With no power to change my circumstances, my boss felt like an enemy to me. On days when I felt overcome with anger, I would sing the words of Psalm 23 as a way to yield my vengeful thoughts to Jesus. And while I cannot say I always managed to yield my enemy-anger to God, the psalms invariably became the go-to therapeutic aid for my heart and mind.

So, are enemies "flesh and blood" or are they not? Can we call someone an enemy or are we forbidden to do so? Do our enemies know what they're doing or don't they? Are the broken and dark forces in this world *real* enemies or is it only that we "experience" them as enemies? And what exactly are we supposed to do with the enemy language of the Psalter from the perspective of the life, death, and resurrection of Jesus?

The first thing is that Jesus never denies the reality of enemies. Enemies are real and they come in all forms: human, societal, natural, demonic. Nor does Jesus tell his disciples to avoid using enemy talk. For Jesus, enemy talk rightly describes the world as it is. And in the first three Gospels he quotes Psalm 110:1 without feeling any need to correct the psalmist, "The LORD says to my lord, 'Sit at my right hand until I make your enemies your footstool.'" Enemies indeed.

How then might these facts inform our life of faith? At the very least it means that we cannot pray for enemies in the abstract. For the psalmist, there are only concrete enemies—those who do enemy-like things. For Jesus, likewise, there is no generic enemy. There are only particular enemies that behave in God-denying, image-of-God-abusing ways. At times they are religious leaders; at other times they are Roman rulers or even his closest friends. Always this includes Satan.

As the Psalter sees it, we pray the psalms of enmity to name the corrosive nature of life-destroying enemy-activity.[22] Such activity includes senseless evil, abusive conduct, neglect to love, and god-awful disasters and diseases. The psalms refuse to minimize or ignore these things. They refuse to let evil have the last word in history, and that refusal requires honest expression:[23] "Make it right, oh Lord!" "Don't let them trample on me!" "Be my refuge!"

The second thing is that Jesus commands us to love our enemies. He calls us to bless those who curse us. He tells us to be merciful, just as our Father in heaven is merciful. This, of course, echoes what God has willed all along. Exodus 23:4 says, "When you come upon your enemy's ox or donkey going astray, you shall bring it back." Proverbs 24:17 adds, "Do not rejoice when your enemies fall, and do not let your heart be glad when they stumble."

Loving our enemies requires an extraordinary amount of humility. Every cell in our broken hearts resists it. With the psalmist, we want God to strike down our enemies. Loving our enemies also requires that we acknowledge our own tendencies to behave in enemy-like ways. We, too, dehumanize. We, too, use and abuse. We, too, withhold love and judge without mercy. We, too, act unjustly and remain indifferent to the suffering of others.

In the end, the psalms ask us to humbly say all these things to God and in the presence of God's people, so they can be *with* us, *for* us, in the hour of trial and temptation. For followers of Jesus, whose word remains final, the call is clear. We name our enemies and we love them. We expose them and we release them. We rebuke them and we serve them. It's a twofold act that only the Spirit of God can make possible in our lives, lest we become foolish or succumb to despair.

QUESTIONS FOR REFLECTION

1. Who in your life has been like an enemy to you? What happened and how did it make you feel?
2. How does the enemy language of the psalms make you feel? Does it frighten you? Do you relish it? Does it confuse you? Why?
3. Do you have an experience of God delivering you from an enemy?
4. In what ways do you find this enemy language in the psalms helpful to vent your feelings? In what ways do you feel it might feed a broken desire in you or make it easy for you to behave wrongly or unfaithfully?
5. Entrusting one's enemies to God is difficult. What things might be helpful to you to do this important work?
6. What role might your community play in helping you to name your enemies and to love them, to expose them and to release them, to rebuke them and to serve them?

EXERCISES

1. Read Psalm 18. Read it once to become familiar with the text. Read it a second time and imagine yourself as the psalmist writing it. Read it a third time and imagine yourself praying it on behalf of somebody whom you know is in a similarly difficult place.
2. The psalmists use vivid language to describe their experience of enemies. It's like being shot at by a gigantic army, or like being an animal pursued by hunters, or like being attacked by rapacious

wild beasts or poisonous snakes. Write down other metaphors or images that express your own experience of enemies.

3. Jim Cotter uses lively language to describe modern-day enemies in light of Psalm 109. Write down your own list of "woes" as it relates to enemies—for example, "Woe to the sex slave trader." "Woe to the womanizer." "Woe to the abuser of authority." After writing this list, pray for each of them that God would intervene and make things right.

4. Taking Psalm 139:21–24 as an example, write a prayer that you might pray together: one half of the prayer expressing anger at enemies, the other half of the prayer asking God to search our own hearts. Consider ways in which we, too, behave like an enemy; ways we, too, use and abuse others, withhold love and judge without mercy, commit sins of omission and commission.

5. Using Psalm 18 or 58 as an example, write a prayer in which you petition God to make things right, to defend the weak, to rescue the needy, to vindicate the innocent, to be a refuge for the victims of enemy violence. Consider singing a song together that gives expression to this prayer.

6. While Jesus wants us to resist our true enemies—Satan, death, the "principalities and powers" (Eph. 6:12)—he also wants us to love our perceived enemies. Consider one thing you might do as a group to serve, in Jesus' name and with the same generous grace that Jesus exhibits, those whom you may experience as enemies.

PRAYER

Lord Jesus, you who ask us to do the impossible—to bless our enemies, to pray for those who persecute us, to love those who seek us harm—we pray that you would do the impossible in us: change our hearts. Help us to love our enemies as you love them. Help us to remember who our true enemy is: Satan, death, and the spiritual forces of evil. Perform also a miracle in our enemies by your Spirit. In your sovereign might, restrain the power of evil. Let your kingdom come on earth as it is in heaven. In your strong name we pray. Amen.

10

JUSTICE

Give justice to the weak and the orphan;
maintain the right of the lowly and
the destitute.

—PSALM 82:3

"Cursed be anyone who deprives the alien, the orphan,
and the widow of justice." All the people shall say, "Amen!"
—DEUTERONOMY 27:19

INJUSTICES IN THE WORLD

On October 2, 2006, a dairy-truck driver entered a one-room school-house in the Old Order Amish community of Nickel Mines in Pennsylvania. The driver, Charles C. Roberts IV, first demanded that all the boys leave the room; he then ordered the eleven girls to line up facing the chalkboard.

The girls had a clear sense of the danger they faced, seeing all the instruments of violence before them: the stun gun, the nails, the bolts, the wrenches, the rope, the plastic ties to bind their feet, and the chains and clamps for restraint. Shortly before Roberts opened fire, two sisters requested they be shot first so that the others might be spared. He ignored their request. Instead he killed five girls and wounded seven before killing himself. One of the sisters was wounded; the other was killed.

The names of the girls who were killed were Naomi Rose Ebersole, seven; Marian Fisher, thirteen (one of the sisters who did not survive); sisters Mary Liz Miller, eight, and Lina Miller, seven; and Anna Mae Stoltzfus, twelve.

Janice Ballenger, the deputy coroner in Lancaster County, Pennsylvania, shaken up by the event, said afterward, "There was not one desk, not one chair, in the whole schoolroom that was not splattered with either blood or glass."[1]

On June 7, 1998, three known white supremacists murdered a forty-nine-year-old father of three in Jasper, Texas. The father, a black man, had accepted an early morning ride home with the three men. After attacking him, they dragged him to his death behind their truck, later dumping the man's mutilated remains in the town's segregated African American cemetery. Afterward they went to a barbecue. The name of the man who was killed was James Byrd Jr.[2]

To date, more than 250,000 people have been displaced from northeast Nigeria on account of the violence caused by the Islamist extremist group Boko Haram.[3]

In early January 2019, two men and nine teenage boys were rescued from bonded-labor slavery at an urban factory near Chennai, India.[4]

On January 31, 2019, the Roman Catholic Church in Texas released the names of almost three hundred priests who it said had been credibly accused of child sex abuse over nearly eight decades.[5]

During the late 2018 trial of Joaquín Guzmán Loera, the Mexican drug kingpin known as El Chapo, nearly every level of Mexican government was implicated in bribes, including the presidency.[6]

In 2017, the CDC found the first genetic link from Legionnaires' disease to the lead-contaminated water supply in Flint, Michigan; such lead exposure in children included the possibility of impaired cognition, behavioral disorders, hearing problems, and delayed puberty.[7]

By the time Hurricane Harvey left the Gulf of Mexico in August 2017, an estimated thirty thousand people had been displaced from their homes. Nearly a trillion gallons of water had fallen over the city of Houston, and the poor were hit the hardest.[8]

No True Faith Without Justice

The fact that injustices occur every day is obvious to anyone who reads the daily news. Injustices happen to individuals, people groups, and entire countries; they mar systems and institutions. Injustices take place in our own homes and in nature as a whole. The book of Psalms understands this. The psalmist says this about the wicked in Psalm 10:

> In arrogance the wicked persecute the poor. . . .
>> those greedy for gain curse and renounce the LORD.
>
> they lurk that they may seize the poor;
>> they seize the poor and drag them off in their net.
>
> They think in their heart, "God has forgotten,
>> he has hidden his face, he will never see it."
>
>> (vv. 2–3, 9, 11)

The psalmists pray repeatedly for justice because they understand that a world full of broken people, dark forces, and harsh conditions generates injustice everywhere and always. Where there is enemy talk in the psalms, there is also justice talk. Where there is injustice talk, there is also a plea for a Just Judge to make things right or, as philosophers might put it, to give people what they are due.[9]

Many Christians, unfortunately, do not see this as clearly as the psalmists see it. The psalmists see structural injustice within society, where Christians, perhaps especially evangelicals in the West, may see only personal guilt. The psalmists see wickedness that pervades institutions and cultures, while Christians may see only the need for the forgiveness of individual sins.

The psalmists see powerless people who are oppressed by the powerful, and so they pray for justice (Pss. 37; 82; 113); Christians see only Psalm 51 with its plea for mercy.[10] Writes C. S. Lewis, "Christians cry to God for mercy instead of justice; *they* [the psalmists] cried to God for justice instead of injustice"[11] (emphasis original).

It isn't that mercy and justice are opposed in the Psalter; they belong together intimately, integrally. But while many Christians give justice half the attention they give to mercy, the Psalter devotes twice as much space to justice as it does to mercy. This is not because mercy matters less than justice but because a world that violates justice violates God's fundamental purposes for that world.[12]

As we shall see in this chapter, in the psalms there is no true worship without justice, no faithful prayer that leaves out justice, and no genuine faith that takes justice less seriously than God takes it. There is no account of God that makes justice secondary to his nature or an afterthought to his redemptive, restorative work in the world. There is likewise no account of human beings in the psalms that allows justice to remain a concern only of other people, rather than of all humanity.

THE PSALMS OF JUSTICE

In the psalms there is no generic idea of justice; there is only God's idea of justice.[13] Psalm 89:14 says this: "Righteousness and justice are the foundation of your throne; steadfast love and faithfulness go before you." Psalm 111:7–8 adds, "The works of his hands are faithful and just;

all his precepts are trustworthy. They are established forever and ever, to be performed with faithfulness and uprightness."

But for the psalmist, it is not simply that God cares about the abstract idea of distributive and retributive justice; it is that God *loves* justice. Psalm 37:28 declares, "For the LORD loves justice; he will not forsake his faithful ones." Psalm 99:4 proclaims, "Mighty King, lover of justice, you have established equity; you have executed justice and righteousness in Jacob."

In the psalms the Lord is king. As king, the Lord stands sovereign over all of creation, sovereign throughout all eternity, sovereign over the nations and over the people of Israel. There is nowhere that God's justice should remain absent (Pss. 33:5-9; 96:11-13). It should be manifest at every level of reality—locally, globally, and cosmically (Ps. 97:6). Psalm 85:10-11 articulates this comprehensive vision of justice:

> Steadfast love and faithfulness will meet;
>> righteousness and peace [*shalom*] will kiss each other.
> Faithfulness will spring up from the ground,
>> and righteousness will look down from the sky.

God wants justice for human beings precisely because he *loves* human beings. Writes Nicholas Wolterstorff, "God desires that each and every human being shall flourish, that each and every shall experience what the Old Testament writers call *shalom*"[14] (emphasis original). Shalom, or a deep sense of well-being, is God's original gift to the cosmos and its final goal. It is what God has promised to creation and what he will fulfill in the new creation.

As the book of Psalms sees it, God isn't the only one who's in the business of making justice happen; human beings are entrusted with this work too. This is certainly the case with individuals in positions of power and rule. Israel's king prays this in Psalm 72:

> May he judge your people with righteousness,
>> and your poor with justice.

> May he defend the cause of the poor of the people,
> give deliverance to the needy.
>
> (vv. 2, 4)

But it's all our business. Psalm 106:3 stresses that we are blessed when we do justice: "Happy are those who observe justice, who do righteousness at all times." Psalm 15 is even more insistent. The ones who get to abide in God's house are those who do justice "no matter what the cost" (v. 4 CEV). For the psalmists, justice is what humans *have* to do. But it is also what humans *get* to do (Ps. 101:1–5). About Psalm 82 Eugene Peterson says this:

> God is presented as judge. But he does not reserve the work exclusively to himself. He shares it. This is surprising, for it is work that requires high intelligence and stalwart virtue. Also, it is work that if done badly reflects adversely on the Judge himself and calls into serious question whether anyone is minding the store: "all the foundations of the earth are shaken."[15]

But the ones who conduct their affairs with justice "will never be shaken" (Ps. 112:5–6 NASB). They will be blessed, says the Lord. Such is the calling of all the faithful, not just some of the faithful.

What exactly does it look like to do justice? The Psalter shows us. Justice shows no partiality. It maintains the rights of the weak and it rescues the needy (Ps. 82). It rejects the use of arrogant words and the desire to take advantage of the vulnerable (Ps. 94). The just do not kill the innocent (Ps. 10); they refuse to speak out of two sides of their mouth (Ps. 28); they're not bloodthirsty (Ps. 139); they're not greedy (Pss. 10; 73); they're not conniving (Ps. 94); they don't love violence (Ps. 11).[16]

Those who love justice actively reject all systems that oppress people (Ps. 58).

Who, in the psalms, are the recipients of justice? All people alike require the kind of justice that God has established. But who are those who need it most? They are the "Quartet of the Vulnerable."[17] This includes widows, orphans, poor, and resident aliens. In Israel, these four groups represent the most lowly members of society and therefore the most vulnerable to injustice (1 Sam. 2). The Psalter gives special attention to them:

> He raises the *poor* from the dust,
>> and lifts the *needy* from the ash heap,
> to make them sit with princes,
>> with the princes of his people.
> He gives the *barren woman* a home,
>> making her the joyous mother of children.
>
> (Ps. 113:7–9, emphasis added)

> Father of *orphans* and protector of *widows*
>> is God in his holy habitation.
> God gives the *desolate* a home to live in;
>> he leads out the *prisoners* to prosperity,
>> but the rebellious live in a parched land.
>
> (Ps. 68:5–6, emphasis added)

> The LORD watches over the *strangers*;
>> he upholds the *orphan* and the *widow*.
>
> (Ps. 146:9, emphasis added)

Psalm 103 includes what might be regarded as the blanket term for this quartet: the "oppressed." And it is for them that the Lord works justice day and night (Pss. 10:14–18; 37; 103:6; Isa. 1:17). Bob Ekblad, in his book *Reading the Bible with the Damned*, offers this insight, "Marginalized people are surprised when the psalms use language and images that evoke their life situations of oppression."[18] In Psalm 146 we hear echoes of Jesus' own words in the Gospels. It is the Lord "who executes justice for the oppressed; who gives food to the hungry. The

LORD sets the prisoners free; the LORD opens the eyes of the blind. The LORD lifts up those who are bowed down; the LORD loves the righteous" (Ps. 146:7–8).[19]

Jesus is the perfect justice of God. Hearing these words we are reminded yet again of the central place justice holds in the work of God in the world. We are reminded yet again of the responsibility the people of God carry to be just as God is just. We are to do justice, to love mercy, to walk humbly with our God (Mic. 6:8). While many Christians often excel at two out of three of these qualities, God would have us exhibit all three. Jesus shows us how.

In Luke 13, Jesus heals an old woman who has been crippled since birth. The woman is small and relatively insignificant, like a mustard seed or a dash of yeast. Yet in her encounter with Jesus, she takes central stage in God's redemptive work. As readers of the story we bear witness to the repeal of Satanic domination (the true enemy of Israel), the heart of God for Sabbath day (mercy, justice, shalom), and the dramatic restoration into community of one who was formerly an outsider.

In Matthew 12, Jesus asks the members of a synagogue, "Is it lawful to cure on the sabbath?" (v. 10). Hearing no answer, he reminds them of their just care of animals. "How much more valuable is a human being than a sheep!" he tells them (v. 12). Jesus commands a man with a withered hand to stretch out his hand, and it is immediately healed. When Jesus hears that the Pharisees wish to destroy him in light of this apparent contravention of the Sabbath, he leaves the synagogue, saying no more.

But the Gospel writer does not remain silent. He makes the meaning of Jesus' deeds manifestly clear. Matthew writes, "This was to fulfill what had been spoken through the prophet Isaiah" (12:17). How had Isaiah described the beloved Servant of the Lord? As one who fulfills the justice of God: "I have put my spirit upon him; he will bring forth justice to the nations" (42:1). This servant, the prophet adds, will bring "justice to victory" (Matt. 12:20).

In Luke 4, Jesus finds himself again in a synagogue, after having recently emerged from the wilderness, where Satan had sought to tempt him to deny his identity as God's beloved servant. Jesus stands up to read from Isaiah 61 and declares that the prophet's words are fulfilled in him. In him, God will release the captives, give sight to the blind, set the oppressed free, and bring good news to the poor.

This is God's work of justice. It's also what Jesus commands his disciples to do—especially concerning the Quartet of the Vulnerable, which according to Jesus includes not just widows, orphans, poor, and strangers in the land but also women, the physically ill and malformed, Gentiles and Samaritans, tax collectors, and those engaged in morally questionable professions.

Jesus not only speaks about justice, he also shows us a beautiful picture of justice on the cross (Rom. 3 and 5).[20] And he shows us the way in which mercy and forgiveness are integral to God's commitment to justice. For while justice gives people "what they're due," mercy and forgiveness do not (Ps. 103:12).[21] Mercy shows compassion where none can be claimed; forgiveness offers grace to one who could not be free or at peace without it.

In delivering us from sin that disfigures the human heart and disrupts relationship between human beings, Jesus sets us on the path of life, where we're freed to do justice, to love mercy, and to walk humbly with God.[22] Through these actions Jesus invites us to discover a deep communion with God and a rich communion with others. He invites us to discover how treating our neighbor justly is *precisely the way* to love our neighbor.[23]

CONCLUSION

As we learned in the previous chapter, prayer against our enemies is not a passive thing. We not only pray; we also do justice. We do not simply vent or bemoan the tragic losses that daily mark our world; we also stand up for the poor, the needy, the widowed, the orphaned, the vulnerable, the alien, the stranger, and all who are oppressed.

As the Psalter sees it, prayer and worship require something of us: doing justice. It requires something of all who align themselves with the God of the Psalter, the God of our Lord Jesus Christ, the Just Judge, the Righteous King, the Messiah who brings justice to victory, the Good Shepherd who defends the vulnerable with his rod and his staff.

The psalms demand that we live as citizens of God's peaceable kingdom, and they invite us to enact the justice of such a kingdom. Justice is the way we make things right, put things back, give people their due *in Jesus' name*. And faith would always have us believe that God will make all things right in the end—will make "the justice of [our] cause shine like the noonday" (Ps. 37:6).[24]

But at times there are things that have been lost or destroyed by injustice that are impossible to put back. "Put it all back!" we cry in our desire for justice. But as Donald Shriver reminds us, "Often 'it' is gone forever."[25] What's gone forever? A daughter. A father. One's health. One's land. One's retirement fund. One's innocence. One's dignity. One's future.

When the Amish families lost their daughters to a senseless killing, they didn't get their daughters back. Nor was there justice in court, because the man had killed himself. But they didn't choose to do nothing. They didn't succumb to bitterness or despair. They chose instead to forgive. For the Amish, this was not the hard part.[26] Built into their cultural DNA, forgiveness is what they have done for four hundred years; it belongs to the warp and woof of their common life.[27]

The hard part was the work of pardon and reconciliation. This would take time. Processing the grief would take time—months, even years. And it would not come easily. But they would not be required to do this on their own. They would do it together. They would remind each other that Charles Roberts IV, too, "had a mother and a wife and a soul."[28] They would remind each other that Charles stood before a just God. And they would welcome the help of others.[29]

Doing justice and loving mercy make us vulnerable. We don't always get the justice we deserve (and certain communities will know that fact more acutely than others). And the mercy we offer may be rejected or misunderstood. As the psalms see it, we can do justice and mercy only with God's help. We can do it only with the help of those who love justice as God loves it. We can do it only *together*. And we can do it only if we see justice and mercy as *all* of our business.

We do justice. We do mercy. We walk humbly with God. And, with W. E. B. Du Bois, we trust also "in the ultimate justice of things," in the "God of Right," in the Last Judgment, and in a "boundless justice in some fair world beyond," where all wrongs shall be made right, all the falsely accused shall be vindicated, and all manner of things shall be well.[30]

QUESTIONS FOR REFLECTION

1. What are ways in which you have experienced injustice? What happened? How did it make you feel? How has it affected the way you thought or felt about God?

2. In what ways have you witnessed injustice in your community, city, country, or around the globe? How has it made you feel?

3. What injustices do you feel strongly about? What injustices do you wish you cared more about?

4. How do you feel about the injustices in our world? Sad? Angry? Numb and ambivalent? Overwhelmed and exhausted? What aspects of justice make you feel uncomfortable? What are the tensions you feel?

5. How is your idea of God affected when you read about all the injustices in the world that never seem to be made right? How do the psalms help form your understanding of the character and work of God as it relates to justice?

6. In what ways might the language of the psalms help you articulate your thoughts and feelings about injustice? In what ways might these psalms convict, confirm, challenge, or complement what you have thought about justice and injustice?

7. What is one story of justice toward the "Quartet of the Vulnerable" (widows, orphans, poor/needy, strangers in the land) that has encouraged you? What is one story about justice in general that you wish to share with others?

8. Who are individuals or groups or movements you admire in their work for justice? What is one thing you want to learn from them? What is one thing you might wish to adopt for yourself as an action or commitment to justice?

EXERCISES

1. Read Psalm 37 once a day for a week. Read it while reviewing the day's news, with its instances of justice and injustice. Pay attention to the specific movements within the psalm. How does it begin? How does it end? What does it tell us about the character of God? What does it tell us about the world in which we live? What might it be saying to you personally?

2. Read Psalm 113, Isaiah 61, and Luke 4, one after the other. Read them once a day for a week. Pay attention to the individual contents of each passage and how the three passages are "talking to each other." What do these three biblical texts tell us about the character of God? What do they tell us about the world? What might they be saying to you personally as it relates to justice?

3. Choose one of these activities to do as a group:
   - Watch and discuss a video from the International Justice Mission website (www.ijm.org). Read, pray, or sing a psalm of justice together after your discussion.
   - Support and participate in a work of justice in your community. Read through the resources on the Christian Community Development Association website (https://ccda.org) to get an idea of possibilities.
   - Read a nonfiction book related to justice. Consider the

following: Kent Annan, *Slow Kingdom Coming: Practices for Doing Justice, Loving Mercy and Walking Humbly in the World*; Annie Dillard, *Pilgrim at Tinker Creek*; Bob Ekblad, *Reading the Bible with the Damned*; Bethany Hanke Hoang and Kristen Deede Johnson, *The Justice Calling: Where Passion Meets Perseverance*; Timothy Keller, *Generous Justice: How God's Grace Makes Us Just*; Martin Luther King Jr., *Strength to Love*; John M. Perkins, *Let Justice Roll Down*; Jean Vanier, *Becoming Human*; Mike and Danae Yankoski, *Zealous Love: A Practical Guide to Social Justice*; Malala Yousafzai, *I Am Malala: The Girl Who Stood Up for Education and Was Shot by the Taliban*; Elie Wiesel, *Night*.

- Read a fiction book related to justice. Consider the following: Isabel Allende, *The House of Spirits*; Margaret Atwood, *The Handmaid's Tale*; Ray Bradbury, *Fahrenheit 451*; Octavia Butler, *Kindred*; Ralph Ellison, *Invisible Man*; Khaled Hosseini, *The Kite Runner*; Zora Neale Hurston, *Their Eyes Were Watching God*; Sue Monk Kidd, *The Invention of Wings*; Harper Lee, *To Kill a Mockingbird*; Toni Morrison, *Beloved*; George Orwell, *Animal Farm*; Dr. Seuss, *The Lorax*; John Steinbeck, *The Grapes of Wrath*; Kurt Vonnegut, *Slaughterhouse-Five*; Alice Walker, *The Color Purple*.

- Watch a movie related to justice. Consider the following: *The Mission, Even the Rain, Reparando, BlacKkKlansman, The Hate U Give, Do the Right Thing, Selma, Hidden Figures, The Killing Fields, Hotel Rwanda, Twelve Years a Slave, To Kill a Mockingbird, Shawshank Redemption, 13th, Planet Earth, The Boy Who Harnessed the Wind, Erin Brockovich, Secret Sunshine, God Grew Tired of Us.*

4. Invite someone to your community who exemplifies God's concern for justice. Welcome their help as it relates to your thoughts, feelings, and actions about justice and injustice. Welcome their insights about how justice is both personal and social, both individual and

systemic, both explicit and implicit, both communal and institutional, both *your* business and *my* business.

5. Commit to reading the psalms of justice (Pss. 9; 68; 72; 82; 85; 103; 106; 109; 111; 140) over a course of months. Prepare a "liturgy" of confession and repentance for ways you may have been explicitly or implicitly involved in systems or cultures of injustice. Discuss how you may want to engage in the work of pardon, reconciliation, and restitution in your community.

PRAYER

"Be with us, O God, as we struggle for a more just world, yet remind us that our actions so often tighten the mesh that binds the oppressed. Keep us from pride in our own strength, and keep us from despair when evil seems entrenched. Renew our trust in your good purposes for us all. Give us the gift of discernment that we may know when to strive in the power of the Spirit, and when to be still and wait for your deliverance. Come in your good time, but come soon! Amen."[31]

11

DEATH

Precious in the sight of the Lord *is the death of his faithful ones.*

—Psalm 116:15

It is important to be prepared for death, very important; but if we start thinking about it only when we are terminally ill, our reflections will not give us the support we need.

—Henri Nouwen[1]

The Waters of Death

On the morning of August 28, 2017, I pedaled madly down my street in the town of Pecan Grove, which sits just southwest of Houston, Texas. Sheets of rain lashed at my marine-blue REI jacket as I raced along on the mountain bike that had once belonged to a police officer. At times the water rose to my knees, soaking my shorts. Halfway to my destination the rear brake pad fell off, leaving me with only my front brake to navigate the sloshing waters.[2]

My wife had asked me to check on the condition of the streets so we could make an informed decision whether to stay or to leave in the face of Hurricane Harvey, a Category 4 hurricane that would officially become the wettest tropical cyclone on record in the contiguous United States. Nearly a trillion gallons of water fell over Houston by the time Harvey left the Gulf Coast. Seeing that only one exit on the opposite side of our neighborhood remained untouched by the floods, I realized we had to leave, and leave now.

I'd already had one argument with Phaedra earlier that morning. Both of us had felt the pressure of the moment as well as the unpredictability of the storm's effects. We had a five-year-old daughter and a four-month-old son. We could not afford to make a poor decision. Our lives depended on it.

As a child I experienced the 1976 earthquake in Guatemala, which resulted in twenty-three thousand deaths, so I had a vivid sense of the presence of death. People had already died in Houston too. A thirty-four-year-old police officer had drowned in his patrol car. A beloved high school coach had been taken by the floodwaters. Four children and their great-grandparents were swept away into the Greens Bayou, their bodies never to be recovered.

In my theology class at Fuller Theological Seminary, I teach my students about the doctrine of Providence. God, I tell them, protects creation against a reversion to the chaos of Genesis 1:1, secures the life of creation against all the forces of destruction, and, by the power of the Spirit, ensures creation's good end through the death and resurrection of Jesus.

But it was one thing for me to say that in class, standing at the lectern with a coffee in hand, as the air conditioning kept the room at an even temperature. It was another thing for me to believe it in the middle of an argument with my wife, with the wind rattling our windows while we watched, with an increasing sense of dread, as the floodwaters covered our backyard.

Where exactly was this God who remained sovereign over life and death? Where was the "Great Rescuer" I'd read about in my daughter's copy of *The Jesus Storybook Bible*? What was the good news for neighbors who would experience the loss of life and property and livelihood? And how were we to face our mortality faithfully in conditions that caused us to feel utterly faithless?

Larger questions surfaced for us. Was our death something we should fear or seek to escape? Was our death something we should think about only at the end of our lives, however that end comes? How do we talk about the dead honestly, truthfully? And how might the psalms help us think faithfully about dying, death, and the dead?

THE PSALMS OF DEATH

In the Psalter, death exists in a shadowy underworld called Sheol, where chaos and lifelessness rule. For the psalmist, the threat of chaos surrounds him on every side. Above the earth are the heavenly waters, kept in place by "the firmament" (Ps. 104:1–4, translation mine). Here on earth is the "storm" chaos. Below the earth are the waters of "the deeps" (Ps. 33:7), which always threaten flooding. Further below is the chaos of the "Pit" (Ps. 69:15), a shadowy domain of darkness and nothingness, while all around the psalmist lie the waters of the sea (Ps. 135:6–7), with its life-devouring monsters.

While chaos always poses a threat to life, *Sheol* is the abyss of death that threatens to extinguish life. But in contrast to Canaanite mythology, where death—in the figure of "Mot," the king of the underworld—has to be conquered repeatedly (in the cycles of winter and spring), in Israel's faith, God stands as the decisive victor over death, as well as over all the cycles of nature. In the psalms, death is a very real power, but it is not a god. God is *God*. Yahweh redeems the psalmist from the "Pit" (Ps. 103:4) and to him "belongs escape from death" (Ps. 68:20).

Yet while this may represent the good news of Israel's theology, things are much different at an existential level. In the psalmist's experience, death is like an enemy that entraps its prey (Ps. 18:4–6); none can escape from its clasp. Death is also like a ravenous creature whose appetite is insatiable; it greedily devours human lives (Ps. 69:15). Death seizes people suddenly and unexpectedly (Ps. 116:3). It appears like a phantom shepherd, escorting the dead to the grave (Ps. 49:14). Death rises up like an ocean that swallows human beings whole (Ps. 69:15). And it is a place of utter darkness, where a person is forever forgotten (Pss. 31:12; 88:12).

Death also confronts the psalmist with his creaturely nature. As Walter Brueggemann summarizes things, life in the Psalter is terminally limited.[3] In the words of Psalm 89:48, "Who can live and never see death? Who can escape the power of Sheol?" Psalm 90:10 goes so far as to put an endpoint on our life: "The days of our life are seventy years, or perhaps eighty, if we are strong, even then their span is only toil and trouble; they are soon gone, and we fly away." The Psalter is soberly realistic about life on earth.

In the view of Psalm 49:10, death is the great equalizer: "When we look at the wise, they die; fool and dolt perish together and leave their wealth to others." What the psalms would remind us again and again is that we are mortals. Our days are like grass. We flourish like a flower, but when the wind passes over it, the flower disappears, "and its place knows it no more" (Ps. 103:15–16). We do not have life in ourselves. Life comes to us as a gift, and death shows us our creatureliness: from dust to dust.[4]

Within the context of the psalms, death is a reality that comes not just at the end of our life, but that also visits us in the middle of our life. Israel's faith is profoundly focused on this world. It embraces the good life that God has established in creation here and now. In contrast to Egyptian theology, Israel does not speculate on the afterlife or institute rituals providing amenities for the entombed, like for the pharaoh.[5] Israel's idea of *Sheol* is more like nonlife than afterlife, and what the psalmist fears is the loss of life *today*. The British poet and priest Malcolm Guite gives voice to the melancholy nature of this idea in his poem "Finished":

> *For I am incomplete, my mirrors show*
> *No more than flaws and fragments as they pass,*
> *The selves I lose, that mock me as they go,*
> *And leave me trembling by the darkened glass.*
> *I do not see the face that once I had*
> *Nor can I see the one I will become,*
> *Flitting between a shadow and a shade*
> *I was, I was, I whisper, not I Am....*[6]

Anything that depletes life—as with sickness or natural disasters—is like a death (Pss. 38:3; 91:5–6; 102:11). Anything that diminishes life, such as the experience of oppression, or that corrupts life, as with sin, or that warps and distorts an aspect of life, as with depression or madness, is like death (Ps. 88:4–5). Anything that mutes life, like the experience of enforced silence, is death. Anything that reduces life to an alienated existence, such as an individual losing community, or that decimates life, such as with imprisonment or the attack of an enemy, is described as an experience of death (Ps. 102).[7]

For this reason, the faithful must always *choose* life, not death, and they must choose life against all the forces of death. God himself urges the faithful to do so: "Choose life!" (Deut. 30:15–20 CEV). This is why the psalmist implores God to keep him in life. If human beings have been created to "walk before the LORD in the land of the living" (Ps. 116:9), as well as to praise the living God, what is the point in going to *Sheol*?

> What profit is there in my death,
>   if I go down to the Pit?
> Will the dust praise you?
>   Will it tell of your faithfulness?
>
> (Ps. 30:9)

The worst outcome that the psalmists might imagine for themselves is Yahweh turning his face away from them. For it, too, would be like death

(Pss. 104:29; 143:7). So in Psalm 80, the psalmist prays not just once but *three* times on Israel's behalf that Yahweh will let his face shine on them so they might be saved. In the context of a passage like Job 19:25–26, which Psalm 103:17 hints at, such a vision of God's face results in life everlasting:

> For I know that my Redeemer lives,
>> and that at the last he will stand upon the earth;
> and after my skin has been thus destroyed,
>> then in my flesh I shall see God.

In the Psalter only God is immortal. Only God can venture in and out of the realm of death untouched by its devastation. Only God can rescue human beings from death-inducing chaos and from the dark realm with its tenacious grasp. Unlike Baal's battle with Mot in Canaanite theology, which ends in a stalemate, in Israel's theology, God remains sovereign over death (Ps. 139:8). And in contrast to the general ancient Near Eastern views of the cyclical nature of death, pictured in the gods of death, Yahweh's power over life is "from everlasting to everlasting" (Ps. 90:2).[8]

It is the Lord who lifts the psalmist "up from the gates of death" (Ps. 9:13). It is the Lord who delivers the psalmist from death "so that I may walk before God in the light of life" (Ps. 56:13). It is the Lord who restores the psalmist "to life from among those gone down to the Pit" (Ps. 30:3). It is the Lord who stands sovereign over "storm chaos" (Ps. 89:9–10), and who defeats "monstrous chaos" (Ps. 74:12–15). It is the Lord who ransoms the psalmist "from the power of Sheol" (Ps. 49:15). Or, as it says in Job 7:21, in Samuel Terrien's translation:

> Thou wilt look for me in the deepest darkness just before dawn,
> but . . . thou wilt not find me!⁹

And even if the psalmist were to attempt to flee from the Lord by hiding himself in death and darkness, the Lord would be there, too, as a comforting, rescuing presence. In the words of Psalm 139:7–12:

Is there anyplace I can go to avoid your Spirit?
>to be out of your sight?
If I climb to the sky, you're there!
>If I go underground [to *Sheol*], you're there!
If I flew on morning's wings
>to the far western horizon,
You'd find me in a minute—
>you're already there waiting!
Then I said to myself, "Oh, he even sees me in the dark!
>At night I'm immersed in the light!"
It's a fact: darkness isn't dark to you;
>night and day, darkness and light, they're all the same to you.

>(THE MESSAGE)

While the language of the psalms may involve a measure of ambiguity about the nature of death and the lot of humanity after death, in Christ we discover the definitive defeat of death and the unambiguous gift of life in the one who calls himself the Resurrection and the Life (John 11:25). Instead of death swallowing up humans, as the psalmist describes it, Jesus is the one who swallows up death once and for all (1 Cor. 15:54–57; Isa. 25:8).

Instead of death consuming us with fear, Jesus absorbs death into himself, along with its curse and its pain, and thereby frees us from the dread of death. Instead of being an enemy against which we are helpless, in the context of the New Testament, death is a conquered enemy (1 Cor. 15:26; Rev. 21:3–4). And whereas the psalmist sees the constant threat of the life-sucking powers of death, Saint Paul sees Jesus as the one who destroys death and brings "life and immortality to light through the gospel" (2 Tim. 1:10).

Significantly, in a way that reflects the singular power of God in the psalms, in Matthew 8:23–27 Jesus rebukes the storm and, in Mark 6:47–51, he walks upon the sea as the Lord of wind and water and of all the forces of chaos in heaven and on earth and under the earth. And whereas the psalmist fears drowning in the deathly waters of chaos, in Revelation 20:14 we see how death is "thrown into the lake of fire." Satan, likewise, as "the dragon, that ancient serpent," is thrown into the "Pit," a "lake of fire and sulfur" (Rev. 20:2, 10).

For the follower of Jesus, yes, death wounds us, and we grieve those losses, but it does not cause us to despair. For there is always hope in the one "who gives life to the dead and calls into existence the things that do not exist" (Rom. 4:17). Death is real—but it is not final. Death induces decay and deprivation in our lives, but Jesus, "the Prince of life" (Acts 3:15 NASB), counters all the deathly effects of sin by the power of his Spirit (Rom. 8:10–11; 2 Cor. 4:10–11). Death still stings, without a doubt, but its sting no longer crushes us. As Paul writes:

> "Death has been swallowed up in victory."
> "Where, O death, is your victory?
> Where, O death, is your sting?"
>
> (1 Cor. 15:54–55)

One last thing bears mentioning here: while the psalms in particular and the Old Testament in general speak honestly about the dead, Christians frequently do not. In the testimony of the biblical authors, Abraham uses his wife, Sarah, to save his skin, Moses murders a man out of anger, Samson beds a prostitute, Saul commits suicide, David commits adultery, and Solomon cannot control his sexual appetites; and the psalms describe jealousy, idolatry, "wanton cravings," child sacrifice, and ingratitude as failures of Israel (Ps. 106). There is no photoshopping or tidying up here.

Yet when Christians give their eulogies for the dead, at worst, they use phrases such as, "they have gone to a better place" or "they're like an angel watching over us." At best, but still short of truthful speech, Christians produce a highlight reel of the deceased person's life so that its listeners walk away comforted "by the good that she did in her life" or relieved that "he wasn't such a bad man after all." To speak in these ways is to fail to speak fully faithfully.[10]

How then should Christians speak a "good word" about the dead? They should speak in a way that offers listeners a chance to encounter afresh the grace of God—that despite the flawed, broken nature of the person's life, the grace of God appeared in all sorts of surprising ways. Christians should remind those listening that God's grace is offered to all: the great and the small, the saint and the sinner, the ordinary and the extraordinary. And when we do so, I suggest, we also bear witness to ourselves, to those still living, who may wonder how the grace of God will show up in the places where we most need it.

In our communities of faith, we must learn how to speak honestly and truthfully about dying, death, and the dead.[11] We must remind each other in our practice of the Lord's Supper, for example, what it means to die a "good" death and to live a "good" life. We must speak honestly today in our practices of testimony-giving so we will bear honest witness about our deaths when that day comes. And we must lament the brokenness of our lives now so we will be able to lament our broken lives at death—and discover that God's grace embraces us here too.

CONCLUSION

According to the Population Reference Bureau and the World Factbook, 106.60 people die every minute, while approximately 55 million die in an average year.[12] The World Health Organization reports that one person will commit suicide about every forty seconds, while another person will die in armed conflict every one hundred seconds.[13] And over the course of this day of writing, about two thousand of my brain cells will die and never come back.[14]

Death is a reality that confronts us daily. It surrounds us on every side. It marks our bodies from the start with a kind of inescapable death-clock built into our genes, and no human can escape it. We dread it; we fear the incompleteness of our lives, of all that we *might* have accomplished under different circumstances; we seek to postpone it or to protect ourselves against it; and we write stories to make sense of it. And, if we would let it, death might also cultivate the virtue of humility in us.[15]

In the context of the psalms, death appears like a watery monstrous force. It pulls us into the underworld of *Sheol*, and it confronts us daily with our mortality, reminding us that we are but "dust." But the psalms also remind us that God stands sovereign over death and that, while we may be like "grass" that withers, God invites us to be like a tree "whose leaf does not wither" (Ps. 1:3 NIV)—a "tree of life." Such a gift of life, a "fountain of life" (Ps. 36:9), comes from God, not from ourselves, and it comes to us now in the midst of life, not just at the end of life.

By the time Hurricane Harvey left the Gulf of Mexico, $125 billion of property damage was sustained. An estimated 30,000 people were displaced from their homes and 107 deaths were confirmed. The hurricane officially became the worst disaster in Texas history.[16] Destruction was visible throughout the Houston area and, like all tragedies of this sort, people would struggle to make sense of the irrational nature of death.

For me personally, barely ten minutes after my family exited our neighborhood, the floodwaters closed over the last way out. As a mass of churning waters rushed by us on either side of the I-10 highway, I struggled to make sense of this "stormy chaos." Thousands would lose their homes and livelihoods. For many it would feel like death in the midst of life. God would rescue many of us from the worst, but not all. Many would escape death, but not everybody.

In the moment, all I could do was pray with the psalmist that God would not forget our mortality, and that he would be the God the Psalter proclaims to us repeatedly: a God of life in the face of death.

QUESTIONS FOR REFLECTION

1. What emotions do you feel when you think about death, whether your own death or the death of loved ones? How are these emotions mirrored in the psalms that describe death?

2. How did your family of origin or church community or subculture talk about death—or not talk about it? In what ways does our society shelter us from the dying and shut us off from the dead? What might we be losing because of it?

3. How would you describe your feelings toward God when tragedies happen? How do you respond when people ask, "Where was God?" or "How could a good God allow this to happen?" How does Psalm 30 help you to process your feelings?

4. When the psalmist repeatedly describes human beings as "dust" and "grass" as a way to remind us of our mortality, how does that make you feel? Does your life feel too short or too fleeting?

5. What experiences have you had that could be described, with the psalmist, as "death in the middle of life"?

6. Can you recall people you have known personally or read about who modeled healthy ways of facing their own death or the death of a loved one? How might have their ideas about God informed their thoughts?

7. In her book *The Art of Death: Writing the Final Story*, Edwidge Danticat states, "We write about the dead to make sense of our losses, to become less haunted, to turn ghosts into words, to transform an absence into language."[17] How does this resonate with your experience of eulogies at funeral services?

EXERCISES

1. Read Psalms 69 and 88. Read them several times. Meditate on them. Pray through them. Consider memorizing a portion of them to carry in your heart as a way to maintain a lively conversation with God throughout the day.

2. Make a parallel list contrasting the Psalter's understanding of death and the New Testament language about death. What feelings and thoughts do you have when you look at the two lists?

3. As a prayerful exercise anticipating your own death, write down instructions for your funeral or memorial service. What elements are most important to you? What do you want said about yourself that will help people see the grace of God in your life in the face of all the good and bad, all the harmful and helpful, all the faithful and unfaithful?

4. As a group, discuss all the ways our culture avoids the reality of death, tries to prolong life artificially, or turns death and dying into a money-making industry. How might Christians become a countercultural witness to a biblical view of life and death?

5. Celtic believers many years ago spoke of the holy act of preparing for "a good and peaceful death." As a group, discuss what you think that might mean. How does this relate to Christians who have suffered an untimely or violent death, or who have suffered physical persecution before their death? Where does that fit with a good God?

6. Read Psalm 139 together and share your thoughts about the language of God's watchful care, of death and dying and darkness, of wickedness and enemies, and of God searching our own hearts for traces of "wicked ways."

PRAYER

Wounded Christ, you who have gone to the monstrous depths and swallowed death whole, robbed it of its sting, tasted its bitter finality, and conquered it once for all, we pray that you would free us from the fear of death, comfort us in the losses that we experience on account of death, infuse our hearts with the hope of your resurrected life, and grant us the serenity to face our own death in humility and peace. In your name we pray. Amen.

12

LIFE

*Sing G*OD *a brand-new song!*
Earth and everyone in it, sing!
*Sing to G*OD*—worship G*OD*!*
　　—PSALM 96:1–2 THE MESSAGE

Author of life divine,
who hast a table spread,
furnished with mystic wine
and everlasting bread,
preserve the life Thyself hast giv'n,
and feed and train us up for heav'n.
　　—CHARLES WESLEY[1]

THE GOOD LIFE

According to the Myers-Briggs personality test I'm an INTJ; in the Enneagram I'm a 5. It means, among other things and on the downside of my personality, that I'm driven to be productive, I hate to waste time,

I resent inefficiency, and I get aggravated when I'm interrupted. It means that I like to engineer my future with ten-year plans, which I do as a way to protect myself from the unpredictable and the uncontrollable. More positively, perhaps, it means that I always wish to make the most of life.

On April 10, 2018, my older sister Christine was in a near-fatal car accident in Austin, Texas. While she was standing on the side of the road, a Chevy Silverado truck hit her at full speed, sending her flying through the air before she hit the ground unconscious.[2]

In that brief moment, my sister suffered direct trauma to her brain, her carotid arteries were dissected, her liver was split in two, her lungs were punctured, her facial bones were broken into pieces like "potato chips" (as the surgeon put it), her eye sockets were shattered, her hearing in both ears was damaged, her feet and ankles were crushed by the truck wheels, and her sense of taste and smell were destroyed. Rushed to the hospital, she spent five weeks in the ICU and another three at a rehab facility.

Knowing that we were needed close at hand, my family left our home in Houston and moved into my sister's home in Austin. For five weeks, ten of us lived under the same roof: my family of four, my sister's four children, and both my parents, while my brother-in-law Cliff kept vigil at the hospital. My younger sister Stephanie spent her daytime hours at the house, leaving only at night to take care of her two boys. Scores of people from the church community provided critically needed support.

During this time, I saw my nieces and nephews struggle with the specter of losing their mother, my brother-in-law become physically ragged, and my small children fall repeatedly through the cracks. I saw my parents feel the burden of old age. Phaedra and I slept in bunk beds, in separate bedrooms, and struggled to stay connected. I managed only two hours of work on any given day, causing me to fall behind on all my projects, and I struggled against the instability of our days.

While my older sister fought for her life in the hospital, we fought to stay hopeful at home. Though we prayed for the miraculous power of God to restore my sister to fullness of life, we feared the worse. We feared, at worst, death, and therefore the loss of a wife and mother, along with a sister and daughter. We feared a permanently disfigured body. We feared the depletion of resources, the waste of potential, and the loss of a future.

What we feared, ultimately, was the loss of *shalom*, what the psalms describe as a deep sense of well-being marked by a fullness of life (Pss. 29:11; 72:7). Among other things, such a life includes physical vitality (Ps. 104:30), plentiful food (Ps. 104:28), meaningful work (Ps. 104:23), deep community (Ps. 107:41), a purposeful future (Ps. 103:17), and a place in the world to call home (Ps. 126:6). God not only gives "food from heaven in abundance" (Ps. 105:40), but he also gives "food from the earth, and wine to gladden the human heart, oil to make the face shine, and bread to strengthen the human heart" (Ps. 104:14–15). He gives food in abundance (Ps. 65:10–11)!

When the king prays for God's blessing in Psalm 21, he asks for "length of days forever and ever" (v. 4). In the face of violence and the threat of death, the psalmist prays that the Lord will redeem his life (Ps. 72:14) and not take him away "at the midpoint of my life" (Ps. 102:24). He prays that God will put him on "the path of life" and grant him "eternal pleasures at your right hand" (Ps. 16:11 NIV).

For the psalmist, "God's Yes is spoken in the midst of life."[3] In other words, this life is good. In fact, to use the language of Genesis 1, it is *very good*. And it is not just that God gives the gift of richly generative life once, at birth, to kickstart the psalmist into existence. It is that God *continuously* sustains the psalmist's life, and in the face of death and destruction, God rescues the psalmist and gives him the gift of a new life—one that begs for a new song.

THE PSALMS OF LIFE

What the psalms assume throughout is that God is the author, preserver, and protector of life. According to the Psalter, the Lord is "the fountain of life" (Ps. 36:9) who "preserves" our life (Ps. 86:2). In the face of danger, the psalmist prays, "O guard my life, and deliver me" (Ps. 25:20). He claims God as the "upholder of my life" (Ps. 54:4). He experiences the Lord's precepts as life-giving (Ps. 119:93). The Lord sustains the psalmist by day, while at night "his song is with me, a prayer to the God of my life" (Ps. 42:8). In Psalm 119 he links the experience of life directly to God's work and character:

- Give me life according to your promise (v. 154).
- Give me life according to your justice (v. 156).
- Preserve my life according to your steadfast love (v. 159).

God is the source of all that is, and apart from him nothing has life. In the language of providence, God protects creation against a reversion to the "formlessness and emptiness" of Genesis 1:2 (translation mine). He enables creation to flourish in all its beauty and variety, and he guarantees creation's good, pleasing, and perfect end. Against all claims to self-sufficiency or "self-made" status, the psalms assert the Lord's "generous, life-initiating, life-sustaining gift of vitality without which no creature can live."[4]

The psalms also reckon with the fragile and fleeting nature of life as well as with all the forces that threaten life. Eugene Peterson translates Genesis 1:2 as "a soup of nothingness, a bottomless emptiness, an inky blackness" (THE MESSAGE). The rest of the Old Testament characterizes this "watery abyss" as a chaos: a place of disorder marked by violent forces and evil monsters that endanger life. It is also a life that is here one day and gone the next.

The psalmist experiences this reality at an existential level. His soul is filled with troubles, and his "life draws near to Sheol" (Ps. 88:3). He sinks into deep darkness (Ps. 44:19). Like a frightened child at night, he sees terrors all around him, and like a woman caught in the sex-slave trade, he hears the whispers of wicked men who "plot to take my life" (Ps. 31:13). Like a man in a midlife crisis, he prays to know "how fleeting my life is" (Ps. 39:4). He knows his "days are like grass" (Ps. 103:15), transient and ephemeral. And with echoes of the word that a priest speaks on Ash Wednesday, he knows that he is dust (Ps. 103:14), and to dust he will one day return (Ps. 90:3).

He also, however, knows that the Lord is the one who raises us up from the dust (Ps. 113:7) and protects our life (Ps. 64:1). The Lord delivers us from the dread of death (Ps. 55:4). The Lord is the one who not only tames the forces of chaos (Ps. 104:7) but also turns the terrifying monsters into household pets (Ps. 104:26). As Peterson translates Psalm 104:24–26:

> What a wildly wonderful world, GOD!
> You made it all, with Wisdom at your side,
> made earth overflow with your wonderful creations.
> Oh, look—the deep, wide sea,
> brimming with fish past counting,
> sardines and sharks and salmon.
> Ships plow those waters,
> and Leviathan, your pet dragon, romps in them.
>
> (THE MESSAGE)

Though we may be like a flower in a field, which soon withers and dies and "its place *remembers* it no more" (Ps. 103:16 NIV, emphasis added), the Lord is the one who, in faithful love, "*remembers* that we are dust" (v. 14 NIV, emphasis added), and whose love remains, from everlasting to everlasting, with those who fear him, those who keep his covenant (Ps. 103:17–18).

In the psalms God does what no one else can do, the presumptions of modern medicine and the near godlike powers of technology notwithstanding: he gives life and takes life. This becomes manifestly clear in Psalm 104. As John Goldingay points out, there is a pattern at work in verses 27–30 that illuminates its meaning.[5] Whereas verses 1–26 describe God's sovereign work in creation, in these four verses the psalmist focuses on God's power to give and to take, not just the basic nourishment required for life, but life itself.

- God *gives* the gift of food that sustains life (vv. 27–28).
- God *withdraws* the gift of food that sustains life (v. 29a).
- God *withdraws* the gift of breath (v. 29b).
- God *gives* the gift of breath (v. 30).

When God takes away our breath (*ruach* in the Hebrew), we die (Ps. 146:2–4). Yet when God breathes his Spirit in us, his *ruach*, we live (Gen. 2:7), and by it we flourish.[6] It is also God's *ruach*, not insignificantly, that renews a heart (Ps. 51:10–12). It is similarly noteworthy that the term "create" (Ps. 104:30a) from the Hebrew *barah*, corresponds to the term "renew" (v. 30b). Within the context of the Old Testament, only God creates in this manner.[7]

And it is not just once that God makes life possible. As Bernhard Anderson remarks, "In the Hebrew text, the verbs refer to continuing actions." God creates life—and then *keeps* creating life. If he stopped being a life-giving God, creation would cease to exist. Anderson proposes a translation of Psalm 104:28 that captures this sense well: "When you give to them (not once but again and again), they gather it up (not one time but frequently)."[8]

One last observation is this: humans do not get preferential treatment. Their fate, in the words of Ecclesiastes 3:19–20, is the same fate as animals: "They all have the same breath, and humans have no advantage over the animals; for all is vanity ["mere breath"]. All go to one place; all are from the dust, and all turn to dust again." Like all God's creatures, the human (the *Adam*) is made from the dust (the *adamah*). All creatures, in this view, are equally vulnerable. In Psalm 104, humanity "stands alongside other creatures in dependence and alongside other creatures in grateful, amazed doxology."[9]

Just as the experience of life often calls for a song (Ps. 104:33), so the experience of new life calls for a new song. To state that the Psalter is full of songs is to state the obvious. It's a songbook after all! What may need stating more explicitly, however, is that the people of Israel are fundamentally a singing people. Wherever life happens, songs naturally erupt. Whenever new life is experienced, it calls for a new song.

But while the instinct of many today will be to interpret the language of "new song" as simply a warrant for new musical compositions, I suggest that this meaning represents only one possible interpretation of the phrase, which appears six times in the Psalter (33:3; 40:3; 96:1; 98:1; 144:9; 149:1). The "new song" of the psalms is not just about new melodies, it is also about the experience of a new grace and a new future.

The psalmist writes a new song for a new day. This is the first sense of the phrase, "Sing to the Lord a new song." Psalm 33:1–3 illustrates this sense well:

> Rejoice in the LORD, O you righteous.
>> Praise befits the upright.
> Praise the LORD with the lyre;
>> make melody to him with the harp of ten strings.
> Sing to him a new song;
>> play skillfully on the strings, with loud shouts.

As the Jewish translator and critic Robert Alter notes, this phrase is "the composer's self-advertisement: God is to be celebrated not with a stock item from the psalmodic repertoire but with a freshly composed piece."[10] A similar sense is at work in Psalms 96:1 and 144:9. Matthew Henry, writing in the early eighteenth century, introduces the reader to a slight variation on this idea. Summarizing Psalm 149:1, he observes:

> We must sing a *new song*, newly composed upon every special occasion, sing with new affections, which make the song new, though the words have been used before, and keep them from growing threadbare.[11] (emphasis original)

Here we encounter, then, a dual sense for the idea of "freshly composed." The psalm itself is freshly *composed*, while it is also *freshly* composed. The new song refers not just to a new musical composition but also to an outburst of new affections. On this understanding, the psalmist invites the reader to give voice to a fresh experience of God by means of a fresh outburst of praise, a "new song."[12]

The psalmist also writes a new song in response to a new grace. This is a sense that we discover especially within what Walter Brueggemann calls the psalms of disorientation.[13] These are psalms that describe experiences of weakness, suffering, grief, or death. Psalm 40:1–3 says this:

> I waited patiently for the LORD;
>> he inclined to me and heard my cry.
> He drew me up from the desolate pit,
>> out of the miry bog,
> and set my feet upon a rock,
>> making my steps secure.
> He put a new song in my mouth,
>> a song of praise to our God.
> Many will see and fear,
>> and put their trust in the LORD.

How might Psalm 40 help us understand the idea of a "new song"? On the one hand, the new song points to the *psalmist's* experience of God's gracious deliverance. God's deliverance from the pit issues into a new grace: the experience of solid ground under the psalmist's feet (v. 2). The deliverance also issues in the gift of a new song (v. 3). In this sense, the new song recounts the psalmist's experience of God's work of redemption, generous provision, and instruction.

On the other hand, the new song points to a new experience of *God's* enduring graciousness. In Psalm 40, God appears in past, present, and future tenses: "Many, LORD my God, are the wonders you have done" (v. 5 NIV); "You are my help and my deliverer" (v. 17b); "Be pleased, O LORD, to deliver me; O LORD, make haste to help me" (v. 13). While the psalmist's experience of disorientation may not change, he can nonetheless cling by faith to God's faithfulness.

What we discover here is a subjective and objective dimension. The "new song" refers both to the psalmist's experience of new grace arising out of an experience of disorientation and in the *middle* of disorientation. The "new song" likewise refers to the possibility of experiencing *the God we have always known* in a new way (vv. 1–10), as well as the *God I did not know could be this way*, that is, gracious in this exact manner (vv. 11–17).

The psalmist writes a new song to make sense of a new future. This final sense of "new song" is what we encounter in Psalm 149, written either during Israel's exile in Babylon or just after exile.

In Psalm 149:1, the psalmist tells the reader to sing a new song. What sort of song is this? It is the song of a new story that beckons from the future.[14] In other words, this is a new song that announces the end of exile, the end of being homeless, the end of feeling disoriented.[15] The new song in this way announces the final coming of God for the sake of the final restoration of God's people.

For as long as God tarries to bring about the fulfillment of his promises, however, the psalmist encourages the reader to sing a new song—a song of the future. This future vision, which elicits the psalmist's praise, involves a new story for God's "faithful" (v. 5). The psalmist's goal, then, is not to generate new music, since the point is not a musical one but rather a theological one. The new song is a new story that God will write. It is a new reality that God's people are to *sing themselves into*.

For the follower of Jesus to sing a new song in this sense is to sing of our new creation. This is how Saint Augustine understood the meaning of the new song.[16] "Humankind has aged in sin," he writes, "but is made new through grace. It is right, then, that all who are renewed in Christ, all those in whom eternal life has begun, should sing a new song."[17] The act of singing itself, as Augustine saw it, brings about real change in the Christian. To sing this new song is to *become* like Christ and to *act* like Christ.[18]

To sing a new song is not to sing a "new thing" or the "next thing." It is to sing in light of the reality of God's good future, made present to Christ's people by his Spirit. This is the same life-giving Spirit who makes us partakers of Christ's ever-renewing resurrected life (Rom. 8): a life that belongs to the new creation (2 Cor. 5:17; Gal. 6:15), where humanity is not simply alive (a *nephesh hayah*) but "hyperalive, excessively alive," as Jeremy Begbie describes it.[19]

CONCLUSION

During my sister Christine's convalescence in the hospital, I saw first-hand not just the reality of suffering and death but also signs of God's life. I saw fractured relationships become reconciled. I saw unbelievers watch with curious interest at the way in which the body of Christ sacrificially served my sister's family. I saw a dear friend, who had been far from God, break down weeping, crying out to God to heal my sister.

I saw myself also freed, at least for a spell, from the pressure I put on myself to measure my worth by my achievements, to "make the most of my life" in terms of my productivity. And I learned from the psalms that to make the most of life was to entrust my life, and my sister's life, utterly to God, as frightening as that has felt at times because of the way it has made me feel vulnerable and exposed.

While there is still pain and much that cannot be recovered in my sister's life, including the time that the locusts have eaten, I have seen the grace of God become manifest in our lives. I have witnessed God breathe new life into shattered bones. I have watched God give hope to despairing minds and peace to fearful hearts. I have seen God heal parts of my sister's body, while other parts have remained as yet unhealed. And I have witnessed her beautiful spirit choosing to praise God for his mercy and goodness despite it all.

I have seen, finally, those who sowed in tears receive the gift of wholehearted, full-throated songs—new songs!—that do not blink away from death but stare it in the face, all in the name of the one who "renew[s] the face of the earth" (Ps. 104:30 NLT), the one whose face is "like the sun shining in all its brilliance" (Rev. 1:16 NIV), and the one who gives us a brand-new life and "everything to live for, including a future in heaven—and the future starts now!" (1 Peter 1:3 THE MESSAGE).

QUESTIONS FOR REFLECTION

1. At what points in your life have you felt most fully alive? What were the circumstances of your life that enabled you to feel this way? What are the things in your life that help you feel God's pleasure when you're doing them?

2. Whether you know your Myers-Briggs or the Enneagram personality test profile, how does the way you are essentially wired affect the way you approach life? Is it more intellectual, emotional, relational, sensory, pragmatic, activist, or otherwise? What might be the downsides of your personality as it relates to the vision of life that the psalms present to us?

3. Have you had any family crises or major losses that make you very thankful for life itself? In what way?

4. In what way might the psalms remind you of God as the "fountain" of your life, or as the "protector" and the "preserver" of your life? In what way might the psalms speak to a place in your life that feels "formless and void"?

5. How might the Psalter's idea of a "new song" as a "new creation," which we can experience here and now, inform the way you live your life and go about your work and relationships?

6. In what ways do you feel the tension between the good gifts of modern science and technology to promote life and the words of the psalmist that our days "are like grass" and that we will one day "turn back to dust"? How do we think about the goal of living a full life versus a long life?

7. How do the multiple senses of "new song" in the Psalter change the way you think about singing a new song?

EXERCISES

1. Read Psalm 104. Read it several times. Meditate on it. Pray through it. Consider memorizing a portion of it to carry in your heart as a way to maintain a lively conversation with God throughout the day.
2. Based on the psalms of this chapter, write your own brief psalm (say, six verses max) in which you express the themes of life, using Hebrew parallelism as an aid.
3. As a group, share how the psalms have been a comfort or provided wisdom during a personal or family crisis.
4. Take the idea in the psalms that God both gives and withdraws the breath of life and write a personal or communal prayer that gives expression to it.
5. Write down fifty things, however small or big, simple or grand, you are grateful for in your life. Consider sharing this list with a friend and bearing witness to one another of God's gift of life to you.
6. Explore with others ways in which you might incorporate the Psalter's multiple senses of "new song" into your practices of prayer and worship. Explore ways that your community might sing itself into a "new future" and a "new creation" that God makes available to us now by the Spirit of Christ.
7. Read Charles Wesley's hymn "Author of Life Divine," and discuss as a group its similarities and differences to the psalms of life (Pss. 33; 36; 54; 103; 104).

Author of life divine,
who hast a table spread,
furnished with mystic wine

and everlasting bread,
preserve the life Thyself hast giv'n,
and feed and train us up for heav'n.

Our needy souls sustain
with fresh supplies of love,
till all Thy life we gain
and all Thy fullness prove,
and strengthened by Thy perfect grace,
behold without a veil Thy face.[20]

PRAYER

Divine Creator, you speak and creatures come into being, you breathe and the universe comes to life. From nothing—make something. From emptiness—make full. From the old—make new. From that which is dead—make alive. And while we humbly accept that you shall one day take our breath away and return us to the dust of the earth, from which we were made, in hope we anticipate the day on which your Spirit shall breathe fully and finally the abundant life of the resurrected Christ in us. Amen.

13

NATIONS

We cannot say "God bless Africa" and stop there. We must add, "and may Africa fear and honour you."

—SAMUEL NGEWA[1]

The God who called Abraham in order to be a blessing to all nations is the God who governs the histories of all nations.

—CHRISTOPHER WRIGHT[2]

WHO IS MY NEIGHBOR?

Growing up in Guatemala City as a child, I attended the Instituto Austriaco Guatemalteco. My parents put my sisters and me in this private Austrian school because they felt it would broaden our horizons. This meant we would speak English at home, Spanish with our friends, and German at school. It meant we would learn not just about the history and culture of America but also of Latin America and Europe.

This being the case, it is not surprising that as a child I felt a pull to the Foreign Service. Having met the former US ambassador to Paraguay, Clyde Taylor, in high school, I became excited at the thought of a globe-trotting life. While my older sister felt drawn to serve God in cross-cultural missions, following in our parents' footsteps, my desire lay with the State Department: working in embassies around the world, learning languages, engaging in diplomatic and cross-cultural exchanges.

In college, I studied international relations. During the summer after my sophomore year, I studied at Georgetown University, taking courses in international politics and international economics. While living in Washington, DC, I worked as an assistant to the economic counselor at the Chilean Embassy, where I kept track of how many canned vegetables Chile exported during the third quarter of the previous year. In my junior year, I studied abroad at the University of Würzburg, improving my German.

In the spring of my senior year, I took the Foreign Service exam. Out of the seventeen thousand people who took the exam, I was one of the two thousand invited to the second-round interview exams. A few weeks later, in Dallas, I found myself miserably failing the interview, because in every scenario the two official diplomats gave me as a test of my judgment, I chose to support the local government's welfare over the imagined US administration's morally questionable policy. In no case could I imagine myself consciously harming the good of another country.

Six months later, much to my surprise, I found myself in seminary in Vancouver, British Columbia.

My whole life I have felt the push-pull of my American identity in relation to my love for the global community.[3] I am proud to be a Texan, but I always come alive when I travel to another country. I feel rooted deeply in my home in Austin, and I cherish the Southern hospitality that marks this part of the world, with its idiosyncratic sounds and tastes, and yet I struggle regularly with a regret that Phaedra and I have not raised our children overseas, like each of us was.

At best, my third-culture-kid identity has helped me to appreciate the bonds that humans share across geographic, linguistic, and cultural lines. At worst, my neither-here-nor-there identity has caused me to feel displaced. Some days I feel strongly that America is the best country in the world. Other days I feel embarrassed by American arrogance and its aggressive presence on the international stage. Like many with hearts broken by sin, I feel unduly proud of my nation and prejudiced against other nations.

The place of the nations in the psalms comes down to one basic question, which will be familiar to all human beings in all times and places: *Who is my neighbor?* This is a question God asks of both globalists and nationalists, both the global north and the global south, both "my people" and "your people," both the Western and the Eastern church. In the Psalter the nations appear at the beginning (Ps. 2) and at the end (Ps. 149). Just as Psalms 1 and 150 provide the outer frame to the Psalter, so Psalms 2 and 149 provide the inner frame. There is nothing coincidental about the role of the nations in the book of Psalms.

The nations feature prominently in the psalms because they represent a fundamental concern of Holy Scripture.[4] They appear first in Genesis 10, with its description of the families that descend from Noah's sons; and they appear at the end in Revelation 21:24–27, with the nations that bring their splendor into the city of God. In Genesis the nations are scattered, whereas in Revelation they are gathered and healed by the leaves that grow on the tree of life, which sits on either side of the life-giving river that flows from the throne of God.

The nations are likewise no minor concern of the Psalter; they appear repeatedly throughout. Egypt, Edom, Babylon, Moab, Philistia, Midian, Assyria—these are just some of the nations that factor into the Psalter's vision of faithful life and prayer. In Psalm 87, for instance, symbolic representatives of the whole world appear in a register of nations, about whom the Lord says, "they know me." This includes the west (Egypt), the east (Babylon), the north (Tyre), and the south (Ethiopia).

Such intimate knowledge of the nations points to God's universal re-creative and redemptive purposes.[5]

How do the nations in the Psalter connect to God's good purposes for all the earth? How do they become participants and antagonists to these divine purposes? How do they figure in the work of God's chosen king? And how might the psalms relate the role of the nations to a life of faith? It is these questions that we explore in this chapter.

THE PSALMS OF THE NATIONS

One of the dominant concerns of the psalms is the charge to bless the nations. While Psalms 1 and 3 involve the blessing of the individual and Israel, respectively, Psalm 2:12 extends the blessing of God to "all who take refuge in him." In Psalm 66:8, the psalmist charges all the peoples of the earth to "bless our God." Psalm 67:5–7 clarifies that the nations' praise of God is intimately linked to God's blessing of the nations. Because of God's goodness to all, the psalmist in Psalm 145 prays that "all [God's] works" (v. 10) might bless him.

As Christopher Wright observes in *The Mission of God*, all nations' histories are under God's sovereign control. Nothing any nation does surprises God; nothing they do, no matter how destructive or self-destructive, can undermine God's desire to bless all of creation. As Wright summarizes things: "The God who called Abraham in order to be a blessing to all nations is the God who governs the histories of all nations. The God who called Israel to be his treasured possession and priestly kingdom is the God who can say 'the whole earth is mine.'"[6]

The joyful noise of the faithful erupts from "all the nations," because all the nations belong to God. Christopher Wright offers four helpful observations about this idea that worship arises from the whole earth and across every people group. "The anticipated praise of the nations for YHWH," he writes, "is said to occur: (1) in response to his mighty acts in general; (2) in response to the justice of his sovereign cosmic rule in particular; (3) in response to his restoration of Zion (which will be for the nations' benefit); and (4) as part of the outpouring of the universal praise of all creation."[7]

We see these ideas embodied, for example, in the language of Psalm 66:4, "All the earth worships you; they sing praises to you, sing praises to your name." Because God is the one who makes the nations, the psalmist reasons that all "shall glorify your name" (Ps. 86:9). The whole earth and all the nations sing to the Lord a new song, because of the mighty deeds that the Lord performs "from day to day" (Ps. 96:1–3). The Lord who judges all with righteousness "has revealed his vindication in the sight of the nations" (Ps. 98:2–9).

As Creator of the universe, God puts the nations of the earth under his sovereign care and rule. This includes "all the families of the nations" (Ps. 22:27) and "all the inhabitants of the world" (Ps. 33:8). "The LORD looks down from heaven," the psalmist continues, "[and] he sees all humankind. From where he sits enthroned he watches all the inhabitants of the earth—he who fashions the hearts of them all, and observes all their deeds" (vv. 13–15). What saves any nation is not their strength but rather their fear of the Lord and "hope in his steadfast love" (v. 18).

The nations of earth, like the nation of Israel, can become antagonists of the good purposes of God in the world. When Psalms 7 and 9 say that the Lord judges the nations with equity and the peoples with righteousness, no distinction is made between Israel and the nations of the world. All remain accountable to God's will for creation. In Psalms 110 and 137, the psalmist prays that God will execute judgment among the nations. In Psalms 44 and 106, the psalmist reckons with God's judgment of Israel.

Psalm 149 represents one of the more challenging psalms on this point and so deserves a bit of extra commentary. The psalmist opens with an invitation to sing to the Lord a new song. He then instructs Israel to be glad in its Maker, who adorns the humble with victory, and to praise him with song and dance. Then, halfway through what appears to be a rather buoyant hymn, the language shifts to a darker key: "Let the high praises of God be in their throats and two-edged swords in their hands, to execute vengeance on the nations and punishment on the peoples" (vv. 6–7).

What exactly is going on here? Is God giving Israel a license to unbridled warfare? Is vengeance ceded to the hands of humans? Does the psalmist endorse xenophobia and institutionalized revenge? The first thing to be said here is that Yahweh is the avenger, not Israel (Judg. 11:36; Isa. 47:3, 59:17; Ezek. 25:17). The Psalter assumes this fact all throughout. The Lord is in charge of vengeance, not human beings (Ps. 94:1). Whatever judgment is involved in this psalm is fundamentally Yahweh's, not Israel's. The final victory is Yahweh's, not Israel's.[8]

Second, according to the psalms, vengeance is necessary as a means to defeat evil and rectify injustice, because the oppression of the afflicted will never cease until "the wicked" are defeated once for all.[9] This is ultimately the psalmist's word of hope. God's justice is required, the psalms argue, wherever people suffer unjustly. Sometimes it is Israel who commits injustice. Other times, as in this case, it is the "nations," a term which here functions as shorthand for all peoples who wickedly commit injustice.[10]

Third, the Lord chooses who will carry out the divine sentence against the nations. What had been assigned to King David in Psalm 2:9 is now, in Psalm 149, assigned to the "faithful ones" (Mic. 4:13; Zech. 10:5; 12:6). Yet it is only as the people reflect God's steadfast love that they can properly carry out their duty as divine representatives.

Finally, whereas in Psalm 148:11 the kings join in the cosmic praise of God, in Psalm 149, these false monarchs who fail to do justice and keep peace deserve only divine rebuke. And whereas the faithful exult in God's glory (chabod), here the nobility (nichbadot, the "glorious ones") deserve only to be put "behind bars for good" (Ps. 149:8 THE MESSAGE).

There is no doubt that Psalm 149 involves a hard word for the nations. But it also involves a good word, and not just for the "faithful ones." In the psalms, God's judgment includes mercy and becomes an invitation to receive mercy (Isa. 30:18; 55:6–7). The psalmist pairs them integrally: "Great is your mercy, O LORD; give me life according to your justice" (Ps. 119:156). As James Mays observes, "Something wonderful and strange is afoot here, the lowly becoming the warriors who fight for the kingdom and inherit the earth."[11]

The nations, when they exhibit the love and justice of God, can also become participants in the good purposes of God in the world.[12] Psalm 67:1–5 shows us how:

> May God be gracious to us and bless us
> > and make his face to shine upon us, *Selah*
> that your way may be known upon earth,
> > your saving power among all nations.
> Let the peoples praise you, O God;
> > let all the peoples praise you.

> Let the nations be glad and sing for joy,
> > for you judge the peoples with equity
> > and guide the nations upon earth. *Selah*
> Let the peoples praise you, O God;
> > let all the peoples praise you.

As scholars point out, this is priestly language. In Israel, the priest would speak the official word of blessing over the people. In this psalm, it is God the heavenly Priest who blesses the nations. The psalmist takes the declarative and turns it into a prayer of petition: may God bless us. But the psalmist then casts his glance beyond the borders of Israel and prays that all the nations would praise God. In the final words of the psalm, the psalmist echoes Genesis 1:

> The earth has yielded its increase;
> > God, our God, has blessed us.
> May God continue to bless us;
> > let all the ends of the earth revere him.

(Ps. 67: 6–7)

Here the psalmist petitions God to bless the whole earth. The corresponding sign of divine blessing is economic well-being: good harvests, plentiful food, abundant variety (Lev. 25:19; Ezek. 34:27; Zech. 8:12–13). The psalmist prays for the nations just as Aaron the priest prays for Israel (Num. 6:23–26). In their direct encounter with God, the nations participate in God's good purposes (Ps. 138:4–5). They also participate in God's purposes because they have participated in the work of God in Zion (Ps. 102:13, 15–16, 21–22). And one day, as the psalms might imagine, the words of Isaiah 19:24–25 will be fulfilled:

On that day Israel will be the third with Egypt and Assyria, a blessing in the midst of the earth, whom the LORD of hosts has blessed, saying, "Blessed be Egypt my people, and Assyria the work of my hands, and Israel my heritage."

A true king will someday rule the nations. That true king's name is Jesus, and he will come as a blessing to the nations. Psalm 2 is the key text. As James Mays points out, in ancient Near Eastern societies, the king, whose power derived from the deity, served three functions: he provided security against enemies; he was responsible for justice and order; and he promoted the well-being of the people as an expression of divine blessing.[13] In Psalm 2, God's chosen king is identified, and here, in Psalm 72:1–4, 12–14, the king's vocation is described:

Give the king your justice, O God,
    and your righteousness to a king's son.
May he judge your people with righteousness,
    and your poor with justice.
May the mountains yield prosperity for the people,
    and the hills, in righteousness.
May he defend the cause of the poor of the people,
        give deliverance to the needy,
        and crush the oppressor.

> For he delivers the needy when they call,
>> the poor and those who have no helper.
> He has pity on the weak and the needy,
>> and saves the lives of the needy.
> From oppression and violence he redeems their life;
>> and precious is their blood in his sight.

The king's vocation, thus, is to mirror God's vocation as King of creation. In Psalm 72:17b, we see the outcome of the work of a true king: "May all nations be blessed in him; may they pronounce him happy." When the true king fulfills his calling, all the nations of the earth receive the blessing of God, which in turn prompts the people to bless the Lord (vv. 18–19).

In the Gospels, when Jesus is baptized, the heavens open up and the voice of the Father speaks, saying, "You are my Son, the Beloved; with you I am well pleased" (Mark 1:11; Luke 3:22). This language, mirroring Psalm 2:1, signals to the reader that the promises of Psalm 2 are finally fulfilled, and it names Jesus as the true King, the true Son of God, the true representative of faithful humanity. This is the King who will unite, save, and bless the peoples of the earth, not alienate them or exploit them or crush them. Mays explains:

> If psalm and Gospel are right—if God lays claim on the nations through the Son, and Jesus is the Son—if that is true, then Jesus is the one offer of God to human history. There is no other divine plan, no other strategy of heaven, to meet our needs and to save us from the consequences of human folly and wickedness. There is only Jesus.[14]

This is the good news that the nations of the earth have been waiting to hear.[15] In Luke 2:30–32, Simeon takes the Christ child in his arms and praises God saying, "for my eyes have seen your salvation, which you have prepared in the presence of all peoples, a light for revelation to the Gentiles and for glory to your people Israel." We hear this language again in the response of Paul and Barnabas to the synagogue leaders:

> When the non-Jewish outsiders heard this, they could hardly believe their good fortune. All who were marked out for real life put their trust in God—they honored God's Word by receiving that life. And this Message of salvation spread like wildfire all through the region. (Acts 13:48–49 THE MESSAGE)

The psalms assert repeatedly that the Lord's steadfast love is offered to all peoples. In goodness the Lord satisfies the desire of every living thing. The Lord is just and near and merciful to all who call on him in truth. The Lord hears the cry of the needy and watches over all who love him. The reason the nations can welcome the blessing of Israel's God is not just because this God is the Creator of all, but because this God can be trusted to protect the nations from their enemies, secure their well-being, and bless them, in fulfillment of the primordial calling of humanity.

This, the Gospels tell us over and over, is the work that Jesus embodies as the true King, the New David, the Greater Son, the one through whom all the nations shall be blessed. "In *this life*," Mays concludes, "we receive the blessing of God's reign by faith as spiritual gifts through the Christ: justice in the form of justification by grace, well-being in the form of salvation, and peace in the form of reconciliation with God."[16] Around this life will one day gather representatives from every tongue, tribe, and nation (Rev. 7:9).

CONCLUSION

As someone who often feels torn by his twin affinity for both the global community and his hometown of Austin, the psalms offer me an answer to the question, Do I have to choose between my nation and the nations of the earth, my geopolitical neighbors? The answer is not either/or. It is not that God blesses *either* my nation *or* the nations of the world. The blessing of God does not come as a zero-sum game, as if the blessing of God could come only to *my* family, *my* people, *my* nation, but not to *your* family, *your* people, *your* nation. Instead, in the Psalter, the answer is both/and. Blessing comes to me and my neighbor alike.

God would have me bless both my nation and the nations of the earth in Jesus' name, because the nations are in fact my neighbor. And God himself will bless the nations that do justice, choose peace, practice righteousness, protect the weak, and walk humbly with God. In the end, and at the end of God's purposes for this aeon, as Chris Wright helpfully explains, the hope is that the nations of the world will have been registered in God's city, blessed with God's salvation, called by God's name, and joined with God's people in praise of the Everlasting Desire of nations.[17] The psalms, in this sense, could well be called "the music of missions," and they invite us to join in its multilingual song with all our hearts, wholly open to the God of the nations.[18]

QUESTIONS FOR REFLECTION

1. In what way does this chapter broaden your understanding of the Psalter and of God's concern for all the nations of the world? Did anything surprise you?

2. In what way does Psalm 87 parallel the ministry of Jesus in his healing of the Syrophoenician woman in Mark 7:24–30?

3. How would you compare the psalms of the nations (Pss. 2; 18; 66–68; 72; 87; 96–98; 148–149) with the language of Revelation 5?

4. How might you read the psalms in a way that helps you to hear the heart of the global church's joys and sorrows? What is one thing you could do to feel how the global church experiences the psalms or perhaps to join in its culturally unique praise of God through the psalms?

5. Why do you think psalms singing has been so meaningful for the oppressed in the global church throughout the centuries?

6. What missional venture might the psalms call you to take on in this season of your life to serve the nations of the earth in Jesus' name?

7. In what way might the psalms of the nations help you to pray for the nations of the earth as your neighbor in Jesus' name?

EXERCISES

1. Read Psalm 66. Read it several times. Meditate on it. Pray through it. Consider memorizing a portion of it to carry in your heart as a way to maintain a lively conversation with God throughout the day.

2. Read Psalm 67 out loud. Read it a second time, calling to mind specific nations of the world that you would have God bless. Take the same Psalm 67 and try to re-create it musically, remembering how this echoes the Aaronic blessing of Numbers 6:23–27. In other words, write a new song of the nations as you consider Psalm 67 as a hymn of God's blessing.

3. Share as a group your response to Isaiah 19:23–25. Have someone read out loud the fuller context of Isaiah 19. Explore together ways in which this text might inform how you think, feel, and talk about the nations of the world.

4. Consider how your practices of congregational song, in general, or psalms singing, in particular, might bear witness to a watching world of the God who enables "every tongue and tribe and people" (Rev. 7:9, translation mine) to be uniquely and beautifully itself, while also unified in mutual care and respect.

5. Read and discuss as a group Psalm 91, along with news headlines from around the world. Read and pray the words of the psalm, one of the most oft-used psalms by Christians in the global church, as a way to identify with their struggles.

6. Read and discuss as a group one of these two books: Stephen Breck Reid, *Listening In: A Multicultural Reading of the Psalms* (Nashville: Abingdon Press, 1997), or Christopher J. H. Wright, *The Mission of God: Unlocking the Bible's Grand Narrative* (Downers Grove, IL: InterVarsity Press Academic, 2006).

PRAYER

May the leaders of the nations rule with justice and mercy.
Amen. Lord have mercy.
May justice be the shield and defender of all peoples of the world.
Amen. Lord have mercy.
May the nations have peace and the people be blessed.
Amen. Lord have mercy.
May the flocks and the herds prosper in the nations and the fish abound in our lakes.
Amen. Lord have mercy.
May the fields be fertile and the harvest plentiful in the nations.
Amen. Lord have mercy.
May we and our enemies in the nations of the world turn toward peace.
Amen. Lord have mercy.
May the love of the Father touch the lonely, the bereaved, and the suffering in the nations.
Amen. Lord have mercy.
May the path of the world be swept of all dangers.
Hallelujah. The Lord of mercy is with us.
Amen.[19]

14

CREATION

Praise GOD from earth,
> *you sea dragons, you fathomless ocean deeps;*
Fire and hail, snow and ice,
> *hurricanes obeying his orders;*
Mountains and all hills,
> *apple orchards and cedar forests;*
Wild beasts and herds of cattle,
> *snakes, and birds in flight;*
Earth's kings and all races,
> *leaders and important people,*
Robust men and women in their prime,
> *and yes, graybeards and little children.*
> > —PSALM 148:7–12 THE MESSAGE

When [God's] hand was opened by the key of love, the creatures came forth.
> > —THOMAS AQUINAS[1]

VOICING CREATION'S PRAISE

Some years back, my wife and I visited the small village of Glencoe in western Scotland. We chose it chiefly because of its proximity to the West Highland Way, a popular walking trail that runs ninety-six miles across the Scottish Highlands. Formed into a U-shape by an ice-age glacier, the trail narrows sharply at a point called the "Pass of Glen Coe." This pass is famous not just because it served as a location for *Monty Python* and *Harry Potter* movies but also because of its stunning geography.

Lying between the six-mile-long notched ridge of Aonach Eagach and the truncated spurs of Bidean nam Bian, the glen is an ice-worn valley mantled with screes and debris from the mountains. As the Scottish National Heritage describes the area, the peaty flats of the lower glen stand in sharp contrast to the towering precipices and water-falls around them. The region includes rugged mountains that soar from the flat valley floor as well as waterfalls, vertical outcrops, and hanging valleys.[2]

During our three-mile hike up Stob Mhic Mhartuin, Phaedra and I played a game we have often played during our walks in nature. It's a game I learned in seminary called the "Divine Game of Pinzatski." Conceived by Arthur and Ellen Pinzatski, the game calls for one person to point out an object in nature that the other person must then, as best they can, state what the object might say about God and why. I'd point to, say, a bit of green moss, and Phaedra would say, "The gentleness of God," and explain why she thought so. Or she'd point to a boulder-strewn cut in the mountain, and I'd say, "God's severe mercy," and explain why I thought so.

Playing this game over the years has taught us to pay attention to the details in creation and to see that there's no such thing as generic moss but rather things like Perthshire beard moss and woolly hair moss; that rocks are not just rocks but can be volcanic or sedimentary. It has taught us to hear the voice of the Maker in the things he has made—that moss and rocks do in fact praise God in their own unique language. It has also taught us to re-see ourselves as humans, how small we are yet how well-loved we are, too, in this "theater of God's glory," as John Calvin described the world. And it has taught us to see what the psalmist saw long ago, in Calvin Seerveld's translation of Psalm 19:1–4:

> The heavens are telling the glory of God.
> The very shape of starry space makes news
>   of God's handiwork.
> One day is brimming over with talk for the next day,
> and each night passes on intimate knowledge
>   to the next night
> —there is no speaking, no words at all,
> you can't hear their voice, but—
> their glossolalia travels throughout the whole earth!
> their uttered noises carry to the end of inhabited land![3]

The Psalter opens with an echo of the first chapters of Genesis, and it closes with a vision of the entire cosmos at praise. Before humans arrive on the scene, creation is already at praise. Once humans enter the stage of history, creation supplies the proper context for a faithful life. In the psalms, creation enacts the praise of God and summons us to faithful praise. Hill and dale, fire and frost, along with amoeba, atom, Asiatic black bear, and Arcturus, twenty times the size of the sun, all rejoice in the Lord, and their praise extends to the "ends of the world" (Ps. 19:4 NIV).

The theme of creation brings this book to a provisional close. Here we see how God ravishes us with his creation and so summons faithful praise from the human heart. Here we see how creation invites us to participate in its joy in God, and in giving ourselves willingly to this joy, we discover our true purpose as creatures made in the image of a joyful God: to faithfully reflect the divine image in all contexts of our created life as royal representatives of our Creator-King.

The Psalms of Creation

The first thing the psalms tell us about creation is that it is a gift of God's wisdom, made possible by God's word and breath, for the sake of creation's joy. In contrast to the theology of surrounding Canaanite peoples, the God of Israel does not propagate the world through a physical act of begetting. Yahweh does not require divine intermediaries to create heaven and earth. Nor does the Lord create out of mere necessity; the Lord does not *have* to create the cosmos, he *chooses* to.

In Psalm 104:24 the psalmist writes, "O Lord, how manifold are your works! In wisdom you have made them all; the earth is full of your creatures." This is similar to the language that we find in Proverbs 8 and Jeremiah 51:15, where "wisdom" takes center stage in God's creative acts.[4] Psalm 36:5 draws our attention to the fact that love likewise marks God's creative work: God's love "extends to the heavens, your faithfulness to the clouds." Psalm 33:5 adds that "the earth is full of the steadfast love of the LORD." In the verse that follows, the psalmist notes that the heavens were made "by the word of the LORD" and "by the breath of his mouth" (Ps. 33:6). All things have been created by his "command" (Ps. 148:5 NIV).

In asserting this, the psalmist would remind us that human beings make nothing original in the world. They only make something *of* the world that God has already made, from top to bottom, from quark to quasars. We ought not, moreover, put our ultimate trust in human beings, who are only mortals. The psalmist writes: "When their breath departs, they return to the earth; on that very day their plans perish" (Ps. 146:4). It is God whom we should trust. It is by God's power and breath that we have our being.

In the psalms, wisdom, power, and love feature largely in God's work of creation. But the psalmist declares that it is for the sake of joy that God makes the world. "Those who live at earth's farthest bounds are awed by your signs," the psalmist writes in Psalm 65:8, and then adds, "you make the gateways of the morning and the evening shout for joy." All throughout the Psalter, creation raises its joyful praise. The rivers clap their hands and the mountains sing for joy (Ps. 98:8). The valleys shout with gladness, the trees sing, and the fields make merry (Ps. 96:10–13). God, in short, creates *for* joy.

"God created the world," writes Ellen Davis, "including and even especially humanity, for the sake of God's own pleasure."[5] God creates in freedom, yes, not out of any necessity that lies outside of his character. But God also creates *in* joy (Ps. 104:31). "These two, freedom and delight," Davis adds, "belong together, in divine play just as in children's play."[6] In Psalm 104:26, for instance, God does not merely observe the Leviathan, God also plays with the Leviathan, as with a pet. In Psalm 104:15, God makes food not just for basic sustenance, but also "to make joyful the human heart."[7] God's joy is full and overflowing.

A second thing the psalms assert about creation is that nothing in creation is divine; only God is divine. All the forces of nature have been tamed and harnessed by God. Everything has its place. All things have a rhythm and a purpose. Over against the common assumption of ancient Near Eastern societies, the stars are not gods, the psalmist argues. Instead, God "determines the number of the stars; he gives to all of them their names" (Ps. 147:4).[8]

Day and night are not deities at war with each other. Instead, God himself establishes a daily rhythm for human and animal life to coexist, during the day and over the course of the night. In the words of Psalm 104:19–23, "The moon keeps track of the seasons, the sun is in charge of each day. When it's dark and night takes over, all the forest creatures come out. . . . When the sun comes up, [the young lions] vanish, lazily stretched out in their dens. Meanwhile, men and women go out to work, busy at their jobs until evening" (THE MESSAGE).

God also establishes a seasonal rhythm for planting and harvesting work. In God's order there is a place for sun and moon and all the elements of earth.[9] Earthly and heavenly bodies, furthermore, are not sentient; they are simply objects that testify to God's glory. And their praise is both a chorale and an antiphonal song. In Psalm 89:5, creation raises its voice like a choir: "GOD! Let the cosmos praise your wonderful ways, the choir of holy angels sing anthems to your faithful ways!" (THE MESSAGE). In Psalm 19:1–2, creation performs a call and response song, *day to day, and night to night.*

Third, in an echo of Genesis 1 and 2, the psalms remind us what it means to be human. Humans are infinitesimally small things in creation yet crowned with God-like glory. Psalm 8 is the key text here. The psalm opens with an acclamation of praise: "LORD, our Lord, how majestic is your name in all the earth!" (NIV). In the context of Israel's life, this is how one would address a royal figure. This verse, thus, presents God as King whose glory rises above the heavens and supersedes all human glory.

In verse 3, when the psalmist looks up at the "macro-skies, dark and enormous," he wonders why the God of the universe should pay attention to "my micro-self" (THE MESSAGE). With an estimated four hundred billion stars and more than one hundred billion planets in the Milky Way galaxy, and with about seventy-five billion tons of living things on Earth, why bother with humans? We are weak and frail, made from organic earth (the *humus* in Latin). Like all creatures, we are mortal, here one day, gone the next. In Jim Cutter's translation of Psalm 8:

> When I look at the heavens, even the work of your fingers,
> the moon and the stars majestic in their courses—
> the eagle riding the air, the dolphin ploughing the sea,
> the gazelle leaping the wind, the sheep grazing the fells—
> who are we human beings that you keep us in mind,
> children, women, and men that you care so much for us?[10]

Yet God "crowns" us like kings and queens, with honor and glory (Ps. 8:5). It is not the monarch alone to whom God gives the privileges of royalty. God elevates *all* human beings to a royal status. Yet while we may feel astonished at our singular status, the psalmist reminds us that it is still all about God: *God* cares for us; *God* makes us; *God* crowns us;

God sets us up as rulers; *God* puts everything under our feet. The glory that Psalm 8:1 ascribes to God-King is now applied to human beings—and yet it remains *God's* glory to give and to receive.

The psalmist reminds us not only of our royal identity but also of our royal responsibility: to exercise dominion over the works of God's hands in a way that models God's dominion of creation. The language of Psalm 8:6–8 resembles the language of Genesis 1 and 2: God makes human beings rulers of "all sheep and oxen, and also the beasts of the field, the birds of the air, and the fish of the sea, whatever passes along the paths of the seas." Just as the king is to rule God's people lovingly, so human beings are to rule creation lovingly, as God rules it, in love.

The idea here is that God has called humans to care for and cultivate the earth, to make something *in* it in order to make something *of* it. In the context of the Psalter, the psalmist asks God to "watch" (*shamar*) over him (Ps. 16:1), to "keep" (*shamar*) him (Ps. 17:8), and to "preserve" (*shamar*) his life (Ps. 86:2). In Psalm 2:11, the psalmist urges the kings of the earth to "serve" (*avad*) the Lord with reverence. This is the same vocabulary that we find in Genesis 2:15, with its charge "to till [*avad*] and to tend [*shamar*] creation."[11]

Significantly, the first term, *avad*, often appears in contexts where humans are charged to "serve" or "worship" God. The second term, *shamar*, suggests the idea of "watching over," "keeping," or "preserving."[12] The point of the psalms, with their Genesis perspective, is this: we "till" and "serve" creation *for God's sake*; we "tend" and "watch over" creation *in God's name.* Our royal dominion, therefore, is qualified by our priestly calling: to offer the things of God in love to all of creation and, in turn, to offer all the things of creation back to God in love.[13]

We can do this work faithfully only when we know "that we are working with the grain of God's creation purposes."[14] What are those purposes? They include a life marked by joyful praise, wonder-filled thanksgiving, care-filled stewardship of creation, hopeful work of restoration and reconciliation, gracious communion with others, and faithful living. And we can succeed at this work only because we are confident that Christ himself has faithfully performed this human vocation in obedience to his Father, the Maker of heaven and earth, and by the power of the life-giving Spirit.

Because Christ stands at the center of creation, the created realm can become a source of near-infinite delight for human beings. In Christ alone, we see how well-beloved the creation is. In Christ crucified and resurrected, we see how truly broken the creation is. And in Christ ascended, as the firstborn of creation who gives us the Spirit to whet "our appetite by giving us a taste of what's ahead" (2 Cor. 5:5 THE MESSAGE), we see how creation is bound in hope for new creation.

In Christ, we perceive *all* of creation's purposes: "that this life is the theater of sin and grace, death and life; that history matters and moves in a direction; that the structures of things, including the stars, had a beginning and may have an end; and that all creatures—animate and inanimate—stand before God."[15] In Christ, we perceive how "mysteriously well-pleasing [creation] is to God."[16] In Christ, we see how creation is fundamentally an expression of grace, and that God invites us to live in light of that grace, which is to say in light of God's economy of abundance.

One of the ways we choose to live in such an economy is by adopting a "Sabbath" mentality. This means we do not see the seventh day of rest as a "recuperation after a toilsome and well-done job."[17] Nor do we see Sabbath as an onerous obligation or an added-extra to God's work. We see Sabbath rather as a festive day on which God savors his work, delighting in it fully. "Strictly speaking," Karl Barth explains, "creation is crowned only when God in His joyful Sabbath rest looks back upon it and down on what He has created."[18]

As it relates to Adam and Eve, our primordial parents, Barth reminds us that Sabbath is the first divine action that humanity witnesses. Sabbath, not Monday, then, is the first day of our week. On this understanding, human life begins "with a holiday and not an imposed task; with joy and not with toil and trouble."[19] It begins on a day of grace. And God continually invites human beings to enter utterly into the grace of creation, marked by an economy of abundance where there is always enough.[20]

CONCLUSION

The psalms of creation bring these things to our attention repeatedly. While the praise of creation is a duty, it is also a delight and a "royal waste of time," to borrow Marva Dawn's phrase, which she uses to describe the fundamental nature of worship.[21] God provides us with "grain"—but he also "crowns the year" with his bounty. Creation bears witness to its God-ordained purposes, but its witness is never minimalist or merely pragmatic; instead, "one day is brimming over with talk for the next day."[22] God charges us to till and to tend creation, not as indentured servants but as royal agents crowned with divine privileges to make something of the world that God so loves.

It is true, of course, that we frequently fail to live out our proper calling. Instead of caring for creation, we despoil it, and when we do so, damaging and squandering its resources, "the earth's ability to praise is diminished," as Kathryn Schifferdecker rightly notes.[23] Instead of accepting our mortality, we seek to become like gods, and thereby warp our human nature. In refusing our place in the created order, we become restless and disoriented. In our rejections of the Creator, we settle for idols that dehumanize us. And rather than perceiving God's economy of abundance, in faith, we see only an economy of scarcity.

In an economy of scarcity, we fear that there will not be enough— not enough time, not enough energy, not enough friends, not enough opportunity, not enough resources, not enough goodness. At root is the fear that there will not be enough of God. Instead of delighting in creation, we detach ourselves from it through our devices and appliances. Instead of living in grace, we give in to our tendencies toward violence, exploitation, commoditization, tight-fisted greed, self-sufficiency, and a pathological anxiety; the limits of our mortality, we fear, are robbing us "of our best life now."[24]

I feel all these things regularly. I continually worry about my advancing age and all the things I may not accomplish before my death. I rarely feel that anything I achieve is enough. I struggle to take the time to truly rest or to be present to the things nearest me: my breath, my body, my wife, my children. I fail to trust God in certain basic areas of my life and frequently feel terrified about all the unknowns in my future. I fight the addictive pull of social media and all the ways it makes it easy for me to refuse in-the-flesh relationships. And I think about praising God but often don't actually do it.

The psalms would, of course, help me, if only I would let them. They would tell me to look up: to see how big the cosmos is and how small I am, and how good it is that I am small but glory-crowned. They would tell me to look down: to see my hands and feet that have been made to till and to tend creation in love. They would tell me to look at my Maker: to see how wise, powerful, good, and generous he is.[25]

And they would tell me to look around me as I play the Divine Game of Pinzatski: to see the lilies of the field and the birds of the air, and the moss and the rocks as well, how they neither worry nor uselessly toil, and instead invite me to delight in a gracious Creator in whom there is always enough—*more* than enough. And if I had ears to hear, I would hear creation's symphonic song of praise, as Isaac Watts beautifully describes it in his hymn "The Heav'ns Declare Thy Glory, Lord":

> *Sun, moon, and stars convey Thy praise*
> *round the whole earth, and never stand:*
> *so when Thy truth began its race,*
> *it touched and glanced on ev'ry land.*[26]

QUESTIONS FOR REFLECTION

1. What is one way the psalms of creation (Pss. 8; 19; 24; 33; 95; 104; 139; 145; 147; 148) have changed your perception of creation?
2. In what ways do you feel connected with nature, the physical world, the nonhuman world? In what ways do you feel disconnected from these things?

3. What is one way you might try to get out in nature more often? What would help you do this successfully and consistently?

4. Reading the news of the week, how does it reflect the fact that the relationship between humans and the nonhuman creation is damaged?

5. In what way do Psalms 8 and 19 echo or expand on the language of Genesis 1 and 2?

6. What are some of the unique flora, fauna, or geological properties of your area? How might they be offering up the praise of God "in their own language"?

7. How does the specific language of Genesis "to till and to tend the earth," which the Psalter uses in relation to our service and worship of God, support or challenge your understanding of the idea of being good stewards of God's creation?

8. In what way does the statement, "While creation's praise is a duty, it is also a delight and a royal waste of time," change the way you think about your own praise of God?

EXERCISES

1. Read Psalm 148 or 150. Read it several times. Meditate on it. Pray through it. Consider memorizing a portion of it to carry in your heart as a way to maintain a lively conversation with God throughout the day.

2. Write down the ways the Psalter's view of creation contrasts with that of our contemporary society. Write down the ways in which they overlap.

3. Explore as a group the biodiversity in your immediate region. What kinds of trees and flowers grow uniquely there? What birds and animal life are most common? What foods grow most naturally? Then praise God for the unique wonder of your part of the earth.

4. Explore with your community a few ways in which you might practically become good stewards of creation around you.

5. Play with your group the Divine Game of Pinzatski. Take twenty to thirty minutes to wander about outside, individually or in pairs, then come back and share which objects in nature brought a specific trait of God to mind.

6. When we read the psalms of creation, it is as if they are urging us, over and over again, to get out into creation as often as possible. List ways you can be more intentional about regularly getting out into nature to walk through it, smell it, see it, hear it, taste it, touch it, and know thereby the joy of creation and the joy of God.

7. Discuss as a group this affirmation: "The first thing the psalms tell us about creation is that it is a gift of God's wisdom, made possible by God's word and breath, for the sake of creation's joy."

8. Read and discuss as a group one of these books: Leah Kostamo, *Planted: A Story of Creation, Calling, and Community*; J. Matthew Sleeth, *The Gospel According to the Earth: Why the Good Book Is a Green Book*; and Douglas and Jonathan Moo, *Creation Care: A Biblical Theology of the Natural World*.

PRAYER

Maker of heaven and earth, all your creatures, animate and inanimate, stand before you. In Christ, who stands at the center of creation, we see how mysteriously well-pleasing it is to you. In Christ, the mediator of the whole world, we see how broken it is. And in Christ, the firstborn of creation, we discover its final destiny: new creation! May we take pleasure in your creation as you take good pleasure in it. May we care for the earth as you lovingly care for it. And may we offer up all the creative work of our hands in praise of you, in service of our neighbor, and in anticipation of that day when the cosmos shall be made forever alive. In the Triune Name. Amen.

CONCLUSION

Every act of love is a risk of the self.
—Eugene Peterson[1]

*The psalmist is brutally honest about the explosive joy
that he's feeling and the deep sorrow or confusion, and
it's that that sets the Psalms apart for me. And I often
think, gosh, well, why isn't church music more like that?*
—Bono[2]

During her years among the Benedictines at Saint John's Abbey in Collegeville, Minnesota, the author Kathleen Norris discovered a very different God from the one that she had encountered as a child growing up in Hawaii. Church, in her early years, meant two things: dressing up and singing. Mainly it meant "sitting up straight," being "good," thinking "holy thoughts," putting on "a good face," and "doing it right." In praying the psalms regularly with Benedictine brothers and sisters as an adult, however, she discovered a different kind of church:

Experiencing the Psalms in this way allowed me gradually to let go
of that childhood God who had set an impossible standard for both

> prayer and faith, convincing me that religion wasn't worth exploring
> because I couldn't dress up and "do it right." . . . You come to the
> Bible's great "book of praises" through all the moods and conditions
> of life, and while you may feel like hell, you sing anyway. To your
> surprise you find that the Psalms do not submerge or deny your true
> feelings, but allow you to reflect on them, right in front of God and
> everyone.[3]

Here in the pages of the Psalter she discovered a faith that counter-acted what one writer has called the "true religion" of America: optimism and denial. Here she encountered a faith that defeated "our tendency to try to be holy without being human first."[4] Here she found a faith that refused to let us become numb to reality or ignore the tangled matters of the heart. Here was a faith that offered up stories that resonated with human experience in a way that was faithful, rather than faithless, to God. Here she came across a tonic to narcissism and the possibility of genuine transformation.

This is, of course, what Christians have discovered about the psalms throughout the centuries. John Calvin in the sixteenth century discovered in the psalms "the anatomy of all the parts of the soul." The fourth-century pastor Athanasius commended the psalms to a young person as the place to "learn about yourself," precisely by encountering God afresh. For scholars and pastors today, the psalms are the "saving help that God provides *in the midst of life's dangers*"[5] (emphasis original). The psalms direct the heart to Jesus. They serve as the Spirit's chief medicine to cure the heart's ills. And they help us pray to God in a way that is "both personal and honest."[6]

In his comment on Psalm 84:2, Augustine of Hippo describes the movements of the heart of faith in a way that feels surprisingly familiar to contemporary people: "Here we desire, there we receive; here we sigh with longing, there we rejoice; here we pray, there praise; here we groan, there exult."[7] What the heart longs for, he remarks, is a home: "even the sparrow finds a home, and the swallow a nest for herself" (Ps. 84:3). And what sort of home would the heart make for itself? Augustine answers: a home that by God's grace might rise by loving.[8]

Thus it is, in the end, that the psalms might form us in the love of God if we would let them. And as Eugene Peterson reminds us, the love of God would open our eyes.[9] In love, we would see what has been there all along but been overlooked in haste or indifference. In love, we would see that what has been distorted by selfishness can be seen truthfully, carefully. In love, all opportunities for intimacy would no longer appear as blurred threats on our alleged autonomy but rather become blessed invitations to know and to be deeply known. Peterson explains it this way in his comment on Psalm 45:

> Love penetrates the defenses that have been built up to protect against rejection and scorn and belittlement, and it sees life created by God for love. When we look through eyes diseased by self-love, we see neither beauty nor virtue. We stumble in a blurred, unfocused, misshapen world and complain that it is ugly or threatening or boring.[10]

The only thing that would heal our hearts from all forms of dehumanizing self-love is the love of God in Christ, which the Spirit sheds abroad in our hearts and communicates to us, among other ways, through the words of the psalms. Nan Merrill captures this idea in her paraphrase of Psalm 37:39–40:

> The saving grace of the upright comes
> from the Beloved;
> Love is their refuge in times of
> trouble.
> Love leads the way and they arrive
> home safely,
> delivered from those who tempt them
> with power.
> Love invites all to open their hearts.[11]

This is, of course, risky business. We risk being hurt, rejected, misunderstood, deceived, left out, and left behind. Yet this is precisely why the psalms are invaluable to the follower of Jesus and to the one who would live in faith, hope, and love.

The psalms invite us to risk the love of God and neighbor and of the world that surrounds us with the reassurance that we do not venture this risk alone. We venture it together with an extraordinary company of fellow pilgrims across the ages.

We would dare to tell our secrets to the community of God because we are confident, or, at the very least, we hold on to some shred of faith, that the steadfast love of God stands behind and before us, above and below us.

We would dare to let the psalms teach us how to pray, because we trust that in them, we discover that Jesus himself, the one who knows every grief and every joy of the human heart, both enables and embodies our own prayers.

In reading the poetry of the psalms, we would discover that it is through these musical, metaphor-rich words, which force us to slow down and pay attention, that we encounter God as both intimately familiar and strangely mysterious.

In singing the psalms, we would discover that we are not alone. We are not the first to feel the sadness of loss, the anger of injustice, the confusion and disorientation of doubt, or the I'm-so-happy-I-could-pop joy of rescue and redemption. We would discover, likewise, a way for all things to be told in community, both those things that we would gladly announce from the hilltops and those things that we might prefer to keep secret, so that God might heal us and lead us "in the way everlasting" (Ps. 139:24).

In praying the psalms, we would recognize the voice of others, in different circumstances than ours, perhaps, who cry out to God, "How long?" Here we would find permission to lay open before God our griefs and infirmities, which we might be ashamed to confess before others.

We would find a way to pray angry prayers without being overcome by our anger, and how to curse in context, how to hate without sinning, how to cuss without cussing at all the damnably awful things that mark our broken world.

We would also find a powerful desire to join the trees and the mountains in their shouts for joy. Like the birds of the air, we, too, would make merry; we, too, would clap our hands with the rivers. Like all of creation, we, too, would yearn with painful hope for the sweet fullness of joy to be made manifest.

With a freedom that we never suspected was ours, we would choose to believe the words of the Psalter, which enjoin us to name our enemies and to expose them and to rebuke them and, in Jesus' name, to love them and to release them and to serve them.

We would choose to do justice. We would not simply bemoan the tragic losses or the ungodly acts of injustice. We would also stand up for the poor, the needy, the widowed, the orphaned, the vulnerable, the alien, the stranger, and all who are oppressed—and bring them all before God in prayer, asking him, in mercy, to be a Just Judge who makes *all* things right.

We would pray these things with open eyes. We would pray these things knowing that many of our prayers might never be fulfilled in our lifetime, and that death, like a monstrously terrifying force, confronts us daily with our mortality, reminding us that we are but dust. And yet we would also pray that, though we may be like grass that withers, God would make us to be a life-giving tree, deeply rooted in the "fountain of life," in the God who is the Author of life that is truly life.

We would pray and sing and read and recite and meditate on all these words of the psalms, but never as a purely solitary act. We would pray them with peoples from every tongue, tribe, and nation. We would pray them with the company of the faithful from every time in history and from all the cultures of the earth.

And along with all sorts of peoples, in all kinds of circumstances, we would join the praise of creation—the praise of angels and archangels, of morning stars and fathomless ocean depths, of sea dragons and herds of cattle, of fire and hail, of apple orchards and cedar forests, of "robust men and women in their prime, and yes, graybeards and little children" (Ps. 148 THE MESSAGE). We would join creation's inarticulate praise, and we would offer up our own articulate praise of God, the Creator and Re-Creator of all things.

How long would we join creation's praise? As the psalms see it, as long as we live and breathe and have our being, and as long as God lives, which is forever and ever, world without end.

The Psalter opens with echoes of Genesis and it closes with a symphony of cosmic praise. In William Brown's words, "Psalm 1 begins the pilgrimage and anticipates the destination."[12] To see the psalms in this way is to see ourselves on "the way." We do not, of course, walk this way alone. We walk alongside others who seek to remain faithful to God. We walk through these one hundred and fifty poems, Christ's own prayer book, in the hope that we will perceive the shape of faithful prayer, faithful witness, faithful living, faithful friendship, and faithful work.[13]

We walk this way, ultimately, with Jesus, for whom these psalms are his heart song. And like Jesus, we read and sing and pray the psalms along "the way" out of love. The gospel of John tells us that Jesus does everything so the world will know that he loves his Father (John 14:31), who in turn loves the Son (John 15:9), and whose Spirit makes the love of God ours as well (Rom. 5:5). This being true, then, Jesus also prays the psalms for love's sake.

With Jesus and in Jesus' name, we, too, would pray the psalms, trusting that they will open up a space in our hearts to give and to receive the steadfast love of God, from whom no secrets are hidden. We, too, would pray with the psalmist that God's steadfast love will meet us in our hour of need (Ps. 59:10). We, too, would pray, "I love you, O LORD" (Ps. 18:1), with whatever faith we could muster. And we, too, would pray the words of Psalm 31:23–24 in the hearing of all creation:

> Love GOD, all you saints;
>> GOD takes care of all who stay close to him,

But he pays back in full
　　those arrogant enough to go it alone.
Be brave. Be strong. Don't give up.
　　Expect GOD to get here soon.

(THE MESSAGE)

AFTERWORD

In the sixth chapter of his second book, the prophet Samuel describes how King David brought to Jerusalem the ark of the covenant, said to contain the stone tablets of the Ten Commandments and to represent the presence of the divine. We are told that to the delight of his troops and the astonishment of passersby, David danced like a dervish before the Lord almost butt naked.

It is a striking image of joy and humility, and as good a definition of being a singer as I can offer. To sing—to really, really sing—the soul has to kind of expose itself. That's when the real connection is made—with the ear, and the ear with the spirit.

I love gospel music with its ecstatic shouts and stomps and hand-claps, with its crescendo endings where you no longer know if you're still in this song—or in another one. Someone explained to me that gospel music is a step of faith, because, while you might not be feeling so good about the world around you or about your personal circumstance, you begin to sing the gospel song in the belief that it will take you to a new place, the one you need to get to. So many of the psalms are just like that: prayers that haul you toward that place you need to be.

And yet . . .

Those are not the psalms that I hold closest. The psalms I hold on to longest and tightest are a communication from a darker territory, from a place of pain or abandonment, from a place of fear and doubt. This is less gospel and more blues. But it's when David is at his lowest ebb, when he is feeling the most distant from his God, that he discovers how to renew that relationship, how to start the conversation again.

It is a conversation in which the dialogue is brutally honest, a conversation not about where he'd like to be but about where he is right now. Like that place he was in described in Psalm 22, that nowhere place, some hideout cave in the borderlands of a kingdom he'd thought he was destined to lead; that kingdom now being led by his best friend's father, King Saul, who wants to see him dead.

"My God, my God, why have you forsaken me?" (Ps. 22:1). In the cave of despair, the blues saves us. The brutal honesty of the psalms asks: "How long LORD? wilt thou hide thyself for ever?" (Ps. 89:46 KJV). Even to the point of rage, David assails the silence: "Answer me when I call!" (Ps. 4:1).

The ache and the abandonment and the being afraid ring true for so many of us, not least the performer. The complexity of the Psalter is what's missing in so much "religious" music—and what's so appealing to the artist. David Taylor's take is "open and unafraid" alright. He really goes there, exposing himself before God in the most beautiful way. He might have called the book *Naked*, because if you don't find your own self feeling a little exposed here, it might be time to take some armor off.

The Psalms see right through us. See right into us.

If we famous people make ourselves known in lots of annoying and self-aggrandizing ways, "making yourself known" has a whole other meaning in the Scriptures. "Now I know in part," writes the apostle Paul, "But then shall I know even as also I am known" (1 Cor. 13:12 KJV). As we sing or read the psalms, they let us both know and be known.

The singer does not sing the song. It is the song that sings the singer, the song that sings me. That's what the singer lives for: the moment of being sung, the moment of being known. And to find themselves being sung, being known, is my prayer for readers of this book.

For anyone who steps inside these psalms: let yourself be sung.

Bono

ACKNOWLEDGMENTS

So many people deserve to be thanked for this book.

Many thanks to Bishop Todd Hunter, Brian and Tamara Murphy, Jeff Williams, Lauren Hance, John Goldingay, and Andy Dearman for their comments on the book and for their generous encouragement along the way. I am also grateful to Emily Scherer for allowing me to work in such a beautiful space, The Guild, in Richmond, Texas, where I wrote the bulk of this book.

Most especially I wish to thank my parents, Bill and Yvonne Taylor, Geno Hildebrandt (along with his good friends Gary Carlile, Dr. George Pryor, and Ron Morgan), Matt Dampier, Peter Coelho, Howard Morrison, Clint Wilson (along with his group of readers), Brian Moss, Jeanmarie Tade, and Johnie Wood for their substantial feedback on specific chapters and for their excellent suggestions for revisions and improvements.

I am equally grateful for the many opportunities I've had to try out the ideas of this book on audiences around the country. This includes the Laity Lodge Retreat Center (with special thanks to Steven Purcell), St. George's Episcopal Church in Nashville, Tennessee (with special thanks to Clint Wilson), the adult Sunday School class at Christ the King Presbyterian Church in Houston, Texas (with special thanks to Taylor Leachman), the small group at First Baptist Church of Richmond, Texas (with special thanks to Joyce Trigger and John Lockhart), Houston Baptist University's Honors College (with special thanks to Philip Tallon), the Hutchmoot Conference (with special thanks to Andrew and Pete Peterson), the Redemptive Presence Conference (with special thanks to Mike Cosper), the Lumen Lecture at Berry College (with special thanks to Jonathan Huggins), and the Brehm Center conference on "Worship, Theology and the Arts in a Divided World."

To Andrea Heinecke, my sincerest thanks for believing in the potential of this book. To Webster Younce, a profound thanks for shepherding the manuscript to its final form and for posing the hard questions that would give this book a fighting chance to succeed with readers. To the fabulous team at Nelson Books, a huge gratitude: Sujin Hong, Rachel Tockstein, Shea Nolan, and Jamie Lockard. To Jan Peterson, thank you for your hospitality, your laughter, and your generous friendship. To Blythe and Sebastian, set your hope always in your Good Shepherd and know that you are an incalculable blessing to me. To Phaedra Jean, thank you for being my faithful co-pilgrim "on the way." And to Eugene and Bono, thank you for everything.

RECOMMENDED
RESOURCES

For readers who wish to explore the psalms further, here are a few resources that might serve as good starting points. I've arranged them according to basic categories to help simplify the process of choosing where to start. It goes without saying, of course, that this list is suggestive rather than exhaustive. Many good resources exist online, and I encourage you to take advantage of them.

A. Introductions to the Psalms

1. Bernhard W. Anderson, *Out of the Depths: The Psalms Speak for Us Today.*
2. Walter Brueggemann, *The Message of the Psalms: A Theological Commentary.*
3. C. Hassell Bullock, *Encountering the Book of Psalms: A Literary and Theological Introduction.*
4. Nancy deClaissé-Walford, *Introduction to the Psalms: A Song from Ancient Israel.*
5. Denise Dombkowski Hopkins, *Journey Through the Psalms.*

6. Rolf A. Jacobson and Karl N. Jacobson, *Invitation to the Psalms: A Reader's Guide for Discovery and Engagement.*
7. Eugene Peterson, *Answering God: The Psalms as Tools for Prayer.*
8. Carroll Stuhlmueller, *The Spirituality of the Psalms.*
9. John Witvliet, *The Biblical Psalms in Christian Worship: A Brief Introduction and Guide to Resources.*
10. N. T. Wright, *The Case for the Psalms: Why They Are Essential.*

B. Psalms and Prayer

1. John Bell, *Psalms of Patience, Protest and Praise.*
2. Dietrich Bonhoeffer, *Psalms: The Prayer Book of the Bible.*
3. Walter Brueggeman, *Praying the Psalms: Engaging Scripture and the Life of the Spirit.*
4. Mark Futato, *Joy Comes in the Morning: Psalms for All Seasons.*
5. Timothy and Kathy Keller, *The Songs of Jesus: A Year of Daily Devotions in the Psalms.*
6. *The Paraclete Psalter: A Book of Daily Prayer.*
7. Mark Lanier, *Psalms for Living: Daily Prayers, Wisdom, and Guidance.*
8. C. S. Lewis, *Reflections on the Psalms.*
9. Thomas Merton, *Praying the Psalms* and *Bread in the Wilderness.*
10. Eugene Peterson, *Praying with the Psalms: A Year of Daily Prayers and Reflections on the Words of David.*
11. Bruce Waltke and James Houston, *The Psalms as Christian Lament.*
12. Ann Weems, *Psalms of Lament.*

C. Psalms and Worship

1. The Calvin Institute of Christian Worship is an excellent online resource for materials on the psalms. https://worship.calvin.edu/.

2. B. Hurd et al., *Cantaré Eternamente / Forever I Will Sing* (bilingual psalms for the liturgical year).
3. *This Far by Faith: An African American Resource for Worship.*
4. Carlos Rosas, *¡Grita de Alegría! Salmos para el año liturgico.*
5. John Michael Talbot, *Chant from the Hermitage: A Psalter.*
6. *The Anglican Chant Psalter.*
7. *Psalms for All Seasons: A Complete Psalter for Worship,* ed. Martin Tel, Joyce Borger, and John D. Witvliet.

D. Fresh Translations of the Psalms

1. David Adam, *Music of the Heart: New Psalms in the Celtic Tradition.*
2. Robert Alter, *The Book of Psalms.*
3. Ernesto Cardenal, *Salmos.*
4. Jim Cotter, *Psalms for a Pilgrim People.*
5. Zephania Kameeta, *Why, O Lord? Psalms and Sermons from Namibia.*
6. Eugene Peterson, *The Message Bible.*
7. Calvin Seerveld, *Voicing God's Psalms.*
8. Laurance Wieder, *Words to God's Music: A New Book of Psalms.*

E. Biblical and Theological Studies on the Psalms

1. Walter Brueggemann, *From Whom No Secrets Are Hid: Introducing the Psalms.*
2. Walter Brueggemann and William H. Bellinger Jr., *Psalms.*
3. Ellen F. Davis, *Getting Involved with God: Rediscovering the Old Testament.*
4. John Goldingay, *Psalms,* vols. 1–3.
5. William Holladay, *The Psalms Through Three Thousand Years: Prayerbook of a Cloud of Witnesses.*

6. James L. Mays, *Psalms: Interpretation: A Bible Commentary for Teaching and Preaching.*
7. Sigmund Mowinckel, *The Psalms in Israel's Worship.*
8. Patrick Henry Reardon, *Christ in the Psalms.*
9. Nancy deClaissé-Walford, Rolf A. Jacobson, and Beth LaNeel Tanner, *The Book of Psalms.*
10. *Dictionary of the Old Testament: Wisdom, Poetry & Writings,* ed. Tremper Longman III and Peter Enns.
11. *The Psalms in the New Testament,* ed. Steve Moyise and Maarten J. J. Menken.
12. Gordon Wenham, *The Psalter Reclaimed: Praying and Praising with the Psalms.*

F. The Psalms and the Arts

1. William P. Brown, *Seeing the Psalms: A Theology of Metaphor.*
2. Cardiphonia: "Holy Week Devotional through the Psalms of Ascents + Hallel Psalms Compilation," and *The Songs of the Psalter* (2015). Cardiphonia is crowd-sourced effort by worship songwriters to provide a variety of approaches to singing the psalms in the modern church. Largely in the folk-rock vein. https://psalms.bandcamp.com/.
3. *Chichester Psalms* (1965): a choral composition by Leonard Bernstein. https://leonardbernstein.com/works/view/14/chichester-psalms.
4. Fuller Studio, "Bono & Eugene Peterson on The Psalms." https://fullerstudio.fuller.edu/bono-eugene-peterson-psalms/.
5. Anneke Kaai and Eugene Peterson, *Seeing a New Song: Painting the Psalms Connection.*
6. Sandra McCracken: a singer-songwriter who has created several albums on the psalms. https://sandramccracken.bandcamp.com/album/psalms.

7. Psalms and the Psalter: an Eastern Orthodox resource page on singing the psalms. https://www.orthodoxprayer.org/Psalms-Psalter.html.

8. Dwight W. Vogel, "The Work of Singing the Psalms," Discipleship Ministries, The United Methodist Church, https://www.umcdiscipleship.org/resources/the-work-of-singing-the-psalms.

NOTES

INTRODUCTION

1. Denise Dombkowski Hopkins, *Journey Through the Psalms* (St. Louis: Chalice, 2002), 1.

2. Stanley Jaki, *Praying the Psalms: A Commentary* (Grand Rapids: Eerdmans, 2001), 27.

3. The short film can be found here: "Bono & Eugene Peterson: The Psalms," Fuller Studio, April 26, 2016, https://www.youtube.com /watch?v=-l40S5e90KY. Further information about the experience, including additional film footage and specific interviews and essays related to the film, can be found here: "Bono & Eugene Peterson on the Psalms," Fuller Studio, https://fullerstudio.fuller.edu/bono-eugene -peterson-psalms/; "Bono & David Taylor: Beyond the Psalms," Fuller Studio, https://fullerstudio.fuller.edu/bono-and-david-taylor-beyond -the-psalms/; "Bono & Eugene Peterson: The Psalms," Brehm Center, http://www.brehmcenter.com/initiatives/texas/projects/the-psalms/; Andrea Palpant Dilley, "Meet the Man Behind the Bono and Eugene Peterson Conversation," *Christianity Today*, May 20, 2016, https://www .christianitytoday.com/ct/2016/june/bridging-gap-between-church -and-arts.html; and "Bringing a Dream to Life: Alumnus David Taylor on Bono, Eugene Peterson, and the Psalms," Regent College, June 1, 2016, https://www.regent-college.edu/about-us/news/2016/bringing -a-dream-to-life--alumnus-david-taylor-on-bono--eugene-peterson--and -the-psalms.

4. This is how Patrick Henry Reardon orients his entire commentary on

the Psalter in *Christ in the Psalms* (Ben Lomond, CA: Conciliar Press, 2000).

5. This is also largely the case with Laurence Kriegshauser, *Praying the Psalms in Christ* (Notre Dame, IN: University of Notre Dame Press, 2012).

6. For readers who wish to dig deeper, I encourage them to follow the "paper trail" in the endnotes and take advantage of the recommended reading list I include at the end of the book.

CHAPTER 1: HONESTY

1. Walter Brueggemann, *From Whom No Secrets Are Hid: Introducing the Psalms* (Louisville, KY: Westminster John Knox, 2014), xi.

2. Ellen F. Davis, *Getting Involved with God: Rediscovering the Old Testament* (Cambridge, MA: Cowley, 2011), 9.

3. Athanasius, *On the Incarnation* (New York: St. Vladimir's Seminary Press, 1977), 106.

4. Brueggemann, *From Whom No Secrets Are Hid*, xi–xii.

5. Brueggemann, *From Whom No Secrets Are Hid*, 94.

6. Laurance Wieder, "Psalm 139: Recognition" in *Words to God's Music: A New Book of Psalms* (Grand Rapids: Eerdmans, 2003), 174.

7. Eugene Peterson, *Answering God: The Psalms as Tools for Prayer* (New York: HarperCollins, 1989), 3–4.

8. Denise Dombkowski Hopkins, *Journey Through the Psalms* (St. Louis: Chalice, 2002), chapter 1.

9. Walter Brueggemann, *Praying the Psalms: Engaging Scripture and the Life of the Spirit* (Eugene, OR: Cascade, 2007), 7.

10. Calvin Seerveld, *Voicing God's Psalms* (Grand Rapids: Eerdmans, 2005), 51.

11. Eugene Peterson, *Praying with the Psalms: A Year of Daily Prayers and Reflections on the Words of David* (New York: HarperOne, 1993), 62. Cf. John D. Witvliet, *The Biblical Psalms in Christian Worship: A Brief Introduction and Guide to Resources* (Grand Rapids: Eerdmans, 2007), 28; and Bernhard W. Anderson, *Out of the Depths: The Psalms Speak for Us Today*, with Steven Bishop (Louisville, KY: Westminster John Knox, 2000), 95.

12. Jim Cotter, "Psalm 32: Release from the Burden of Sin," in *Psalms for a Pilgrim People* (Harrisburg, PA: Morehouse Publishing, 1998), 68.

13. Carroll Stuhlmueller, *The Spirituality of the Psalms* (Collegeville, MN: Liturgical Press, 2002), 131 ("The honest confession of weakness and dependency by sick persons in the psalms is something of an amazement. . . . The sick person soon collapses into depression").

14. Peterson, *Answering God*, 100; and Hopkins, *Journey Through the Psalms*, 5.
15. Rolf A. Jacobson and Karl N. Jacobson, *Invitation to the Psalms: A Reader's Guide for Discovery and Engagement* (Grand Rapids: Baker Academic, 2013), 56.
16. Peterson, *Answering God*, 100.
17. Athanasius, *On the Incarnation* (New York: St. Vladimir's Seminary Press, 1977), 106–107.
18. Karl Barth, *Church Dogmatics*, vol. 3, bk. 2, trans. Harold Knight, G. W. Bromiley, J. K. S. Reid, and R. H. Fuller (Edinburgh: T. & T. Clark, 1960), 41.
19. Barth, *Church Dogmatics*, vol. 3, bk. 2, 192.
20. Timothy and Kathy Keller describe Psalm 44:23 this way: "'Awake Lord!' is the daring but honest cry." Keller, *The Songs of Jesus: A Year of Daily Devotions in the Psalms* (New York: Viking, 2015), 93.
21. John Goldingay, *Psalms, Volume 1: Psalms 1–41* (Grand Rapids: Baker Academic, 2006), 22–23.
22. Davis, *Getting Involved with God*, 5.
23. N. T. Wright, *Simply Christian: Why Christianity Makes Sense* (New York: HarperOne, 2010), 151.
24. Athanasius, *On the Incarnation*, 103.
25. This is how Bono describes the Psalms in "Bono & Eugene Peterson: The Psalms," Fuller Studio, April 26, 2016, https://www.youtube.com /watch?v=l40S5e90KY.
26. Peterson, *Praying with the Psalms*, 89.

CHAPTER 2: COMMUNITY

1. "Minister for Loneliness Appointed to Continue Jo Cox's Work," BBC News, January 17, 2018, https://www.bbc.com/news/uk-42708507.
2. C. Hassell Bullock, *Encountering the Book of Psalms: A Literary and Theological Introduction* (Grand Rapids: Baker Academic, 2001), 52.
3. These are words Monica Lewisnky said she heard for the first time in a long time. As she writes, "They landed in a way that cracked me open and brought me to tears. Yes, I had received many letters of support in 1998. And, yes (thank God!), I had my family and friends to support me. But by and large I had been alone. *So. Very. Alone.* Publicly Alone— abandoned most of all by the key figure in the crisis, who actually knew me well and intimately. That I had made mistakes, on that we can all agree. But swimming in that sea of Aloneness was terrifying." Lewinsky,

"Emerging from 'The House of Gaslight' in the Age of #MeToo," *Vanity Fair*, February 25, 2018, https://www.vanityfair.com/news/2018/02/monica-lewinsky-in-the-age-of-metoo.

4. "New Cigna Study Reveals Loneliness at Epidemic Levels in America," CIGNA, May 1, 2018, https://www.cigna.com/newsroom/news-releases/2018/new-cigna-study-reveals-loneliness-at-epidemic-levels-in-america.

5. Laura Entis, "Chronic Loneliness Is a Modern-Day Epidemic," *Fortune*, June 22, 2016, http://fortune.com/2016/06/22/loneliness-is-a-modern-day-epidemic/. Rhitu Chatterjee, "Americans Are a Lonely Lot, and Young People Bear the Heaviest Burden," NPR, May 1, 2018 ("Members of Generation Z, born between the mid-1990s and the early 2000s, had an overall loneliness score of 48.3. Millennials, just a little bit older, scored 45.3. By comparison, baby boomers scored 42.4. The Greatest Generation, people ages 72 and above, had a score of 38.6 on the loneliness scale").

6. "Minister for Loneliness Appointed to Continue Jo Cox's Work."

7. Jane E. Brody, "Shaking Off Loneliness," *New York Times*, May 13, 2013, https://well.blogs.nytimes.com/2013/05/13/shaking-off-loneliness/ ("'Is it any wonder that we turn to ice cream or other fatty foods when we're sitting at home feeling all alone in the world?' Dr. Cacioppo said in his well-documented book *Loneliness*, written with William Patrick. 'We want to soothe the pain we feel by mainlining sugar and fat content to the pleasure centers of the brain, and absent of self-control, we go right at it.' He explained that lonely individuals tend to do whatever they can to make themselves feel better, if only for the moment. They may overeat, drink too much, smoke, speed or engage in indiscriminate sex").

8. In the King James Version, for example: congregation (21 times), assembly (4 times), people (122 times), neighbor (10 times), friend (4 times).

9. Cf. John Goldingay, *Psalms, Volume 1: Psalms 1–41* (Grand Rapids: Baker Academic, 2006), 60.

10. Eugene Peterson, *Where Your Treasure Is: Psalms That Summon You from Self to Community* (Grand Rapids: Eerdmans, 1993), 10–11.

11. James L. Mays, *The Lord Reigns: A Theological Handbook to the Psalms* (Louisville, KY: Westminster John Knox, 1994), 32 ("Rightness is a matter of the community's health and well-being [*shalom*], and of acts that create and foster its well-being. Righteousness is the character and condition of the community when things are in order for its

shalom. Righteousness as conduct and activity is what benefits the community, makes things right. . . . Wickedness, the opposite of *sedaqah* [righteousness], designates character and conduct that are adverse and destructive of the community and persons in it").

12. Mays, *The Lord Reigns*, 52.
13. Goldingay, *Psalms*, vol. 1, 59.
14. Bullock, *Encountering the Book of Psalms*, 52.
15. Stanley Hauerwas, "Reflections on Learning How to Speak Christian," ABC Religion & Ethics, August 16, 2010, http://www.abc.net.au/religion /articles/2010/08/16/2984111.htm.
16. Mays, *The Lord Reigns*, 42–43; and James L. Mays, *Psalms: Interpretation: A Bible Commentary for Teaching and Preaching* (Louisville, KY: Westminster John Knox, 2011), 66–69.
17. Bullock, *Encountering the Book of Psalms*, 160 ("The fellow worshipers saw themselves in that or similar situations and entered empathetically into the singer's joy of deliverance. Or the call for the saints to join him in praise and celebration may be motivated by the psalmist's desire to spread the joy and evoke a response of faith from his comrades").
18. Mays, *The Lord Reigns*, 52.
19. John Calvin, quoted in John D. Witvliet, *The Biblical Psalms in Christian Worship: A Brief Introduction and Guide to Resources* (Grand Rapids: Eerdmans, 2007), 41.
20. Reggie Kidd, *With One Voice: Discovering Christ's Song in Our Worship* (Grand Rapids: Baker, 2005). Psalm 22:22: "I will declare thy name unto my brethren: in the midst of the congregation will I praise thee" (KJV).
21. Kidd, *With One Voice*, 126.
22. On the question of what carries over from Old Testament practices of song and music into a New Testament vision for corporate worship, see W. David O. Taylor, "Chapter 1: Musical Instruments in Calvin" and "Chapter 5: The Double Movement of Creation in Worship," in *The Theater of God's Glory: Calvin, Creation and the Liturgical Arts* (Grand Rapids: Eerdmans, 2017).
23. Susan Pinker, "The Secret to Living Longer May Be Your Social Life," TED, April 2017, https://www.ted.com/talks/susan_pinker_the _secret_to_living_longer_may_be_your_social_life.
24. Zephania Kameeta, *Why, O Lord? Psalms and Sermons from Namibia* (Geneva: World Council of Churches, 1986), 26.

CHAPTER 3: HISTORY

1. Quoted in John D. Witvliet, *The Biblical Psalms in Christian Worship: A Brief Introduction and Guide to Resources* (Grand Rapids: Eerdmans, 2007), 4.

2. Ellen F. Davis, *Getting Involved with God: Rediscovering the Old Testament* (Cambridge, MA: Cowley Publications, 2011), 7. For an excellent introduction to the Jewish and Christian use of the psalms throughout history, see Bruce K. Waltke and James M. Houston, *The Psalms as Christian Worship: An Historical Commentary* (Grand Rapids: Eerdmans, 2010).

3. John Goldingay, *Psalms, Volume 1: Psalms 1–41* (Grand Rapids: Baker Academic, 2006), 35 ("The Psalter came into being in something like the form we know it some time in the Second Temple period, in Persian or early Greek times. From the beginning it was presumably among the authoritative resources of the Jewish community, and in this sense the time it came into being is also the time when it became canonical. . . . Although we cannot know when individual psalms were written, we can trace a little of that process whereby the Psalter itself came into being").

4. Bernhard W. Anderson, *Out of the Depths: The Psalms Speak for Us Today*, with Steven Bishop (Louisville, KY: Westminster John Knox, 2000), 17–18 ("For Israel, this ascription ['a psalm of David'] did not necessarily indicate authorship; rather, it signified that the community identified itself with David as it came before God in worship. David was the archetypal figure whose career portrayed both the misery and the grandeur of the people of God. . . . In a troubled time when Israel had no king, the people found in the story of David not only the archetype of their own existence but also the prototype of the coming king who would inaugurate God's dominion").

5. A close reading of the Psalter uncovers a number of "collections" of psalms that have been grouped together in specific ways, either by superscription or by a key word or theme. These collections include: a "Davidic" collection (Pss. 3–41; 51–72; 138–145); a "Korahite" collection (Pss. 42–49; 84–85; 87–88); an "Elohistic" collection (Pss. 42–83); an "Asaphite" collection (Pss. 73–83); a "Songs of Ascent" collection (Pss. 120–134); and a "Hallelujah Psalms" collection (Pss. 111–118; 146–150).

6. The Psalms are the *Tehillim*, the Book of Praise, according to the Hebrew title to the book. They are the *Psalmoi*, the "Songs Sung to a Stringed Instrument," as the Septuagint, the Greek translation of the

Hebrew Bible, describes the 150 poems. And they are the *Psalterion*, as the fifth-century AD Greek manuscript Codex Alexandrinus titled the book, drawing attention to the musical dimension of the psalms—and it is from this title that we get our English term *Psalter*.

7. Goldingay, *Psalms*, vol. 1, 76 ("There is hardly a verse in the Revelation to John that would survive intact if one removed the allusions to the Psalms and other parts of the OT, but there is not a single actual quotation of the OT there"). Cf. Steve Moyise, "The Psalms in the Book of Revelation," in *The Psalms in the New Testament*, ed. Steve Moyise and Maarten J. J. Menken (London: T & T Clark, 2004), 231–46.

8. A great deal of the material in this chapter is drawn from two primary sources: William L. Holladay, *The Psalms Through Three Thousand Years: Prayerbook of a Cloud of Witnesses* (Minneapolis: Fortress, 1993), and Kevin Adams, *150: Finding Your Story in the Psalms* (Grand Rapids: Square Inch Press, 2011).

9. Cited in Massey H. Shepherd, *The Psalms in Christian Worship: A Practical Guide* (Minneapolis: Augsburg, 1976), 37.

10. C. Hassell Bullock, *Encountering the Book of Psalms: A Literary and Theological Introduction* (Grand Rapids: Baker Academic, 2001), 94.

11. For a close reading of Augustine's relation to the psalms, see Jason Byassee, *Praise Seeking Understanding: Reading the Psalms with Augustine* (Grand Rapids: Eerdmans, 2007).

12. Athanasius, *On the Incarnation* (New York: St. Vladimir's Seminary Press, 1977), 104.

13. Augustine, *Confessions*, bk. 9.7.15, cited in Holladay, *The Psalms Through Three Thousand Years*, 166.

14. In an Eastern Orthodox custom, the bishops prayed fourteen prayers while they vested themselves for the Divine Liturgy. Eight of those prayers derive from the Psalter.

15. Gordon Wenham, *The Psalter Reclaimed: Praying and Praising with the Psalms* (Wheaton, IL: Crossway, 2013), 16.

16. Roland Bainton, *Here I Stand: A Life of Martin Luther* (Nashville: Abingdon Press, 1950), 335.

17. Cited in Witvliet, *The Biblical Psalms*, 39–40. See also Bruce A. Cameron, *Reading the Psalms with Luther: The Psalter for Individual and Family Devotions* (St. Louis, MO: Concordia Publishing House, 2007).

18. Holladay, *The Psalms Through Three Thousand Years*, 195.

19. Horton Davies, *Worship and Theology in England: From Andrewes to Baxter and Fox, 1603–1690* (Princeton, NJ: Princeton University Press, 1975), 270, 272.

20. James F. White, *Protestant Worship: Traditions in Transition* (Louisville, KY: Westminster John Knox, 1989), 129.

21. Esther Rothenbusch Crookshank, "'We're Marching to Zion': Isaac Watts in Early America," in *Wonderful Words of Life: Hymns in American Protestant History and Theology*, ed. Richard J. Mouw and Mark A. Noll (Grand Rapids: Eerdmans, 2004), 21.

22. Cited in Mark Noll, "The Defining Role of Hymns in Early Evangelicalism," in *Wonderful Words of Life: Hymns in American Protestant History and Theology*, ed. Richard J. Mouw and Mark A. Noll (Grand Rapids: Eerdmans, 2004), 5.

23. Cited in Brian Brock, *Singing the Ethos of God: On the Place of Christian Ethics in Scripture* (Grand Rapids: Eerdmans, 2007), 74.

24. This is an excerpt taken from a series of selected messages prepared by Edwin Aldrin, Neil Armstrong, and Michael Collins, in "Apollo Expeditions to the Moon: Chapter 11.7," NASA, https://history.nasa.gov /SP-350/ch-11-7.html.

25. Cited in Adams, *150: Finding Your Story in the Psalms*, 119.

26. Adams, *150: Finding Your Story in the Psalms*, 191.

27. Adams, *150: Finding Your Story in the Psalms*, 17–18.

28. U2, "40," Universal Music Group, December 12, 2018, https://www .youtube.com/watch?v=pt9Xc4jO-Yc.

29. Christopher R. Weingarten et al., "U2's 50 Greatest Songs," *Rolling Stone*, June 29, 2017, https://www.rollingstone.com/music/music-lists /u2s-50-greatest-songs-205104/40-201620/.

30. Cited in *Martin Luther: Selections from His Writings*, ed. John Dillenberger (New York: Anchor Books, 1962), 41.

31. One can find the original prayer on the Anglican lectionary website for "The Lessons Appointed for Use on the Sunday Closest to November 16: Year A, Proper 28," in *Book of Common Prayer*, https://www.lectionarypage .net/YearA/Pentecost/AProp28.html.

CHAPTER 4: PRAYER

1. This is something the New Testament scholar Gordon Fee would often tell his students at Regent College in Vancouver, British Columbia.

2. Dietrich Bonhoeffer, "Christ in the Psalms," lecture given to students

on July 31, 1935, quoted in Edwin Robertson, *My Soul Finds Rest in God Alone* (Guildford, UK: Eagle, 2001), 8.

3. Thomas Merton, *Bread in the Wilderness* (New York: New Directions Books, 1953), 38.

4. Thomas G. Long, *Testimony: Talking Ourselves into Being Christian* (San Francisco: Jossey-Bass, 2004), 47.

5. Quoted in Robertson, *My Soul Finds Rest in God Alone*, 9.

6. Eugene Peterson, *Answering God: The Psalms as Tools for Prayer* (New York: HarperCollins, 1989), 4.

7. Cited in Calvin R. Stapert, *A New Song for an Old World: Musical Thought in the Early Church* (Grand Rapids, MI: Eerdmans, 2007), 151.

8. John D. Witvliet, "Part I: The Psalms and the Basic Grammar of Christian Worship" in *The Biblical Psalms in Christian Worship: A Brief Introduction and Guide to Resources* (Grand Rapids: Eerdmans, 2007), 11–12 ("The biblical Psalms are the foundational mentor and guide in this vocabulary and grammar for worship.... If we want to better understand the DNA of the Christian faith and to deepen our worship, there are few better places to begin than with careful and prayerful engagement with the Psalms").

9. James Luther Mays, *Psalms: Interpretation: A Bible Commentary for Teaching and Preaching* (Louisville, KY: Westminster John Knox, 2011), 34 ("The psalms are not only informed by a theology of the reign of the Lord. They are the primary form that language takes in response to the reign of the LORD. In their three principal functions, they define the ways in which human beings live by and in the kingdom. Because 'the LORD reigns,' human beings may and must praise in wonder and joy, pray in dependence and gratitude, and practice the piety of trust and obedience").

10. Walter Brueggemann, *The Psalms and the Life of Faith* (Minneapolis: Fortress, 1995), 68.

11. Peterson, *Answering God*, introduction.

12. Witvliet, *Biblical Psalms in Christian Worship*, 26–28.

13. Witvliet, *Biblical Psalms in Christian Worship*, 26 ("The Psalms teach us that even prayers offered in the first person singular are not always soliloquies").

14. David F. Ford, *Self and Salvation: Being Transformed* (New York: Cambridge University Press, 1999), 127. See also Sigmund Mowinckel, *The Psalms in Israel's Worship*, vol. 1, trans. D. R. Ap-Thomas (Nashville: Abingdon, 1962), 42–46.

15. Cited in William L. Holladay, *The Psalms Through Three Thousand*

Years: Prayerbook of a Cloud of Witnesses (Minneapolis: Fortress, 1993), 165.

16. Cited in Holladay, *The Psalms Through Three Thousand Years*, 165.

17. Ellen F. Davis, *Getting Involved with God: Rediscovering the Old Testament* (Cambridge, MA: Cowley Publications, 2011), 5.

18. Timothy and Kathy Keller, *The Songs of Jesus: A Year of Daily Devotions in the Psalms* (New York: Viking, 2015), viii.

19. Cf. Mark D. Futato, *Joy Comes in the Morning: Psalms for All Seasons* (New Jersey: P&R Publishing, 2004), 59–62.

20. Athanasius, *On the Incarnation* (New York: St. Vladimir's Seminary Press, 1977), 103.

CHAPTER 5: POETRY

1. Eugene Peterson, *Holy Luck* (Grand Rapids: Eerdmans, 2013), xvi.

2. George Herbert, "The Church Porch," in *The Complete English Poems* (London: Penguin Classics, 1991), 6.

3. Dr. Seuss, *Yertle the Turtle and Other Stories* (New York: Random House, 1958), 40.

4. Marilyn McEntyre, "Why Read a Poem at a Time Like This?" Medium, September 15, 2016, https://medium.com/active-voice/why-read-a-poem -at-a-time-like-this-8b1f884de94d#.jpxzwvwbc.

5. John W. Work, *American Negro Songs: 230 Folk Songs and Spirituals, Religious and Secular* (1940; repr., Mineola, NY: Dover, 1998), 24–25.

6. G. K. Chesterton, *Orthodoxy* (San Francisco: Ignatius, 1995), 65–66.

7. C. S. Lewis, *The Seeing Eye and Other Selected Essays from Christian Reflections* (New York: Ballantine, 1986), 174.

8. I show how different kinds and different practices of poetry form in us different ideas of God and of our place in the world in my chapter on poetry and worship in *Glimpses of the New Creation: Worship and the Formative Power of the Arts* (Grand Rapids: Eerdmans, 2019).

9. C. S. Lewis, *Reflections on the Psalms* (New York: HarperOne, 2017), 3.

10. This is an observation I borrow from Carroll Stuhlmueller, *The Spirituality of the Psalms* (Collegeville, MN: Liturgical Press, 2002), 16.

11. Work, *American Negro Songs*, 23.

12. Quoted in Howard Gardner, *Frames of Mind: The Theory of Multiple Intelligences* (New York: Basic Books, 2011), 80.

13. Laurence Perrine and Thomas R. Arp, *Sound and Sense: An Introduction to Poetry* (New York: Harcourt College Publishers, 1991), 148.

14. John Goldingay, *Psalms, Volume 1: Psalms 1–41* (Grand Rapids: Baker Academic, 2006), 348.

15. Gerard Manley Hopkins, "As Kingfishers Catch Fire," *Poetry and Prose* (London: Penguin Classics, 1953), 51.

16. Cynthia Ozick, *Art and Ardor* (New York: Alfred A. Knopf, 1983), 248.

17. Eugene Peterson, "Pastors and Novels," in *Subversive Spirituality* (Grand Rapids: Eerdmans, 1997), 188.

18. Eugene Peterson, "Novelists, Pastors, and Poets," in *Subversive Spirituality* (Grand Rapids: Eerdmans, 1997), 180.

19. Peterson, "Novelists, Pastors, and Poets," 180–81.

20. Reginald Box's book *Making Music to Our God: How We Sing the Psalms* (London: SPCK, 1996), provides a helpful exposition of different ways that the psalms have been sung by Christians, including through chanted, metrical, choral, hymnic, plainsong, and a cappella means.

21. On this point, see W. E. Brown and J. J. Rankin, "Oral Poetry," in *Dictionary of the Old Testament: Wisdom, Poetry & Writings,* ed. Tremper Longman III and Peter Enns (Downers Grove, IL: InterVarsity Press Academic, 2008), 497–501.

22. Francis Hopkinson, "To Thee, my God and Saviour, I," *Hymnary*, https://hymnary.org/text/to_thee_my_god_and_savior_i_hopkinson.

23. Charles Wesley, *Hymns on the Trinity* (Bristol: Pine, 1767), https://divinity.duke.edu/sites/divinity.duke.edu/files/documents/cswt/67_Trinity_Hymns_%281767%29.pdf. I might also recommend Malcolm Guite liturgical poetry, *Sounding the Seasons: Seventy-Seven Sonnets for the Christian Year* (Norwich: Canterbury Press, 2014), and his "Trinity Sunday: A Sonnet," June 2, 2012, https://malcolmguite.wordpress.com/2012/06/02/trinity-sunday-a-sonnet/.

24. Stuhlmueller, *Spirituality of the Psalms*, 7 ("The phrase, 'A Psalm of David,' does not so much intend to certify the authorship of King David himself, as to copyright the psalm for a guild of psalm writers under the patronage of King David and possibly founded by him").

25. See David G. Firth, "Asaph and Sons of Korah," in *Dictionary of the Old Testament*, 24–27.

26. Other general characteristics include ellipsis, the omission of a word within a poetic or grammatical unit where it would otherwise be expected (Ps. 114:4); the use of strophe and stanza (Pss. 13; 19); the use of refrain (Pss. 67; 80); the use of acrostic (Ps. 119; Prov. 31:10–31; Lam. 1–4); an interest in the sound of words, such as rhyme, paronomasia,

alliteration (Ps. 127:1), assonance (Ps. 102:6); and a richer use of imagery and metaphor than is employed in prose or legal passage.

27. E. C. Lucas, "Terminology of Poetry," in *Dictionary of the Old Testament*, 520–25.

28. Helpful resources on biblical poetry include John D. Witvliet, *The Biblical Psalms in Christian Worship: A Brief Introduction and Guide to Resources* (Grand Rapids: Eerdmans, 2007), 76–85; C. Hassell Bullock, *Encountering the Book of Psalms: A Literary and Theological Introduction* (Grand Rapids: Baker Academic, 2001), 36–43; Nancy deClaissé-Walford, *Introduction to the Psalms: A Song from Ancient Israel* (St. Louis, MO: Chalice, 2004), ch. 2; Bernhard W. Anderson, "Chapter 2: The Poetry of Prayer and Praise" in *Out of the Depths: The Psalms Speak for Us Today*, with Steven Bishop (Louisville, KY: Westminster John Knox, 2000); and Rolf A. Jacobson and Karl N. Jacobson, "Chapter 1: Why Is My Bible Repeating Itself? Learning to Understand Hebrew Poetry," in *Invitation to the Psalms: A Reader's Guide for Discovery and Engagement* (Grand Rapids: Baker Academic, 2013).

29. Dietrich Bonhoeffer, *Psalms: The Prayer Book of the Bible* (Minneapolis: Fortress, 1974), 24.

CHAPTER 6: SADNESS

1. Frederick Buechner, *Now and Then: A Memoir of Vocation* (San Francisco: HarperOne, 1983), 46.

2. For a beautiful example of a personal reappropriation of the lament psalms, see Ann Weems, *Psalms of Lament* (Louisville, KY: Westminster John Knox, 1995).

3. Eugene Peterson, *Answering God: The Psalms as Tools for Prayer* (New York: HarperCollins, 1989), 35.

4. Carroll Stuhlmueller, *The Spirituality of the Psalms* (Collegeville, MN: Liturgical Press, 2002), 99.

5. Walter Brueggemann, *The Message of the Psalms: A Theological Commentary* (Minneapolis: Augsburg, 1984), 72.

6. Walter Brueggemann, *From Whom No Secrets Are Hid: Introducing the Psalms* (Louisville, KY: Westminster John Knox, 2014), 19.

7. Stuhlmueller, *Spirituality of the Psalms*, 100.

8. Brueggemann, *Message of the Psalms*, 78.

9. Cited in John D. Witvliet, *The Biblical Psalms in Christian Worship: A Brief Introduction and Guide to Resources* (Grand Rapids: Eerdmans, 2007), 43.

CHAPTER 7: ANGER

1. Kim Phuc Phan Thi, "These Bombs Led Me to Christ," *Christianity Today*, April 20, 2018, https://www.christianitytoday.com/ct/2018/may/napalm-girl-kim-phuc-phan-thi-fire-road.html.

2. Madeleine L'Engle, foreword to *A Grief Observed*, by C. S. Lewis (New York: HarperOne, 2009), 10.

3. Jeffrey Kluger, "The Las Vegas Shooting and Our Age of Anger," *Time*, October 4, 2017, http://time.com/4969640/las-vegas-shooting-anger/.

4. Vanessa Barford, "Why Are Americans So Angry?" BBC News, February 4, 2016, https://www.bbc.com/news/magazine-35406324.

5. J. Todd Billings, "Can Anger at God Be Righteous?" *Christianity Today*, December 28, 2018, https://www.christianitytoday.com/ct/2019/january-february/can-anger-at-god-be-righteous-psalms-suffering.html ("What about psalms that seemed to protest to God, to express anger and fear? I had been taught the Psalms were God's Word given for our own prayer. But I had no way to incorporate the most widespread type of psalm [about 40 percent of the book]—the psalms of lament. When the psalms' melody was in minor, even dissonant keys, I just didn't sing along. I was not alone in my inexperience with psalms of lament").

6. As David Stowe points out, Isaac Watts excluded the curse psalms from his 1719 hymnal, *The Songs of David Imitated in the Language of the New Testament*, for this very reason. Stowe, *Song of Exile: The Enduring Mystery of Psalm 137* (Oxford: Oxford University Press, 2016), 73.

7. C. S. Lewis, *Reflections on the Psalms* (New York: HarperOne, 2017), 22.

8. Walter Brueggemann and William H. Bellinger Jr., *Psalms* (Cambridge, UK: Cambridge University Press, 2014), 262.

9. As Holy Scripture presents things, both the wicked (human beings) and the gods (principalities and powers) threaten the good order of God in the world. Extreme acts of violence, destruction, and death are both demented, where human beings find themselves out of their mind or driven mad, and demonic, where supernatural beings seek to steal, kill, and destroy God's creation.

10. Mary Douglas, *Purity and Danger: An Analysis of the Concepts of Pollution and Taboo* (London: Routledge, 2002), 3–7, 78–85.

11. Douglas, *Purity and Danger*, 117–18.

12. Douglas, *Purity and Danger*, 160–72.

13. Douglas, *Purity and Danger*, 197–200.

14. Geoffrey Hughes, *Swearing: A Social History of Foul Language, Oaths*

and Profanity in English (Oxford: Blackwell, 1991); and Hugh Rawson, *Wicked Words: A Treasury of Curses, Insults, Put-Downs, and Other Formerly Unprintable Terms from Anglo-Saxon Times to the Present* (New York: Crown, 1989).

15. Stowe, *Song of Exile*, 32, 62, 85.

16. Miroslav Volf, quoted in Stowe, *Song of Exile*, 171.

17. Cf. Joel M. LeMon, "Saying Amen to Violent Psalms: Patterns of Prayer, Belief, and Action in the Psalter," in *Soundings in the Theology of the Psalms: Perspectives and Methods in Contemporary Scholarship*, ed. Rolf A. Jacobson (Minneapolis: Fortress, 2011), 93–110.

18. Miroslav Volf, quoted in Stowe, *Song of Exile*, 171.

19. Miroslav Volf, quoted in Stowe, *Song of Exile*, 172.

20. Dietrich Bonhoeffer, *Psalms: The Prayer Book of the Bible* (Minneapolis: Fortress, 1974), 59–60.

21. Aristotle, *The Nicomachean Ethics*, trans. David Ross (Oxford: Oxford University Press, 2009), 36.

22. Eugene Peterson, "Bono & Eugene Peterson: The Psalms," Fuller Studio, April 26, 2016, https://www.youtube.com/watch?v=-l40S5e90KY.

23. Lytta Basset offers this observation: "Holy anger engages with injustice and motivates us to right what is wrong in the world (without losing our dependence upon God)." Cited in Daniel Michael Nehrbass, *Praying Curses: The Therapeutic and Preaching Value of the Imprecatory Psalms* (Eugene, OR: Pickwick, 2013), 155.

CHAPTER 8: JOY

1. Dorothy Day, *The Long Loneliness* (San Francisco: Harper & Row, 1952), 29.

2. Catherine La Cugna, *God for Us* (San Francisco: Harper, 1973), 338–39.

3. Walter Brueggemann, *From Whom No Secrets Are Hid: Introducing the Psalms* (Louisville, KY: Westminster John Knox, 2014), 47.

4. David F. Ford and Daniel W. Hardy, *Living in Praise: Worshipping and Knowing God* (Grand Rapids: Baker Academic, 2005), 92 ("Part of the logic of laughter, poetry and praise is that of intensification and overflow. The intense, pointed delight and the explosion of laughter go together; the poem's concentration and economy let it communicate more widely and with more power. The resurrection of the crucified Jesus Christ is this logic at the heart of Christianity").

5. James L. Mays, *The Lord Reigns: A Theological Handbook to the Psalms*

(Louisville, KY: Westminster John Knox, 1994), 62 ("By its movement, conclusion, and title the book in its shape defines all its contents, the prayers and instruction, as the praise of the Lord. Their literary genre remains, but their function is transposed to another canonical genre.... The making of the Psalter turns out to have been a project to put praise on the scriptural agenda. It was an enterprise that made praise canonical").

6. Rolf A. Jacobson and Karl N. Jacobson, *Invitation to the Psalms: A Reader's Guide for Discovery and Engagement* (Grand Rapids: Baker Academic, 2013), 46–50, 151.

7. Ford and Hardy, *Living in Praise*, 9.

8. Eugene H. Peterson, *The Message: The Bible in Contemporary English* (Colorado Springs, CO: NavPress, 1993), 272.

9. Thomas Merton, *Praying the Psalms* (Collegeville, MN: Liturgical Press, 1956), 12.

10. John Calvin, *Sermon on Job*, trans. Douglas Kelly (Edinburgh: Banner of Truth, 1993), 4:20; 39:8–40:6.

11. I write about this at greater length in my book *The Theater of God's Glory: Calvin, Creation and the Liturgical Arts* (Grand Rapids: Eerdmans, 2017).

12. For the faithful who have experienced God's rescue, "it seemed like a dream, so unreal, so impossible, so beyond explanation, even beyond anticipation. But of course that is in the nature of YHWH's rescue miracles; outside the purview of YHWH, such wonders seem like a fantasy—except in this case it is a lived reality!" Walter Brueggemann and William H. Bellinger Jr., *Psalms* (Cambridge, UK: Cambridge University Press, 2014), 539.

13. "Holy Baptism," in *Book of Common Prayer*, https://www.bcponline.org.

14. Dietrich Bonhoeffer, quoted in Edwin Robertson, ed. and trans., *My Soul Finds Rest in God Alone* (Guildford, UK: Eagle, 2001), 105.

15. Robertson, *My Soul Finds Rest in God Alone*, 106.

16. Robertson, *My Soul Finds Rest in God Alone*, 107.

17. Patrick Kavanagh, quoted in David Ford, *The Shape of Living: Spiritual Directions for Everyday Life* (Norwich: Canterbury Press, 2012), 165.

18. Patrick Miller, *Interpreting the Psalms* (Minneapolis: Fortress, 1986), 66.

19. Walter Brueggemann, *The Message of the Psalms: A Theological Commentary* (Minneapolis: Augsburg, 1984), 167.

20. Eugene Peterson, *Answering God: The Psalms as Tools for Prayer* (New York: HarperCollins, 1989), 123.

21. Ellen F. Davis, *Getting Involved with God: Rediscovering the Old Testament* (Cambridge, MA: Cowley Publications, 2011), 30.
22. Denise Dombkowski Hopkins, *Journey Through the Psalms* (St. Louis: Chalice, 2002), 33 ("Have we become so mechanical and unthinking in our praise that our hallelujahs have become hollow?").
23. C. S. Lewis, *Surprised by Joy* (New York: Houghton Mifflin Harcourt, 1956), 68.
24. Ford and Hardy, *Living in Praise*, 48.
25. Ford and Hardy, *Living in Praise*, 176.

CHAPTER 9: ENEMIES

1. Dietrich Bonhoeffer, "A Bonhoeffer Sermon," trans. Donald Bloesch, *Theology Today* 38, no. 4 (1982): 469.
2. For example, the Houston Police Department union president Joe Gamaldi is quoted, saying, "The ones that are out there spreading the rhetoric that police officers are the enemy, just know we've got your number." Marcy de Luna, "'We Are the Good Guys. We're Trying to Protect Our Community,' Says HPD Union President Joe Gamaldi," *Houston Chronicle*, January 29, 2019, https://www.houstonchronicle.com/news/houston-texas/houston/article/HPD-union-Joe-Gamaldi-officer-shooting-houston-13570291.php.
3. Jay Ambrose, "Liberals Are Enemies of Freedom," *Tribune News Service*, October 11, 2018, https://www.vcstar.com/story/opinion/columnists/2018/10/11/liberals-enemies-freedom/1603402002/.
4. Jason McIntosh, "Republicans Are Enemies of Human Civilization," *Fogknife*, June 19, 2018, http://fogknife.com/2018-06-19-republicans-are-enemies-of-human-civilization.html. See also Roland Vincent, "35 Reasons Conservatives Are the Enemy," Armory of the Revolution, March 25, 2015, https://armoryoftherevolution.wordpress.com/2015/03/25/35-reasons-conservatives-are-the-enemy/.
5. Jim Powell, "How Did Our Friend Iran Become Our Enemy?" *Forbes*, December 22, 2011, https://www.forbes.com/sites/jimpowell/2011/12/22/how-did-our-friend-iran-become-our-enemy/#10ec182f68b0.
6. The Harvard political scientist Samuel P. Huntington wrote: "While wars at times may have a divisive effect on society, a common enemy can often help to promote identity and cohesion among people. The weakening or absence of a common enemy can do just the reverse." Huntington, "The Erosion of American National Interests," *Foreign*

Affairs Journal (September/October 1997), https://www.foreignaffairs
.com/articles/1997–09–01/erosion-american-national-interests.

7. Carol Giacomo, "Iran and the United States: Doomed to Be Forever
Enemies?" *New York Times*, January 20, 2019, https://www.nytimes.com
/2019/01/20/opinion/iran-united-states-trump.html; and Hamid
Dabashi, "Who Is the 'Great Satan'?" *Al Jazeera*, September 20, 2015,
https://www.aljazeera.com/indepth/opinion/2015/09/great-satan
-150920072643884.html ("As an absolute metaphor of the enemy, the
'Great Satan' is embedded in the Islamic Republic itself—its discursive
self-consciousness, its hidden and repressed desires").

8. Lorraine Boissoneault, "The Ballad of the Boombox: What Public
Enemy Tells Us About Hip-Hop, Race and Society," *Smithsonian*,
February 9, 2017, https://www.smithsonianmag.com/smithsonian
-institution/ballad-boombox-what-public-enemy-tells-us-about-hip
-hop-race-and-society-180962095/#DHKDXmBtTcTmVS4L.99.

9. Kory Grow, "Public Enemy Reveal Origins of Name, Crosshairs Logo,"
Rolling Stone, August 18, 2014, https://www.rollingstone.com/music
/music-news/public-enemy-reveal-origins-of-name-crosshairs-logo
-241248/.

10. Walter Brueggemann and William H. Bellinger Jr., *Psalms* (Cambridge,
UK: Cambridge University Press, 2014), 260.

11. Eugene Peterson, *Answering God: The Psalms as Tools for Prayer* (New
York: HarperCollins, 1989), 95.

12. Nancy L. deClaissé-Walford, "The Theology of the Imprecatory
Psalms," in *Soundings in the Theology of Psalms: Perspectives and Methods
in Contemporary Scholarship*, ed. Rolf A. Jacobson (Minneapolis:
Fortress, 2011), 83.

13. J. Clinton McCann Jr., *A Theological Introduction to the Book of Psalms:
The Psalms as Torah* (Nashville: Abingdon, 1993), 119–20.

14. I borrow these images from Erich Zenger, *A God of Vengeance?:
Understanding the Psalms of Divine Wrath* (Louisville, KY: Westminster
John Knox, 1996), 11.

15. Zenger, *God of Vengeance?*, 9–11.

16. Cf. Zenger, *God of Vengeance?*, 12.

17. John Day, "The Imprecatory Psalms and Christian Ethics," *Bibliotheca
Sacra* 159 (2002): 170. Cf. Daniel Michael Nehrbass, *Praying Curses:
The Therapeutic and Preaching Value of the Imprecatory Psalms* (Eugene,
OR: Pickwick, 2013), 160.

18. Jim Cotter, *Psalms for a Pilgrim People* (Harrisburg, PA: Morehouse Publishing, 1998), 240.

19. Peterson, *Answering God*, 98.

20. Peter J. Leithart offers this important observation: "Imprecatory Psalms don't give Christians an excuse to be mean-spirited, vicious, or vengeful. They're not a warrant to be macho and talk trash. God may destroy ISIS enemies by transforming them into allies. Praying the Psalms, we leave the outcome to him and do what Jesus did: entrust ourselves to the Judge who judges justly (1 Peter 2:23)." Leithart, "Teach Us to Pray," *First Things*, April 24, 2015, https://www.firstthings.com/web-exclusives/2015/04/teach-us-to-pray.

21. John Mark Hicks, "Preaching Community Laments: Responding to Disillusionment with God and Injustice in the World," in *Performing the Psalms*, ed. David Fleer and David Bland (St. Louis: Chalice, 2005), 75.

22. Zenger, *God of Vengeance?*, vii–viii, 75.

23. Zenger, *God of Vengeance?*, 75.

CHAPTER 10: JUSTICE

1. Tamara Jones and Joshua Partlow, "Pa. Killer Had Prepared for 'Long Siege,'" *Washington Post*, October 4, 2006, http://www.washingtonpost.com/wp-dyn/content/article/2006/10/04/AR2006100400331.html.

2. Rick Lyman, "Man Guilty of Murder in Texas Dragging Death," *New York Times*, February 24, 1999, https://www.nytimes.com/1999/02/24/us/man-guilty-of-murder-in-texas-dragging-death.html.

3. Bukola Adebayo and Sara Mazloumsaki, "30,000 Nigerians Flee Boko Haram Violence in Two Days, UN Says," CNN, January 29, 2019, https://www.cnn.com/2019/01/29/africa/nigerians-flee-boko-haram-violence-intl/index.html.

4. As reported by the International Justice Mission: "They had been trapped since June 2018, making fried pani puri snacks popular in north India. These impoverished men and boys were recruited from their village with loans of as little as 10,000 rupees (about $140 USD), which they were meant to pay off with their labor. Instead, the factory owner charged them impossible interest rates and controlled their every movement so they could never repay the debt. He verbally abused them and beat them viciously if they slowed down during the 18-hour work days—ensuring they were always afraid of his power." International Justice Mission,

"Scared and Scarred: 11 Rescued from Fried Snack Factory," https://www
.ijm.org/news/scared-and-scarred-11-rescued-from-fried-snack-factory.

5. Liam Stack, "Catholic Church in Texas Names Nearly 300 Priests
Accused of Sex Abuse," *New York Times,* January 31, 2019, https://www
.nytimes.com/2019/01/31/us/priests-abuse-texas.html.

6. Emily Palmer and Alan Feuer, "El Chapo Trial: The 11 Biggest Revelations
from the Case," *New York Times,* February 3, 2019, https://www.nytimes
.com/2019/02/03/nyregion/el-chapo-trial.html.

7. "Flint Water Crisis Fast Facts," CNN Library, December 6, 2018,
https://www.cnn.com/2016/03/04/us/flint-water-crisis-fast-facts
/index.html.

8. Manny Fernandez, "A Year after Hurricane Harvey, Houston's Poorest
Neighborhoods Are Slowest to Recover," *New York Times,* September 3,
2018, https://www.nytimes.com/2018/09/03/us/hurricane-harvey
-houston.html.

9. Nicholas Wolterstorff, "Chapter 7: What Is Justice?" in *Justice in Love*
(Grand Rapids: Eerdmans, 2011).

10. John Mark Hicks, "Preaching Community Laments: Responding to
Disillusionment with God and Injustice in the World," in *Performing the
Psalms,* ed. David Fleer and David Bland (St. Louis: Chalice, 2005), 76.

11. C. S. Lewis, *Reflections on the Psalms* (New York: HarperOne, 2017), 14.

12. According to Dietrich Bonhoeffer, "It is an evil time when the world
lets injustice happen silently, when the oppression of the poor and the
wretched cries out to heaven in a loud voice and the judges and rulers of
the earth keep silent about it, when the persecuted church calls to God
for help in the hour of dire distress and exhorts men to do justice, and yet
no mouth on earth is opened to bring justice." Bonhoeffer, "A Bonhoeffer
Sermon," trans. Donald Bloesch, *Theology Today* 38, no. 4 (1982): 467.

13. Nancy deClaissé-Walford, Rolf A. Jacobson, and Beth LaNeel Tanner,
The Book of Psalms (Grand Rapids: Eerdmans, 2014), 577, 732.

14. Nicholas Wolterstorff, *Justice: Rights and Wrongs* (Princeton, NJ:
Princeton University Press, 2008), 82.

15. Eugene Peterson, *Where Your Treasure Is: Psalms That Summon You from
Self to Community* (Grand Rapids: Eerdmans, 1993), 135.

16. The Nicaraguan poet Ernesto Cardenal captures the spirit of the psalms
on this account in his fresh translations of particular psalms in *Salmos*
(Madrid: Editorial Trotta, 1998).

17. This is a phrase that Wolterstorff uses in *Justice: Rights and Wrongs*, 76.

18. Bob Ekblad, *Reading the Bible with the Damned* (Louisville, KY: Westminster John Knox, 2005), 129.

19. Deuteronomy 24:17 says this: "You shall not deprive a resident alien or an orphan of justice; you shall not take a widow's garment in pledge."

20. Cf. N. T. Wright, "Chapter 3: Evil and the Crucified God," in *Evil and the Justice of God* (Downers Grove, IL: InterVarsity Press, 2006).

21. Wolterstorff, *Justice: Rights and Wrongs*, 24–26, 42; and Nicholas Wolterstorff, *Justice in Love* (Grand Rapids: Eerdmans, 2011), 85–86, see also "Chapter 9: Love as Care" and "Chapter 15: What Is Forgiveness?"

22. Daniel M. Bell Jr., "Deliberating: Justice and Liberation," in *The Blackwell Companion to Christian Ethics*, ed. Stanley Hauerwas and Samuel Wells (Oxford: Blackwell, 2006), 190.

23. Nicholas Wolterstorff, *Journey Toward Justice: Personal Encounters in the Global South* (Grand Rapids: Baker Academic, 2013), 108.

24. A helpful look at the ways in which the world of the psalms might intersect the world of an urban context is Gerald H. Wilson, "Songs for the City: Interpreting Biblical Psalms in an Urban Context," in *Psalms and Practice: Worship, Virtue, and Authority*, ed. Stephen Breck Reid (Collegeville, MN: Liturgical Press, 2001), 231–43.

25. Donald W. Shriver Jr., *An Ethic for Enemies: Forgiveness in Politics* (Oxford: Oxford University Press, 1995), 31.

26. Not everyone thought favorably of their decision to forgive so readily. Jeff Jacoby, "Undeserved Forgiveness," *Boston Globe*, October 8, 2006, http://www.jeffjacoby.com/5858/undeserved-forgiveness.

27. Bob Abernathy, "Amish Forgiveness," PBS, Religion & Ethics NewsWeekly, September 21, 2007, https://www.pbs.org/wnet/religionandethics/2007/09/21/september-21-2007-amish-forgiveness/4295/.

28. Daniel Burke, "Amish Search for Healing, Forgiveness After 'The Amish 9/11,'" RNS, October 5, 2006, https://web.archive.org/web/200610 21051654/http://www.religionnews.com/ArticleofWeek100506.html; and Ann Rodgers, "Nickel Mines Legacy: Forgive First," *Pittsburgh Post-Gazette*, September 30, 2007, http://old.post-gazette.com/pg/07273/821700-85.stm.

29. Donald B. Kraybill, Steven M. Nolt, and David L. Weaver-Zercher, "Chapter 12: Grief, Providence and Justice," in *Amish Grace: How Forgiveness Transcended Tragedy* (San Francisco: Jossey-Bass, 2007).

30. W. E. B. Du Bois, *The Souls of Black Folks* (New York: Penguin, 1996), 213–14 ("Through all the sorrow of the Sorrow Songs there breathes

a hope—a faith in the ultimate justice of things. The minor cadences of despair change often to triumph and calm confidence. Sometimes it is faith in life, sometimes a faith in death, sometimes assurance of boundless justice in some fair world beyond").

31. This is Jim Cotter's prayer for Psalm 37, in *Psalms for a Pilgrim People* (Harrisburg, PA: Morehouse Publishing, 1998), 82.

CHAPTER 11: DEATH

1. Henri Nouwen, *A Sorrow Shared: A Combined Edition of the Nouwen Classics,* In Memoriam *and* A Letter of Consolation (Notre Dame, IN: Ave Maria Press, 2010), 66.

2. A longer version of this story appears in W. David O. Taylor, "When Jesus Doesn't Calm the Storm," *Christianity Today,* August 31, 2017, https://www.christianitytoday.com/ct/2017/august-web-only/when -jesus-doesnt-calm-storm-hurricane-harvey-houston-flood.html.

3. Walter Brueggemann, *From Whom No Secrets Are Hid: Introducing the Psalms* (Louisville, KY: Westminster John Knox, 2014), 124.

4. Hans Schwarz, *Eschatology* (Grand Rapids: Eerdmans, 2000), 257.

5. Carroll Stuhlmueller, *The Spirituality of the Psalms* (Collegeville, MN: Liturgical Press, 2002), 134–37.

6. Used with permission from the author.

7. Cf. Bernhard W. Anderson, *Out of the Depths: The Psalms Speak for Us Today,* with Steven Bishop (Louisville, KY: Westminster John Knox, 2000), 111.

8. Frederick J. Mabie offers helpful background information in his essay "Chaos and Death," in *Dictionary of the Old Testament: Wisdom, Poetry & Writings,* ed. Tremper Longman III and Peter Enns (Downers Grove, IL: InterVarsity Press Academic, 2008), 41–54.

9. Samuel Terrien, *The Psalms: Strophic Structure and Theological Commentary* (Grand Rapids: Eerdmans, 2003), 133.

10. Stanley Hauerwas, "Reflections on Learning How to Speak Christian," *ABC Religion & Ethics,* August 16, 2010, http://www.abc.net.au/religion /articles/2010/08/16/2984111.htm.

11. Cf. Allen Verhey, *The Christian Art of Dying: Learning from Jesus* (Grand Rapids: Eerdmans, 2011), 346.

12. Central Intelligence Agency, "The World Factbook," https://www.cia.gov /library/publications/the-world-factbook/geos/xx.html.

13. Jamie Holguin, "A Murder a Minute," CBS News, October 3, 2002, https://www.cbsnews.com/news/a-murder-a-minute/.

14. Peter Saul, "Let's Talk about Dying," TEDxNewy, November 2011, https://www.ted.com/talks/peter_saul_let_s_talk_about_dying.

15. Matthew Levering makes this point in his excellent book, *Dying and the Virtues* (Grand Rapids: Eerdmans, 2018), 119–34.

16. Hurricanes Irma and Maria followed within a month of Harvey, affecting Florida, Puerto Rico, and much of the Caribbean, respectively, causing between $50 billion and $90 billion in damages. An estimated 1,400–5,740 deaths occurred because of Hurricane Maria.

17. Edwidge Danticat, *The Art of Death: Writing the Final Story* (Minneapolis: Graywolf Press, 2017), 29.

Chapter 12: Life

1. The full text to Charles Wesley's hymn, "Author of Life Divine," can be found at https://hymnary.org/text/author_of_life_divine.

2. The chronicle of my sister's accident and months-long recovery can be read here: https://christchurchofaustin.org/category/christine/.

3. Claus Westermann, cited in Bernhard W. Anderson, *Out of the Depths: The Psalms Speak for Us Today*, with Steven Bishop (Louisville, KY: Westminster John Knox, 2000), 118.

4. Walter Brueggemann, *From Whom No Secrets Are Hid: Introducing the Psalms* (Louisville, KY: Westminster John Knox, 2014), 69, 71.

5. John Goldingay, *Psalms, Volume 3: Psalm 90–150* (Grand Rapids: Baker Academic, 2008), 193.

6. Job 34:14–15 echoes this idea.

7. Isaiah 35 and 42 apply this idea of God's unique creative power to *all* his works—the cosmos, human beings, ecologies, Israel, and so on.

8. Anderson, *Out of the Depths*, 143.

9. Brueggemann, *From Whom No Secrets Are Hid*, 70.

10. Robert Alter, *The Book of Psalms: A Translation with Commentary* (New York: W. W. Norton & Company, 2007), 113.

11. Matthew Henry, *A Commentary on the Whole Bible, Volume 3: Job to Song of Solomon* (Old Tappan, NJ: Fleming H. Revell Company, 1986), 786.

12. Charles Briggs, *A Critical and Exegetical Commentary on the Book of Psalms*, vol. 1, The International Critical Commentary (New York: Charles Scribner's Sons, 1906), 286.

13. Walter Brueggemann, *The Message of the Psalms: A Theological Commentary* (Minneapolis: Augsburg, 1984), 19.

14. Cf. Artur Weiser, *The Psalms: A Commentary* (Philadelphia: The Westminster Press, 1962), 839; Leslie C. Allen, *Psalms 101–150: World Biblical Commentary*, rev. ed. (Nashville: Thomas Nelson, 2002), 397–98; Goldingay, *Psalms*, vol. 3, 737; J. Clinton McCann Jr., *The Book of Psalms*, vol. 4, TNIB (Nashville: Abingdon Press, 1996), 660–62, 1274; and Amos Hakham, *The Bible: Psalms, with the Jerusalem Commentary*, vol. 3 (Jerusalem: Mosad Harav Kook, 2003), 491.

15. Instead of the "old" covenant, God makes a "new" covenant with his people (Jer. 31:31–37). Where Israel bears an "old" name of reproach, God gives her a "new" name (Isa. 62:2). Where Israel labors under an "old" spirit, entangled and corrupted by idolatry, Yahweh promises her a "new" spirit and a "new" heart (Ezek. 11:19; 18:31; 36:26). And in place of the "old" heavens and earth, the Lord will create a "new" heaven and a "new" earth, and "the former things shall not be remembered or come to mind" (Isa. 65:17). Cf. also N. T. Wright's comments about exile in *The New Testament and the People of God* (Minneapolis: Fortress, 1992), 268–79, 299–301.

16. Augustine, *Expositions of the Psalms 121–150*, vol. 3, bk. 20, *The Works of Saint Augustine: A Translation for the 21st Century*, trans. Maria Boulding (New York: New City Press, 2004), 374.

17. Augustine, *Expositions of the Psalms*, 121–50, 492.

18. Augustine argues that the new song of Christ is matched by "the new music of charity." Augustine, *Expositions of the Psalms 73–98*, vol. 3, bk. 18, *The Works of Saint Augustine: A Translation for the 21st Century*, trans. Maria Boulding (New York: New City Press, 2002), 424–25, 459–60. To sing this new song of love is to sing an ever-renewing song "because it never grows old." It never grows old, because we have been caught up in the inertia of Christ's resurrected life (Col. 3:17), a life that belongs to the new creation (2 Cor. 5:17; Gal. 6:15).

19. Jeremy S. Begbie, "Looking to the Future: A Hopeful Subversion," in *For the Beauty of the Church: Casting a Vision for the Arts*, ed. W. David O. Taylor (Grand Rapids: Baker, 2010), 198n6.

20. The full text to Charles Wesley's hymn "Author of Life Divine" can be found at https://hymnary.org/text/author_of_life_divine.

Chapter 13: Nations

1. Samuel Ngewa, comment on Psalm 67:4–5 in the *Africa Bible Commentary*, ed. Tokunboh Adeyemo (Grand Rapids: Zondervan, 2006), 684.

2. Christopher J. H. Wright, *The Mission of God: Unlocking the Bible's Grand Narrative* (Downers Grove, IL: InterVarsity Press Academic, 2006), 467.

3. David Brooks, "Yes, I'm an American Nationalist," *New York Times*, October 25, 2018, https://www.nytimes.com/2018/10/25/opinion/america-nationalism-diversity-trump.html ("Love for nation is an expanding love because it is love for the whole people. It's an ennobling love because it comes with the urge to hospitality—to share what you love and to want to make more love by extending it to others").

4. Duane L. Christensen, "Nations," in *Anchor Bible Dictionary*, vol. 4, ed. David Noel Freedman et al. (New York: Doubleday, 1992), 1037 ("It is clear that 'Israel as a light to the nations' is no peripheral theme within the canonical process. The nations are the matrix of Israel's life, the raison d'etre of her very existence").

5. Walter Brueggemann and William H. Bellinger Jr., *Psalms* (Cambridge, UK: Cambridge University Press, 2014), 376–77.

6. Wright, *Mission of God*, 467.

7. Wright, *Mission of God*, 479.

8. As Walter Brueggeman helpfully observes, in regard to the human and divine dimension of vengeance, "There is no sense of being triumphant, but only of being very sure of God. By the end of such a Psalm, the cry for vengeance is not resolved. The rage is not removed. But it has been dramatically transformed by the double step of *owning* and *yielding*" (emphasis original). Brueggeman, *Praying the Psalms* (Winona, MN: Saint Mary's Press, 1982), 60.

9. Cf. Brueggeman, *Praying the Psalms*, 62–65.

10. James L. Mays, *Psalms: Interpretation: A Bible Commentary for Teaching and Preaching* (Louisville, KY: Westminster John Knox, 2011), 447.

11. Mays, *Psalms*, 448.

12. Walter Brueggemann, *The Message of the Psalms: A Theological Commentary* (Minneapolis: Augsburg, 1984), 151 ("That Yahweh is a royal power serves to destabilize every other royal power and to relativize every temptation to absolutize power. . . . It is Yahweh's character that is decisive for the character of all political authority in Israel—judge, king, and priest").

13. James L. Mays, *The Lord Reigns: A Theological Handbook to the Psalms* (Louisville, KY: Westminster John Knox, 1994), 112.
14. Mays, *The Lord Reigns*, 116.
15. Wright, *Mission of God*, 501.
16. Mays, *The Lord Reigns*, 116.
17. Wright, *Mission of God*, 489. This is certainly the view of Haggai 2:7.
18. W. Creighton Marlowe, "Music of Missions: Themes of Cross-Cultural Outreach in the Psalms," *Missiology* 26 (1998): 452. See also Joan Huyser-Honig, "Why Persecuted Christians Sing Psalms in Pakistan," Calvin Institute of Christian Worship, January 7, 2013, https://worship.calvin.edu/resources/resource-library/why-persecuted-christians-sing-psalms-in-pakistan/; and Philip Jenkins, "Psalm 91: In Every Time and Place," *Christian Century*, January 9, 2018, https://www.christiancentury.org/article/notes-global-church/psalm-91-every-time-and-place.
19. This prayer is adapted from the Eucharistic Service from the Anglican Church of Kenya. For details, go to https://www.reformedworship.org/article/march-2018/kenyan-rite.

CHAPTER 14: CREATION

1. Thomas Aquinas, quoted in Robert W. Jenson, *Systematic Theology*, vol. 2, *The Works of God* (Oxford: Oxford University Press, 1999), 14.
2. "SNH Commissioned Report No.374: The Special Qualities of the National Scenic Areas," Scottish Natural Heritage, 2010, https://www.nature.scot/snh-commissioned-report-374-special-qualities-national-scenic-areas.
3. Calvin Seerveld, *Voicing God's Psalms* (Grand Rapids: Eerdmans, 2005), 8.
4. On this point, see E. C. Lucas, "Wisdom Theology," in *Dictionary of the Old Testament: Wisdom, Poetry & Writings*, ed. Tremper Longman III and Peter Enns (Downers Grove, IL: InterVarsity Press Academic, 2008), 901–12.
5. Ellen F. Davis, *Getting Involved with God: Rediscovering the Old Testament* (Cambridge, MA: Cowley Publications, 2011), 68.
6. Davis, *Getting Involved with God*, 68.
7. Bernhard W. Anderson, *Out of the Depths: The Psalms Speak for Us Today*, with Steven Bishop (Louisville, KY: Westminster John Knox, 2000), 144 ("In Psalm 104, then, we are given a picture of the marvelous order and design of God's creation: a carefully wrought whole in which all creatures, including human beings, have their proper place and times. There is even an element of esthetic enjoyment in this poem, a feeling for the beauty of

God's creation. This experience of beauty, however, is not based merely on human perception. . . . Human enjoyment may be full because God 'rejoices' in the works of creation").

8. Cf. Tremper Longman III, "Psalms 2: Ancient Near Eastern Background," in *Dictionary of the Old Testament: Wisdom, Poetry & Writings*, 593–605.

9. Cf. Rolf A. Jacobson and Karl N. Jacobson, *Invitation to the Psalms: A Reader's Guide for Discovery and Engagement* (Grand Rapids: Baker Academic, 2013), 156–57.

10. Jim Cotter, *Psalms for a Pilgrim People* (Harrisburg, PA: Morehouse Publishing, 1998), 13.

11. The translations of Hebrew terms are drawn from Davis, *Getting Involved with God*, 192–94.

12. Davis, *Getting Involved with God*, 192.

13. This three-session Bible study might be a helpful place for readers to explore this part of our human calling: "Creation Care," *Christianity Today*, December 1, 2007, https://www.christianitytoday.com/biblestudies/c/creation-care.html.

14. John Goldingay, *Psalms, Volume 1: Psalms 1–41* (Grand Rapids: Baker Academic, 2006), 161.

15. Gordon W. Lathrop, *Holy Ground: A Liturgical Cosmology* (Minneapolis: Fortress, 2003), 45.

16. Karl Barth, *Church Dogmatics*, vol. 3, bk. 1, trans. J. W. Edwards, O. Bussey, and Harold Knight (Edinburgh: T. & T. Clark, 1958), 346.

17. Barth, *Church Dogmatics*, vol. 3, bk. 1, 214.

18. Barth, *Church Dogmatics*, vol. 3, bk. 1, 181.

19. Barth, *Church Dogmatics*, vol. 3, bk. 1, 219.

20. Barth concludes his discussion of the Sabbath with a bit of practical news for tired human beings: instead of seeing each week as "being a trying ascent," it should be seen as "a glad descent from the high-point of the Sabbath." Barth, *Church Dogmatics*, vol. 3, bk. 1, 228.

21. Marva J. Dawn, *A Royal Waste of Time: The Splendor of Worshiping God and Being Church for the World* (Grand Rapids: Eerdmans, 1999).

22. Calvin Seerveld, *Voicing God's Psalms* (Grand Rapids: Eerdmans, 2005), 8.

23. Kathryn Schifferdecker, "Creation Theology," in *The Dictionary of the Old Testament*, 68 ("A polluted river cannot praise God with full voice").

24. Walter Brueggemann, *From Whom No Secrets Are Hid: Introducing the Psalms* (Louisville, KY: Westminster John Knox, 2014), 79.

25. On this point, see Christopher R. J. Holmes, "Chapter 5: The Good

Creator," in *The Lord Is Good: Seeking the God of the Psalter* (Downers Grove, IL: InterVarsity Press Academic, 2018).

26. The full text of Isaac Watts's hymn can be found here: https://hymnary .org/text/the_heavens_declare_thy_glory_lord_in_ev.

Conclusion

1. Eugene Peterson, *Where Your Treasure Is: Psalms That Summon You from Self to Community* (Grand Rapids: Eerdmans, 1993), 174.

2. "Bono & Eugene Peterson: The Psalms," Fuller Studio, April 26, 2016, https://www.youtube.com/watch?v=-l40S5e90KY. See also "Bono & Eugene Peterson on the Psalms," Fuller Studio, https://fullerstudio.fuller .edu/bono-eugene-peterson-psalms/.

3. Kathleen Norris, "The Paradox of the Psalms," in *Out of the Garden: Women Writers on the Bible*, ed. Christina Büchmann and Celina Spiegel (New York: Fawcett Columbine, 1994), 222–23. Cf. *The Psalms with Commentary by Kathleen Norris* (New York: Riverhead Books, 1997).

4. Norris, "The Paradox of the Psalms," 225.

5. Rolf A. Jacobson and Karl N. Jacobson, *Invitation to the Psalms: A Reader's Guide for Discovery and Engagement* (Grand Rapids: Baker Academic, 2013), 56.

6. Eugene Peterson, *Praying with the Psalms: A Year of Daily Prayers and Reflections on the Words of David* (New York: HarperOne, 1993), 89.

7. Augustine, *Expositions of the Psalms 73–98*, vol. 3, bk. 18, *The Works of Saint Augustine: A Translation for the 21st Century*, trans. Maria Boulding (New York: New City Press, 2002), 190.

8. Augustine, *Expositions of the Psalms 73–98*, 196.

9. Eugene Peterson, *Where Your Treasure Is*, 171–72.

10. Peterson, *Where Your Treasure Is*, 172.

11. Nan C. Merrill, *Psalms for Praying: An Invitation to Wholeness* (New York: Continuum, 2007), 69–70.

12. William P. Brown, *Seeing the Psalms: A Theology of Metaphor* (Louisville, KY: Westminster John Knox, 2002), 57. Brown adds: "The psalmist has, in effect, placed a tree at the entrance to the Psalter, at the threshold of its refuge and the head of its pathway. . . . Like the freestanding tree-pillars that flank the entrance to the temple demarcating the sanctuary as inviolably holy, so the opening psalm delineates the Psalter as wholly instructive and comprehensively cultic in its scope" (75).

13. Brown, *Seeing the Psalms*, 165.

ABOUT THE AUTHOR

W. DAVID O. TAYLOR is assistant professor of theology and culture at Fuller Theological Seminary as well as the director of Brehm Texas, an initiative that seeks the renewal of the church through the arts. He is the author of *Glimpses of the New Creation: Worship and the Formative Power of the Arts* (Grand Rapids: Eerdmans, 2019) and *The Theater of God's Glory: Calvin, Creation and the Liturgical Arts* (Grand Rapids: Eerdmans, 2017). He is also the editor of *For the Beauty of the Church: Casting a Vision for the Arts* (Grand Rapids: Baker, 2010), and coeditor of *Contemporary Art and the Church: A Conversation Between Two Worlds* (Downers Grove, IL: InterVarsity Press Academic, 2017). His forthcoming book with Baker Academic is provisionally titled *The Glory of the Body: An Introduction to the Physical Body in Worship*. He has published articles in the *Washington Post, Christianity Today, Christian Scholars Review, Books & Culture, Theology Today, Comment Magazine, The Living Church, In Touch Ministries,* and *Image Journal,* among others.

He serves on the advisory board for Duke Initiatives in Theology and the Arts as well as InterVarsity Press Academic's series, "Studies in Theology and the Arts." A pastor for ten years in Austin, Texas, he has lectured widely on the arts, from Thailand to South Africa. In 2016, he produced a short film on the psalms with Bono and Eugene Peterson.

He lives in Austin with his wife, Phaedra, a visual artist and gardener, his daughter, Blythe, and son, Sebastian. He tweets @wdavidotaylor and posts on Instagram @davidtaylor_theologian.